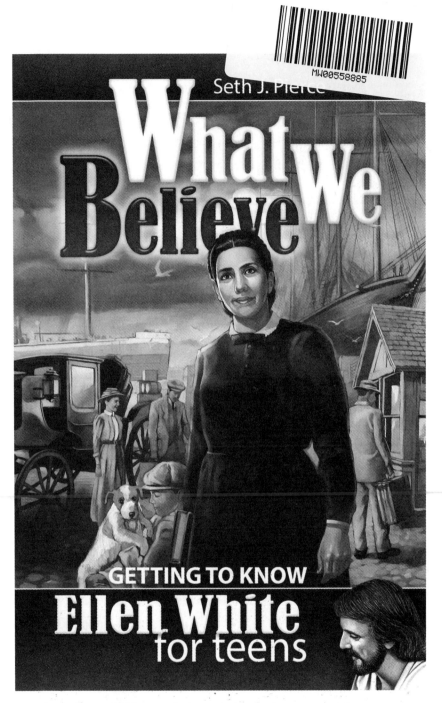

Seth J. Pierce

What We Believe

GETTING TO KNOW

Ellen White
for teens

Pacific Press®
Publishing Association

Nampa, Idaho | Oshawa, Ontario, Canada
www.pacificpress.com

Cover design by Gerald Lee Monks
Cover design resources from Marcus Mashburn
Inside design by Kristin Hansen-Mellish
Photo on page 269 courtesy of the Ellen G. White Estate, Inc.

The author assumes full responsibility for the accuracy of all facts and quotations as cited in this book.

The Ellen G. White Time Line from appendix A originally appeared in *Our Father Cares* (Hagerstown, MD: Review and Herald® Publishing Association, 1991). It is used with permission from the White Estate.

You can obtain additional copies of this book by calling toll-free 1-800-765-6955 or by visiting http://www.adventistbookcenter.com.

Library of Congress Cataloging-in-Publication Data:

Pierce, Seth J.
Ellen White for teens / by Seth J. Pierce.
pages cm. — (Getting to know)
Includes bibliographical references and index.
ISBN 13: 978-0-8163-5828-1 (pbk. : alk. paper)
ISBN 10: 0-8163-5828-1 (pbk. : alk. paper)
1. White, Ellen Gould Harmon, 1827–1915. 2. Adventists—Doctrines. I. Title.
BX6193.W5P54 2015
286.7092—dc23
[B]
2015011379

May 2015

Table of Contents

Dedication

For Madeline, Chloe, and Natalie:
May each of you grow up to be strong women of faith
with powerful voices that point people to Jesus.
I love you always.

Author's Note

Any book featuring Ellen White will probably offend a bunch of people. Whenever we explore important topics we all bring some baggage—things we have always assumed, always been told, and maybe even a few painful experiences. So, let me clarify something before you embark on this journey of printed or digital paper. I am a friend of Ellen's. The goal of this book is not to tear her apart. However, as a friend of Ellen's, I also know she isn't perfect—she is a human being.

I have done my best to respect her incredible ministry and the prophetic voice God gave her. I have also, out of respect for God and Ellen, refused to deify (make a god out of) her. Because the primary target audience of this book is teens, I have spent more time on Ellen's younger years as a teen, young wife, and mother. One challenge I faced in writing this book was to condense the massive quantity of source material for her life and writings. I know some people will be upset that certain things didn't make the cut—but I recommend other sources for further study. This book, as all the volumes in this series, is a stepping-stone for deeper study—though many longtime Ellen friends will find new things in here to enjoy . . . or be offended by.

I have tried my best to steer clear of a defensive/apologetic tone and let her story speak, although a few chapters are spent clearing away what I believe are erroneous ideas about what prophets are and how to interpret their writings. I hope they are helpful. My goal for this book is to provide a starting point and maybe even a way to cleanse the palate from any previous Spirit of Prophecy pain inflicted by "pious" people.

Finally, my prayer is that you will become a friend of Ellen's. You may find her challenging, aggravating, beautiful, confusing, or inspiring—or all of these at the same time—but that's true of anybody we have a close relationship with. Above all, I hope you hear a voice pointing you to Jesus.

Section I: Our Issues

There are a lot of thoughts, opinions, and rants about who Ellen was and how to understand her. Maybe you have heard some of the arguments about her that will be addressed in this section; maybe some will be new. The point here is to drop a little of our "baggage" about her so we can travel light when we get into Ellen's life story.

Chapter 1

Who Cares?

"OK, so what do you all know about Ellen White?"

The question was fairly innocuous—a simple query about a historical person posed to a group of teenagers in a Bible class. I stood at the front of the room, hand at the ready with digital pen to write their responses on the SMART Board. What followed was a torrent of wild answers that scarcely seemed to be about the same person, or any person for that matter.

To my great delight, the students rewarded me with a biographical sketch that belonged in a game of Mad Libs:

"She hated bread."

"Cheese is poison."

"Hated drums."

"Against theater attendance."

"Stopped breathing during visions."

"She was a bazillion years old."

"She loved animals."

"She was anorthex."

"Did you say *anorthex*?" I asked.

"Yes," the student confirmed his answer to the merry bewilderment of the class. "Anorthex."

"A-n-o-r-t-h-e-x?" I suggested.

The student seemed content with my spelling.

"As there is no known spelling of this word in the English dictionary," I continued with a smile, "I think you mean anorexic."

The class laughed. The student corrected his answer, but he liked the new word, so I left "anorthex" on the board. I have no idea what it means, but I'm quite sure it refers to something unpleasant.

The Mad Lib biography continued.

"She looked down on everything."

"Only had a couple years of schooling."

"Wrote a lot of books."

"Didn't like black pepper."

"Very picky."

"Didn't like tea."

"Loved meat."

"She was hit by a rock."

The final offering came from the same student who had invented "anorthex" when he shouted, "She was blind and deaf!"

"That's Helen Keller!" exclaimed several gleefully indignant adolescent historians. Hilarity ensued, effectively ending our game. When decorum was achieved, we all glanced at the list describing their impressions of Ellen White. While some may dismiss these suggestions as a reflection of adolescent ignorance, these students most likely received this picture of Ellen from parents at home or from the pulpit at church. This means that many adults, and the children they interact with, all possess a passionate portrait of an accomplished, incredibly negative, very strange person. A person that many people love to hate.

Haters

Ellen's founding hater was a man named D. M. Canright. Born in 1840 and married to an orphan girl who had been partially raised by Ellen and her husband, this talented man left the Adventist ministry three times, citing Ellen White as the reason. If he were a student in my Bible class, he would have added to our list the words "self-deceived, bitter, and vindictive" to describe her.[1]

Canright could write, and he wrote books filled with these words—words that inspired people like Walter Rea, another minster in the 1980s who also quit the Adventist ministry and wrote a book. Rea's book, *The White Lie,* uses fun words such as "feeble," "sickly," "unschooled," "impressionable," "abnormally religious," "excitable," and "thief" to portray Ellen.[2]

While other former ministers have written books too, a quick perusal online reveals lots of regular people playing Character Assassination Scrabble: "heretic,"[3] "false,"[4] "racist,"[5] "medium,"[6] "liar,"[7] "Freemason."[8]

That last one is my favorite—considering that only males are initiated into Freemasonry.[9] Nevertheless, being a woman and viewed as an integral part of a covert scheme for worldwide domination via a secret society, particularly an all-male one, is a rather impressive credential.

So far, Ellen seems like a pretty awful person.

Super fans

James White, writing in 1845, said marriage is "a wile of the Devil."[10] He must have changed his mind, because James married a gal named Ellen Harmon in 1846 and went on to have four children with her. Knowing how children are made, and given that James (an accomplished writer/speaker) wrote that Ellen was his "crown of rejoicing,"[11] we start to see a different quality to Ellen's persona. Other men were drawn to her as well, since long after James passed away, ending their thirty-five-year marriage, suitors such as Stephen Haskell proposed marriage to her.[12]

Ellen White—thief of hearts?

Her children also seemed to think highly of her. Her son Willie selected the words "kind but firm" in describing how he was raised.[13] And Ellen's grandkids, such as Arthur White, had so many positive words for her that Arthur went on to write a massive six-volume biography of her life.[14]

Arthur wrote that his grandmother "knew how to feed and treat . . . animals with affection. . . . She abhorred any practice that brought pain or discomfort to animals, and she had firm words of disapproval for anyone who misused a horse or abused a cow."[15]

You can tell a lot about a person by the way he or she treats animals, and Ellen extended to the people around her the same kindness she showed to animals.

Gracie White, another grandkid, said, "Never did we feel under a strain or stress in her presence. She had deep blue-gray eyes that were kind and alert. She looked at us with love."[16] Not exactly the words you would choose to describe a tyrannical, judgmental monster.

Another story, this time from granddaughter Mabel Miller, goes like this:

> One morning, my mother helped me pick a handful of our prettiest pansies from our flower garden. Then she let me take them to Grandma Ellen and visit her all by myself. . . . When Grandma Ellen saw me, her face turned into one big smile. She pushed her flat writing board to the side of her chair and held out her arms. I ran straight into them. . . . This morning, she hugged me tightly and thanked me as she took the flowers. . . . She smiled like I had given her the biggest bouquet of flowers from a real flower shop!
>
> "Look at all these smiling pansy faces!" Grandma Ellen said with a laugh. "That's why pansies are one of my favorite flowers. They make me happy. Look Mable! Every pansy is smiling at you." . . . She pulled me closer. "Jesus wants us to be like pansies. He wants us to bring happiness to everyone around us." . . .
>
> I have remembered what my Grandma Ellen told me that day. It was more than eighty years ago now, but whenever I see a pansy, I remember to smile.[17]

Smiling and pansies? Where's the moody, brooding crank who snaps kids' hands with a switch when they pick flowers from the garden?

Historians such as George Knight have uncovered stories where Ellen explicitly avoids being harsh and judgmental:

> Another time Ellen White recalled when some of the children she was caring for in her home were learning how to knit. "One of them asked me, 'Mother, I should like to know whether I am helping you by trying to do this knitting work?' I knew that I [would] have to take out every stitch, but I replied, 'Yes, my child, you are helping me.' Why could I say that they were helping me?—Because they were learning. . . . Never did I condemn them for their failure. Patiently I taught them until they knew how to knit properly."[18]

And these little urchins weren't even her kids!

From outside Ellen's family we have other words describing her in stark contrast to the haters. Look at the following sample from the "webbernet": "right,"[19] "powerful,"[20] "remarkable,"[21] "prophet."[22]

Gaiam Life, a Web site offering advice on everything from diet, eco-travel, and Yoga poses, places her in the "popular author" category and gives several quotes from her writings.[23]

She even has a Facebook page with more than one hundred thousand "likes."[24]

Radio personality Paul Harvey, who passed away in 2009, had his recording "So God Made a Farmer" featured in a 2013 Super Bowl ad that went viral. Google it. On his long-running radio show, Harvey would occasionally quote Ellen and even said, "Ellen White. You don't know her? Get to know her!"[25]

But perhaps the most impressive, and even disturbing, tribute to Ellen White comes from D. M. Canright (her most ardent hater), who attended her funeral in 1915. That's impressive on its own—paying your respects at your nemesis's funeral says a lot about someone. However, Canright's brother says that as D. M. gazed upon Ellen's casket he had tears running down his cheeks and said, "There's a noble Christian woman gone."[26] I can only hope the people who hate me after reading this book will be so gracious at my funeral!

We appear to be dealing with a complex human being who made a lot of people angry and a lot of people happy. Such intense hate on one side, and such love on the other, forces us to place Ellen within the realm of human beings. And a word or two from someone on the same journey, even if we don't always agree, is a valuable source of inspiration. Especially if the words belong to a voice with a unique blessing from Jesus.

The voice

Everyone has a voice—even if they can't speak.

We all have ways we influence people every day—even if it's just with a look or a smile or a frown. Some of us are so adept at this that we can throw our voice around the world and have it heard by people we will never meet. Sometimes the gift is so powerful our voice can influence people to do certain things or change the way they think.

It's like we are X-Men or something.

Ellen's voice is so powerful it still speaks even though she died a hundred years ago. Her books are still in publication, with titles such as *Steps to Christ* translated into 150 different languages. The blockbuster novel series revolving around a young wizard named Harry Potter managed only sixty-seven.

The gift God gave to Ellen gave her the literary fuel to produce fifty thousand pages of manuscript, five thousand articles, and forty books.[27] Personally, including schoolwork going back to kindergarten, I have managed maybe four thousand pages. Most of them unpublishable—except perhaps for Parent's Refrigerator Press.

Far from being manifestos (you know, the kind crazy people write in their backwoods Montana cabin on old typewriters), Ellen's work helped create the world's largest Protestant education system, which includes some seventy-eight hundred schools, ninety-three thousand teachers, and 1.8 million students.

I am one of those students, and you are reading my book—which means Ellen is already influencing you. Yes, that does sound a bit creepy, but get over it and continue reading.

Mrs. White also helped bring to life cutting-edge medical practices that produced such places as Loma Linda University Medical Center, which performed the first successful newborn heart transplant.[28] And for princess fans, the Adventist Florida Hospital Celebration Health is the only medical facility to partner with Walt Disney World Resort as part of Disney's planned community of Celebration, Florida.[29]

It's hard to imagine the ideas of a crabby lady in the nineteenth century—ideas we might think would more likely befit an evil queen rather than a member of the pantheon of Disney princesses—inspiring partnerships with the "Happiest Place on Earth" in a city named Celebration. Some of her less-than-celebratory fans would do well to think about this.

Finally, Ellen was a founding member of the Seventh-day Adventist Church, with roughly seventeen million members worldwide today. You might even be one. This number doesn't even include the millions of non-Adventists who have read her writings or readers throughout the past hundred years who have heard her voice.

If you profess the faith that she helped discover, then her voice should matter to you. Even if you don't profess any faith at all, she is a significant voice in history speaking to a variety of topics in ways that have probably influenced your thinking—and you don't even know it yet, so you should listen to her too.

Her voice matters, and I hope you can begin to hear it in the pages of this book.

ENDNOTES

1. D. M. Canright, letter to A. C. Long, December 8, 1883.

2. Walter T. Rea, *The White Lie* (Turlock, CA: M & T Publications, 1982), 42, 48.

3. http://www.jesus-is-savior.com.

4. J. Mark Martin, ExAdventist Outreach, http://www.ellenwhiteexposed.com.

5. Margie Little, https://www.facebook.com/groups/307882372654283/?fref=ts, June 10, 2014.

6. Hope of Israel Ministries, "Ellen G. White—Messenger or Medium?" http://www.hope-of-israel.org/egwhite.htm.

7. Robert K. Sanders, "*Desire of Ages* Not Inspired," http://www.truthforfables.com/Desire_of_Ages.htm.

8. http://leavethecult.com/2012/08/10/the-seventh-day-adventist-mystery-babylon-connection/. This Web site is now defunct.

9. Edward L. King, "What About Women?" December 2009, *Anti-Masonry Points of View,* http://www.masonicinfo.com/women.htm.

10. James White, *The Day Star,* October 11, 1845.

11. James and Ellen White, *Life Sketches: Ancestry, Early Life, Christian Experience, and Extensive Labors of Elder James White, and His Wife, Mrs Ellen G. White* (Battle Creek, MI: Seventh-day Adventist Publishing Association, 1880), 126.

12. Denis Fortin and Jerry Moon, eds., *The Ellen G. White Encyclopedia* (Hagerstown, MD: Review and Herald® Publishing Association, 2013), 404.

13. William C. White, *Review and Herald,* February 13, 1936.

14. Arthur L. White, *Ellen G. White: A Biography,* 6 vols. (Review and Herald® Publishing Association, 1981–1986).

15. Arthur L. White, "Ellen G. White the Person," *Spectrum* 4, no. 2 (1972).

16. Grace White Jacques, *My Special Grandmother* (Washington DC: Review and Herald® Publishing Association, 1961), 15.

17. Mabel R. Miller, *Grandma Ellen and Me* (Nampa, ID: Pacific Press® Publishing Association, 2000), 13–17.

18. George R. Knight, *Walking With Ellen White* (Hagerstown, MD: Review and Herald® Publishing Association, 1999), 42.

19. Ron du Preez, "A Prophet or a Loss: Dealing With Issues," September 2012, http://advindicate.com/articles/2044.

20. Evan T. Makumbe, https://www.facebook.com/pages/Ellen-G-White-Quotes/178292495596479?fref=ts, June 16, 2014.

21. "Who Is Ellen White?" EllenWhiteDefend, http://www.ellenwhitedefend.com/Bio-Hist/who_is.htm.

22. Martin Weber, "Do You Think Ellen White Has the Same Authority as Paul?" SDA for Me, http://sdaforme.com/FAQRetrieve.aspx?ID=38257.

23. Gaiam Life, "Quote Authors - E," http://blog.gaiam.com/quotes/authors/browse/e.

24. https://www.facebook.com/pages/Ellen-G-White/103780762994147?fref=ts.

25. Paul Harvey, September 25, 1997, quoted in Loren Seibold, "Before Her Time," Seventh-day Adventist Church, http://www.adventist.org/en/spirituality/prophecy/article/go/0/before-her-time/.

26. Jasper B. Canright, letter to S. E. Wight, February 24, 1931.

27. Arthur White, "Ellen G. White®: A Brief Biography," The Ellen G. White Estate, http://www.whiteestate.org/about/egwbio.asp.

28. Richard A. Schaefer, "Perspective on Neonatal Heart Transplantaton," *Legacy: Daring to Care,* http://www.llu.edu/central/info/legacy/chapter3.page.

29. Celebration Health, Florida Hospital, https://www.floridahospital.com/celebration-health.

Chapter 2

Time Travel

One of my wife's guilty pleasures is the lame sci-fi show *Doctor Who.*

Or as I call it, *Doctor Who Cares?*

The premise for this waste of time involves a character named "the Doctor," who happens to be a Time Lord—a time-traveling alien in human form. The Doctor spends his time running around the universe in his TARDIS—a blue British police box (think old-school telephone booth; you may need to Google that for a picture). The TARDIS is a feeling and perceiving ship that escorts Doctor Who through time and space in order to fight bad guys and save various civilizations from ruin. The program first aired in 1963, and for some reason still appeals to people.

I just can't get into it. Not that I have seen it. Nope; I am judging this program purely on hearsay and the forty-five seconds I spent reading about it on Wikipedia. I realize that is a poor analysis on my part, but now I mostly avoid the show out of pride and to annoy my wife.

I do, however, respect the concept of time travel.

In the film *Napoleon Dynamite,* which is *my* guilty pleasure, we are introduced to a character named Uncle Rico. Uncle Rico spends his time reliving his high school football days—videotaping (yes "taping"; you might need to Google that too) himself throwing footballs outside of his van where he lives.

Sad.

He laments some of his choices and wants so badly to go back to the past so he can change the future.

Toward the middle of the film he sits his nephews down and forces them to watch his football movies, to which Napoleon replies, "This is pretty much the worst video ever made." Not deterred by such criticism, Uncle Rico goes online to buy a home-made time machine—essentially a metal box with a T-shaped attachment that goes between the traveler's legs with handles to hold on to. When turned on, the box simply sends electricity shooting through the user. This is not only painful and ineffective, but causes Uncle Rico to walk funny for part of the film.[1]

Most of us aren't dumb enough to hook ourselves up to electrodes on untested devices purchased online. And my guess is you also don't hang out in phone booths waiting for them to morph into a ship and drop you off in the Bronze Age. Yet how awesome would it be to quietly slip in and out of time to fix things in our past?

That test you failed? *Grade changed!*

The girl you asked out who rejected you? *Left her alone.*

That broken leg you got when you tried to parachute out your bedroom window using a blanket? *You read this book instead.*

So much mess could be avoided if we could travel backward in time in order to fix the now—including some of the strange things Ellen White seems to say in her writings.

The spirit of crotchety

I once spent a Sabbath afternoon with a family who refused to allow their children to "play" on the Sabbath. Hymn singing, couch sitting, and maybe nature walking were all fine activities—but playing was certainly not within the scope of God's plan for people's lives on such a holy day. To support their case, they offered me the following quote: "Do not suffer them [children] to violate God's holy day by playing in the house or out-of-doors. You may just as well break the Sabbath yourselves as to let your children do it. . . . God looks upon you as Sabbathbreakers."[2]

Sadly, Sabbath was not a happy day for their children—at least not as happy as it could have been. What kind of foul-tempered woman would ban children from playing? Or worse yet, what kind of God did she serve who would be angered by the innocent joy of little ones frolicking about on a sunny Sabbath afternoon?

It gets better.

When I was in seminary, I rode my bike to class every day to save on gas. Being a graduate student is a special kind of poverty, and since I couldn't eat my books (well, I could, but they were too expensive to digest), riding my bicycle seemed to be the most economical choice to make. But not according to Ellen.

She says, "You would not be purchasing bicycles, which you could do without, but would be receiving the blessing of God in exercising your physical powers in a less expensive way. Instead of investing one hundred dollars in a bicycle, you would consider the matter well, lest it might be at the price of souls for whom Christ died."[3]

A bit heavy handed don't ya think, Ellen? It's just a bike . . . I mean, well . . . *sigh* . . . fine, I'll take the car!

Well, at least I can enjoy music, right? There's nothing like listening to your favorite song in your favorite genre of music, unless it has drums. Mrs. White is often said to have had a deep abiding disgust of percussion—and the evidence goes something like this: "The things you have described as taking place in Indiana, the Lord has shown me would take place just before the close of probation. Every uncouth thing will be demonstrated. There will be shouting, with drums, music, and dancing. . . . A bedlam of noise shocks the senses and perverts that which if conducted aright might be a blessing."[4]

The use of drums is a sign of the end? I guess you better forget playing snare drum in school band and take up the oboe instead.

These three quotes are a mere sample of what many Ellen fans latch on to and quote to perfectly normal people in order to ruin their lives. Well, maybe it's not quite like that, but it is true that many times people will find a phrase in Ellen's writings and make people feel bad for doing things that seem normal and OK. These, along with myriads more, contribute to making Ellen look like a crotchety old woman who declares war on happiness and joy everywhere it may be found.

How did Ellen's kids ever grow up if they lived with such a crotchety lady? No music, no bicycles, and no playing?

No thanks.

Unless . . . unless there is something we are missing. Something in the past.

Thankfully, in order to retrieve what we need, we don't need crystals, DIY Internet contraptions, or even a TARDIS.

All we need is context.

ENDNOTES

1. *Napoleon Dynamite,* directed by Jared Hess (Fox Searchlight Pictures, 2004).

2. Ellen G. White, *Child Guidance* (Nashville, TN: Southern Publishing Association, 1954), 533.

3. Ellen G. White, "We Shall Reap as We Sow," *Review and Herald,* August 21, 1894.

4. Ellen G. White, *Last Day Events* (Boise, ID: Pacific Press® Publishing Association, 1992), 159.

Chapter 3

When, Who, and What

Let's get something very clear—Ellen White doesn't live in your world. She still speaks to it, but physically she stopped thinking and writing in 1915 when she died. Her life spread across the last half of the nineteenth century and into the very early twentieth century—nowhere close to the twenty-first century that you call home. I'm sure you have had a grandparent, or some elderly grandparentesque person, share stories about when they were growing up. Depending on how old they are, the stories can be increasingly strange.

"You know, when I was your age, people didn't have eyes."

What?

Ellen lived about a hundred years earlier than you—meaning her existence included such things as telegrams and horse-drawn buggies instead of smartphones and space travel.

So the task falls on us to do some history (you love history, right?) to figure out the background Ellen White grew up in so that her writings can be understood more easily. So here I offer just a quick survey of some of the differences you would have enjoyed had you grown up with Ellen.

Let's begin with cheese. According to one source, "Unhygienic methods of milk production in her day could be [a] concern, although pasteurization became commercially available in 1882. By 1900, standards had been established in the United States to ensure a reasonably safe milk supply."[1] Basically, if you wanted some cheese, you'd walk into the general store, ask for it, and then the clerk would drag out a moldy hunk of the stuff and lop you off a piece.

I don't know about you, but I prefer medium cheddar instead of moldy cheddar. This could have been a factor in Ellen saying, "Cheese should never be introduced into the stomach."[2] Even as late as 1905 she hated the stuff, but it wasn't until 1916 that a man named James Kraft (of macaroni fame) received a patent on a process that could extend the shelf life of cheese almost indefinitely.[3] I'm not saying cheese is the finest source of health in the universe—simply that it's a different product now than it was in the 1800s.

Another area of Ellen's ire is tea and coffee. She says, "Tea and coffee produce an immediate effect. Under the influence of these poisons the nervous system is excited; and in some cases, for the time being, the intellect seems to be invigorated, the imagination more vivid. . . . Many conclude that they really need them; but there is always a reaction. The nervous system has borrowed power from its future resources for present use, and all this temporary invigoration is followed by a corresponding depression."[4]

While no one can deny the addictive nature of caffeine for many people or that running your life on Starbucks is not a great long-term solution, some studies suggest coffee can have health benefits, such as protecting against Parkinson's disease, type 2 diabetes, and liver disease.

So was Ellen just trying to kill our buzz?

It's interesting to note that studies also point out those health benefits from caffeine occur with small amounts—less than two cups per day—and that unfiltered coffee, such as espresso, appears to elevate cholesterol levels. Plus, adding sugary syrups and whipped cream (creating what my friends call "frou-frou" drinks) loads you up with sweet, sweet fat. As for the "depression" Ellen talks about, consuming a pile of caffeine does set you up for an energy drop later on.[5] To be honest, science seems a little divided over the issue of the java bean. In such cases, perhaps the safest route is to lean on inspiration instead of ever-changing/conflicting reports.

Ellen also dwells on the expense of tea and coffee—even calling them an "idol" in 1879.[6] Remember, UPS didn't show up until 1907 (and they didn't have jets) and FedEx took its sweet time, arriving on the scene in 1971. This meant that any spices, teas, or coffees had to be shipped . . . literally shipped . . . on a boat, from half a world away.

That's expensive.

So expensive that many of the pirates we find so fascinating today had their biggest fights over spices instead of gold. There was a time when cinnamon—the stuff you put in apple pie—was worth more than silver. So, from a budgetary standpoint, tea or coffee was a ridiculous expense—like trying to drink silver. Totally different than spending two bucks on a box of the stuff at Walmart today. However, Ellen's words may apply to those who spend hundreds a month buying six-dollar lattes every day before work. I mean, what difference could you make with an extra 120 bucks a month?

Other questions arise as well: Did they make coffee back then the same way we make it now? Was it more or less healthful? Was its production tied to slavery? Oh, and did you know they used lead—a substance toxic to humans—as a coloring agent for tea? Back in the good old days, "the usual thing was for merchants simply to buy up used tea leaves from hotels, coffee houses and the servants of the rich, stiffen them with a gum solution and re-tint them with black lead."[7] Maybe Ellen's word *poison* wasn't that far off. In her day, they even put acorns in people's coffee grounds and storeroom floor sweepings into black pepper.[8]

And who can blame her for being a little passionate? Average life expectancy was thirty-two years in 1800, forty-one in 1850, and a whopping fifty by 1900. Today, it's in the mid to high seventies—and that's just average. Part of the reason was that the world of medicine in the nineteenth century was like something out of a horror novel set in the Middle Ages.

Everything was backwards.

Fresh fruits and vegetables were suspected of being bad for you. Symptoms such as diarrhea, vomiting, and fever were considered signs of improving health. People thought bathing wasn't healthful. No joke—Ellen actually told people to take baths! "Frequent bathing is very beneficial," she wrote, "especially at night, just before retiring, or upon rising in the morning."[9]

Just how reluctant were the folks in New York City, for example, to dip themselves into some soapy water?

In 1855, the Big Apple had 1,361 bathtubs—and 629,904 residents. The sum of that hygienic equation amounts to a smelly mass of stinky. And they were stinky. Consider these other fun facts of city life in the nineteenth century:

- Most places didn't have indoor plumbing.
- Poor sewage systems resulted in a different kind of water slide running through the streets.
- Horses polluted the dirt roads with their own special kind of pavement that mixed with the sewage and rain.
- Women's fashion included skirts that would drag in the aforementioned muck.
- Little or no refrigeration for such important items as the aforementioned cheese—as well as milk, butter, meat, etc.

And when someone would inevitably become sick, they could be magically whisked away to the hospital—the place you went to die.

In addition to their bizarre anti-vegetable/bathing philosophy, doctors used such techniques as draining your blood and administering medicines containing lethal poisons (think strychnine) to aid in your demise, I mean, recovery. If you were lucky enough to need surgery, you wouldn't have any sort of anesthesia. Maybe a swig of whiskey, but other than that, you would be wide awake as they cut you open or cut things off. One early Adventist theologian had his leg amputated on the family's kitchen table with his mom standing by clasping his hand.[10]

It would be kind of hard to enjoy a meal on the table after that.

Even the way people tried to keep themselves looking presentable was fraught with danger. Ellen breaks it down by saying, "Many are ignorantly injuring their health and endangering their life by using cosmetics. They are robbing the cheeks of the glow of health, and then to supply the deficiency use cosmetics. When they become heated in the dance the poison is absorbed by the pores of the skin, and is thrown into [sic] the blood. Many lives have been sacrificed by this means alone."[11] Hear that, all you lipstick-applying, eyeliner-lining, blush-wearing sinners? You are poisoning your face, your blood, and you are all in grave danger!

Sarcasm.

Truth be told, we sometimes place too much value on external appearances, and we have all watched aspiring models get a little cray-cray with their cosmetics and turn themselves into circus clowns in the name of fashion. But poison? Death? Sounds like a scare tactic to me.

Except it isn't.

Back in Ellen's world there was no government agency monitoring the ingredients people put in their makeup—and one of the favorite ingredients was lead. Lead is a poison, which is why people have stopped using it even in such substances as paint. People were literally applying lead paint to their faces—sometimes even using enamel or lacquer (substances you treat wood with).

Men weren't exempt from the poisons of vanity-inspired products either. Ellen herself was poisoned by applying a hair restorer to her husband's hairless head.[12]

By now you should get the sense that much of the world's way of doing things in the nineteenth century was either unhealthful or lethal. Passionate voices like Ellen's arose to call out awful practices and help people avoid unnecessarily killing themselves with ignorance . . . or stupidity. Reformers like her helped us get to where we are now, and we owe them our thanks.

The lesson of historical context is to always ask, "When?" We need to know when something was written in order to make sense of it—be it the Bible, Ellen White, or that lame text you sent a few years ago professing your love to that boy who turned out to be a bad decision on your part.

There are two more contexts we must look at briefly in order to time travel effectively.

Who?

Not Dr. Who, just the one-word question: Who?

This may come as a heart-stopping shock to your system, but Ellen didn't write to you. Not really.

Certainly she had books and articles designed for a general audience (an audience living in the nineteenth and early twentieth centuries), but much of what she wrote was addressed to certain people, such as "Brother and Sister B," who didn't know how to manage their money.[13] Or "Brother and Sister G," who made poor dietary choices.[14] Or "Brother and Sister H," who had parenting problems and couldn't control their kids.[15] Or Brother and Sister (insert letter of the alphabet here), who had any number of specific problems that you don't necessarily have.

When we see that a piece of writing is addressed to a specific someone, our job is to carefully extract the BIG idea from the passage (making a budget, eating healthfully, and disciplining kids under our care) rather than taking all the specific language she uses and applying it directly to ourselves.

It makes sense, and it makes Ellen not so crazy, when we understand that some of her intense feelings are directed at specific situations and not necessarily at you and me. And as we will see later, some cases included some unsavory characters who needed some strong language in order to stop them from self-destruction.

Finally, we must activate literary context to make our time travel complete.

Collect all the contexts

With fifty thousand pages of writings, Ellen said a lot about a lot. And sometimes she said a lot about one thing, and in order to get the full picture of that one thing, you need to read all she said about that one thing. I mean, if I wanted to find out what you thought about your family, it would be a good idea to check out more than that two-sentence essay you wrote in kindergarten, right?

Otherwise you will be bamboozled when Ellen White blesses eggs in one place and then in another place (in the same book, although to be fair, the book may be a collection of statements she made or wrote at different times) tells people that using them will affect the power of their prayers![16]

You have to "collect the contexts"—gather up everything Ellen wrote on a subject—to appreciate her thoughts. You can remember this by asking: "What?"

What all did she say on a particular subject? What were the specific situations?

Sadly, this is where most people fail miserably. They not only cherry-pick snippets of her writings, but they also choose the strongest language possible in order to make people feel guilty.

Actually, this is one thing that has remained the same in both Ellen's world and ours. Ellen hated it when people took her writings and smacked people around with a few of her sentences taken out of context. She said, "We see those who will select from the testimonies the strongest expressions and, without bringing in or making any account of the circumstances under which the cautions and warnings are given, make them of force in every case. . . . Let the testimonies speak for themselves. Let not individuals gather up the very strongest statements, given for individuals and families, and drive these things."[17]

Ellen went so far as to call those people who delight in finding strong quotes to point out the wrongs of others "vultures" and "buzzards."[18]

Conclusion

Ellen White lived and wrote in a different place and time than you and I live in. While her voice carries weight and power for us, we need to treat her with respect and time travel in order to make sure we understand her correctly. No one likes being misquoted and misunderstood.

So what about the bicycles, playing on the Sabbath, and drums?

Well, I will leave you to do an in-depth study, using the tools we have discussed. However, to relieve a little tension, consider the following:

Bicycles: A hundred bucks back then was equivalent to six months' wages. What does that tell you?

Playing on Sabbath: She writes about this elsewhere, making the point that she was addressing a situation where individuals were trying to have church in the living room where kids were running wild.[19] Also, notice the implications of parents not knowing where their kids are or what they are doing. The emphasis seems to be on those who treat the Sabbath with no special focus or genuine family time.

Drums: This passage specifically mentions something happening in Indiana. You should go find out what was going on; it's pure crazy. It should also be noted that if this passage makes drums bad, the same is true of "music," since it's in the same sentence. Notice the word *bedlam.* Look it up, along with what happened in Indiana, and you will have a better idea what she is talking about.

With simple questions of When? Who? and What? at your disposal, I have no doubt your time-traveling adventures will help clear up a lot of the modern messes people have made by misusing Ellen's work.

ENDNOTES

1. Fortin and Moon, *Ellen G. White Encyclopedia,* 683.
2. Ellen G. White, *Testimonies for the Church* (Mountain View, CA: Pacific Press® Publishing Association, 1948), 2:68.
3. Curt Wohleber, "From Cheese to Cheese Food," *Invention & Technology,* Summer 2001, 8, 9.
4. E. G. White, *Child Guidance,* 403.
5. Donald Hensrud, MD, "Is Coffee Good for Me?" http://mayoclinic.org.
6. E. G. White, "An Appeal for Northern Europe," *Review and Herald,* February 6, 1879, supplement.
7. Reay Tannahill, *Food in History* (New York: Three Rivers Press, 1988), 293.
8. Ibid., 293, 294.

9. E. G. White, *Child Guidance,* 461.

10. While there are many sources for these past realities, a great starting point is George Knight's *Ellen White's World* (Hagerstown, MD: Review and Herald® Publishing Association, 1998), which I drew from for this chapter and for the section about how everything is backwards. Check out pages 30–37, and the whole book for that matter.

11. Ellen G. White, "Words to Christian Mothers," *The Health Reformer,* October 1, 1871.

12. Ibid.

13. Ellen G. White, *The Adventist Home* (Nashville, TN: Southern Publishing Association, 1952), 395.

14. E. G. White, *Testimonies for the Church,* 2:404.

15. Ibid., 4:500.

16. Ellen G. White, *Counsels on Diet and Foods* (Washington, DC: Review and Herald® Publishing Association, 1938), 202, 204, 245. As to prayers being affected, the issue seems to be a family wanting God to bless their health while at the same time eating foods that weren't good for their family.

17. Ellen G. White, *Selected Messages* (Washington, DC: Review and Herald® Publishing Association, 1980), 3:285–287.

18. Ellen G. White, *Manuscript Releases* (Silver Spring, MD: Ellen G. White Estate, 1981–1993), 5:215.

19. E. G. White, *Selected Messages,* 3:257.

Chapter 4

Prophet Problems

First-World problems

Those of us living in relatively wealthy parts of the world find ourselves complaining about a unique set of challenges that makes the majority of the human race gag. We gripe about the dumbest things, which we believe cause us immense suffering.

Like when you wake up and can't find your smartphone to tell you what time it is so you will know whether or not to get out of your comfy bed and get ready to go to school for an education. Hate that stuff!

Remember when your laptop battery ran out? You lost the TV remote? The Wi-Fi stopped working for like two hours? Or when you wanted Chinese food but everyone else at the party voted for pizza? Garbage!

Then there was the time the sweatshirt you wanted went on sale, but it sold out, except for the one on the mannequin, but they wouldn't sell that one to you. True story. It happened to me at Hollister in the Tacoma Mall. I was so mad. Especially because when I found it on eBay later that day, the price was *twice* the sale price in the store. Even though I could afford it, I didn't want to, because I wanted to save that money to buy other stuff.

Life is hard sometimes, am I right?

Our complaints are disgusting in light of the struggles others face. They would make absolutely no sense for people whose daily schedule includes foraging for food, finding fresh water, and dodging bullets. We have no concept of what those people struggle with every single day—just as they cannot imagine having our "problems." In fact, their greatest dream would be to have our problems.

Prophets have their own unique set of challenges—not just in their personal lives, but in how those of us who are not prophets understand them.

What does it mean to be a prophet?

The biblical word for "prophet" simply means "messenger"—not "fortune-teller." While many prophets have "predictive" (future-telling) aspects to their ministry, the vast majority of what they do is to call people out on the stupid stuff they know they aren't supposed to be doing.

The Bible is full of examples of people not following God's explicit commands. So God has to send a special representative to deliver a message. One of the best examples is when King David committed adultery with Bathsheba, got her pregnant, had her husband killed in battle, and then married her in order to cover everything up. God sent a guy named Nathan, with a story about a man stealing a lamb, to confront David. When David was outraged by the act of thievery in Nathan's story, Nathan told David that the story was really about him. Much weeping and mourning ensued, and David was brought back into line with what he knew was right all along.

The apostle Paul talks about the spiritual gift of prophecy: "For to one is given through the Spirit the utterance of wisdom, and to another the utterance of knowledge according to the same Spirit, to another faith by the same Spirit, to another gifts of healing by the one Spirit, to another the working of miracles, to another prophecy, to another the ability to distinguish between spirits, to another various kinds of tongues, to another the interpretation of tongues. All these are empowered by one and the same Spirit, who apportions to each one individually as he wills" (1 Corinthians 12:8–11).

Paul is giving a list of tools that the Spirit gives the church to help it grow and change the world around it. Notice that the source of the gifts is the Holy Spirit. Sometimes people call Ellen the "Spirit of Prophecy" (sometimes abbreviated SOP), when in fact the Holy Spirit is the SOP. Prophets, or messengers, help keep the church on track.

They aren't very popular people.

No one likes being held accountable for their actions—especially when their actions are making a mess. So people did all kinds of awful stuff to God's prophets to keep them quiet. Jeremiah was thrown into a cistern (see Jeremiah 38:6). John the Baptist had his head cut off and served on a platter (see Mark 6:25–28). And they tried to kill Daniel in a lions' den (see Daniel 6:16). Jesus told the Pharisees, "Woe to you! For you build the tombs of the prophets whom your fathers killed" (Luke 11:47).

And Stephen's prophetic voice called out those same leaders who killed Jesus, asking the dangerous question, "Which of the prophets did your fathers not persecute? And they killed those who announced beforehand the coming of the Righteous One, whom you have now betrayed and murdered" (Acts 7:52). They stoned him for asking this question.

Prophets *always* have haters.

While some Christians don't believe the Holy Spirit gives the church these gifts anymore, groups such as Baptists, Pentecostals, Methodists, and Seventh-day Adventists do. Adventists, in particular, see the gift of prophecy as a special gift for the church just before Jesus comes.

Chapter 5

So, How Did Ellen View Herself?

How we view ourselves determines a lot of things, especially when a lot of voices are trying to define us. Whenever we study a person or a group of people, it is important to see what they say about themselves. Ellen White's view of herself shifted over the years—particularly from how she viewed herself when she was your age (which we will discuss in another chapter). She says a lot about her work, but a couple of quotes are key to getting her view of her ministry.

First is how she viewed the process of being inspired by the Spirit to speak and write. I used to think that prophets got messages directly downloaded into their brains or had angels grab their hands and force them to write out things in perfect cursive. But Ellen says, "The writers of the Bible were God's penmen, not His pen."[1]

In other words, God didn't grab Ellen's hands and make her write out stuff. He didn't hijack her vocal cords and make her say things. God respects human freedom and even human expressions. A quick glance at Scripture reveals unique voices in each of the sixty-six books of the Bible. There is the poetry of David, the philosophies of King Solomon, the stories recorded by the Gospel writers, the farming imagery of Amos, and the precise theological expertise of Paul.

Ellen consistently paints a picture of teamwork with the Holy Spirit. She says, "Although I am as dependent upon the Spirit of the Lord in writing my views as I am in receiving them, yet the words I employ in describing what I have seen are my own, unless they be those spoken to me by an angel, which I always enclose in marks of quotation."[2] "While I am writing out important matter, He [the Holy Spirit] is beside me, helping me . . . and when I am puzzled for a fit word with which to express my thought, He brings it clearly and distinctly to my mind."[3]

Her view seems to be the same view expressed in the Bible. The apostle Peter wrote: "For no prophecy was ever produced by the will of man, but men spoke from God as they were carried along by the Holy Spirit" (2 Peter 1:21). What is cool is that no matter how God does it, it's always through human language—meaning that God somehow captures the essence of divine truth in the simple, ever-changing ways human beings communicate.

Ellen goes so far as to say, "The writers of the Bible had to express their ideas in human language." "The Bible is not given to us in grand superhuman language." And even, "Everything that is human is imperfect."[4] This sounds like a pretty honest position—and one that so many people, for whatever crazy reason, refuse to accept.

Which brings us to one of the big issues that seem to cause problems for people trying to understand prophets: Do prophets make mistakes?

ENDNOTES

1. E. G. White, *Selected Messages,* 1:21.
2. E. G. White, "Questions and Answers," *Review and Herald,* October 8, 1867.
3. E. G. White, *Manuscript Releases,* 2:156, 157.
4. E. G. White, *Selected Messages,* 1:19, 20.

Chapter 6

Perfect Prophets

I used to think my parents were perfect—along with the founding fathers of my country, my elementary school teachers, professional baseball players, and especially people in the Bible. When we are younger, it's easy to look up to adults and famous, historical persons we respect and think they had their stuff together.

Actually, they didn't.

And that can be really hard to accept when we have put so much faith in them. Truth is, Bible prophets are as notorious for sinning, being ignorant, and losing their faith as we are.

The great Noah, the only human being deemed worthy to save on the planet, who preached the coming Flood for 120 years to unbelieving people, celebrated his great, heroic ark journey by getting drunk, taking off all his clothes, and passing out (Genesis 9:18–28). Sort of an awful ending to an epic story, isn't it? We don't tell that part of the story to little kids in church. We don't make felts, videos, or coloring books to go along with it either.

Then we have Moses. His journey starts out with being radically saved in a reed basket by Pharaoh's daughter. How can you go wrong with a beginning like that? Moses grows up, kills a slave master in cold blood, then skedaddles out of Egypt. After getting his herding on for forty years, he is greeted by God in a burning bush and told he will be the messenger (remember, "prophet" means "messenger") to let Pharaoh know that God is liberating His people. Moses stutters and tests God's patience by not accepting the role, until finally God says that Moses' brother, Aaron, can help him.

Now, think about this. You have God speaking to Moses (presumably in Hebrew), who in turn will tell his brother, who will then translate the message into Egyptian. The message comes from God and gets filtered through two human beings in two different languages before finally arriving in Pharaoh's ear—not exactly a word-for-word situation here. Nevertheless, the message gets through. You'd think that Moses, the messenger, would now feel powerful and vindicated. Instead, as we read the story of the

Exodus, we find Moses disobeying and forfeiting entry into the Promised Land (see the book of Exodus and Deuteronomy 31:1–6).

The fire-slinging Elijah, who called down a blaze from heaven and then destroyed the evil prophets of Baal, ran like a chicken from the wicked Queen Jezebel. After hiding in the woods for a while, Elijah told the Lord that he (Elijah) was the only one who served God anymore. Nice ego, Elijah! For a prophet, that's a pretty weak observation, because the Lord informed His prophet that there were still seven thousand people who remained faithful (1 Kings 18, 19).

The great prophet Daniel, known for his massive prophetic output concerning how God will work in the future right up until Jesus comes again, included himself in confessing the sins of his people that had led them into Babylonian captivity (Daniel 9:20). He felt sick about his own visions, because he didn't understand them (Daniel 8), and he had his book end with a prophecy that wasn't explained to him (Daniel 12). So much for prophets understanding everything they see and record!

Even John the Baptist, the one who claimed he was the special messenger come to prepare the way for Jesus (John 1:23), the one who baptized Jesus and called Him "the Lamb of God, who takes away the sin of the world" (verse 29), later on had the audacity to send his disciples to ask Jesus, "Are you the one who is to come, or shall we look for another?" (Matthew 11:3). *What?* You baptized this guy, saw the Holy Spirit descend on Him, how can you even think to ask that question?

What makes this incident particularly bizarre is that in the same chapter of Matthew, Jesus called John the greatest prophet of all (verses 10, 11).

What is happening to our perfect prophets?

They are sinful, imperceptive, fallible, and even narcissistic (self-centered). And Ellen seems perfectly at home with this reality as she tells people outright that "in regard to infallibility [being perfect], I never claimed it; God alone is infallible."[1] There you have the devastating reality, my friends—Ellen White has admitted she isn't perfect.

Let the panic and hate mail ensue.

But before you open your browser, hunt down my contact information, and eviscerate me with your angst—let me ask you something: Why do we think we are doing a disservice to Ellen by making her a human being?

ENDNOTE

1. Ellen G. White, *The Ellen G. White 1888 Materials* (Washington, DC: Ellen G. White Estate, 1987), 4:1393.

Chapter 7

Did Ellen Ever Make Mistakes?

The short answer is yes—she is human. But we can expand this question: Do prophets ever make mistakes? You know the answer already. It's the same as asking if people ever make mistakes. It may surprise some people, but everyone from Noah to Ellen White needs a Savior named Jesus.

That is Christianity 101.

To act surprised, or even offended, that Ellen didn't do everything perfectly indicates either a total absence of Bible knowledge or a serious psychosis involving living in some alternate reality where it rains gumdrops and people ride magic carpets to work. Seeing that Ellen makes mistakes actually makes her more in line with the pickier of the prophetic *people* within the pages of Scripture.

To make her, as one of my seminary professors would say, the "vegetarian virgin Mary" is to create a fantasy with serious consequences for sincere people later on. Many people grew up with a spotless, superhuman view of Ellen, and when they learned later on that she had all the trappings of a normal human being, they became disillusioned and haters.

It has been well documented that Ellen and her husband went through rough patches in their marriage. We will look at that more in another chapter, but for now, look at what she wrote to her husband after a season of not getting along so well: "I wish that self should be hid in Jesus. I wish self to be crucified. I do not claim infallibility, or even perfection of Christian character. I am not free from mistakes and errors in my life. Had I followed my Saviour more closely, I should not have to mourn so much my unlikeness to His dear image. . . . Again I say, forgive me every word or act that has grieved you."[1]

So, yes, Ellen made mistakes.

Typos?

Of course the big question is: Did she make any mistakes in her writings? Many people say she did, and naturally, others say she didn't. Some people also say that the Bible contradicts itself, and others say it doesn't. Much of the issue lies not only in how we understand prophets (which we have already talked about) but also in how we understand the nature of prophecies.

One example people love to point out from Ellen's writings has to do with a conference she attended in 1856. Ellen says, "I was shown the company present at the Conference. Said the angel: 'Some food for worms, some subjects of the seven last plagues, some will be alive and remain upon the earth to be translated at the coming of Jesus.' "[2]

Of course all those who attended said conference are now dwelling in a cemetery, so did Ellen make a boo-boo? One way to look at statements such as this is to remember that some prophecies are "conditional." This means that some things in the prophecy will happen *if* other things happen.

For example, remember that runaway prophet, Jonah? God told him to tell Nineveh: "Yet forty days, and Nineveh shall be overthrown!" (Jonah 3:4). Pretty clear, right? Nineveh is going down in forty. Boom! There it is. Game over.

But those doomed people decided to change their ways. Look at this: "And the people of Nineveh believed God. They called for a fast and put on sackcloth, from the greatest of them to the least of them. . . . When God saw what they did, how they turned from their evil way, God relented of the disaster that he had said he would do to them, and he did not do it" (verses 5, 10).

So was the prophecy false? Or was it simply conditional on a certain set of circumstances?

Dating issues

What about dating issues? No, I'm not referring to anyone's tragic love life. There are a host of other books you can check out on that subject. All I can offer here is my sympathy and silent judgment of your character.

What I am speaking of is a favorite area haters love to jump on—the fact that historical dates and observations don't always match modern scholarship. However, Ellen made no claims that her writings on history were to be taken as divinely dictated. It is documented that "in some of the historical matters such as are brought out in *Patriarchs and Prophets* and in *Acts of the Apostles,* and in *Great Controversy,* the main outlines were made very clear and plain to her, and when she came to write up these topics, she was left to study the Bible and history to get dates and geographical relations and to perfect her description of details."[3]

The Spirit led her to the big ideas, and then she used the best resources of her day to fill in the rest. Naturally, people might freak out about this and claim that this is unbiblical. However, we also see moments in the Bible where technical details aren't as specific as we'd like them to be.

A quick example from the awful world of math should suffice. In the Old Testament book of 1 Kings we read: "Then he [Solomon] made the sea of cast metal. It was round, ten cubits from brim to brim, and five cubits high, and a line of thirty cubits measured its circumference" (1 Kings 7:23). Now, if you paid attention during your geometry class, you know as well as I do that to get the circumference of something it must be multiplied by pi—roughly 3.14. So how can you have a circumference of thirty when you are supposed to be multiplying by that crazy pi number?

You can't. It's an estimation.

So what do we do? Panic? Cry? Lock ourselves in a closet with a gallon of ice cream? That's actually not a bad idea at all, but not as an answer to this situation.

Instead, how about remembering that the point of 1 Kings is to chronicle the big flow of Israel's history—not provide specific calculations for your math class.

William C. "Willie" White wrote, "When [*The Great*] *Controversy* was written, Mother never thought that the readers would take it as authority on historical dates or use it to settle controversy regarding details of history, and she does not now feel that it should be used in that way."[4] Again, big picture. Ellen's *purpose* is very clear in her writings.

If I texted you: "hEy frend, downt ordr pIza frum that playss dOWn the STREAT, becz lazzt weak i gut fud pozenening!!" you might be tempted to ignore the message based on my creative spelling—or because as a good friend of mine you know full well it was actually *two* weeks ago I had food poisoning.

However, because you get the big picture, you avoid the lethal pizza down the street in favor of Chinese, which is not only healthier for you, but you find a coupon making it cheaper than pizza—plus you get to eat with chopsticks, so that is pretty sweet. Obviously, you focused on the big idea and received my message.

Changing her mind?

While it is a known fact that it is a woman's prerogative to change her mind at will, without warning, in order to confuse the male of the species, haters will also try to suggest that Ellen changed her theological views over the years. This is true—just like Elijah did (see 1 Kings 19:13–18) and Peter did (see Acts 10). We all grow in our knowledge of God and are able to more fully and clearly articulate the truth.

There was a time Ellen held to something called the "shut door" theory, which was a belief that after 1844 Jesus was no longer saving people. Yet, she grew out of that. Ellen said, "For a time after the disappointment in 1844, I did hold, in common with the advent body, that the door of mercy was then forever closed to the world. This position was taken *before* my first vision was given me. It was the light given me of God that corrected our error, and enabled us to see the true position.

"I am still a believer in the shut-door theory, but not in the sense in which we at first employed the term or in which it is employed by my opponents."[5]

Ellen frequently had experiences where she held one view, then had a vision or an experience, and she changed that view.

Finally, as with any set of writings, we will come across things we simply don't have an answer for. We already saw how Daniel himself didn't always grasp the meaning of his own prophecies. But also consider the disciples, who failed to recognize Jesus even after He told them *three* times about His death (see Luke 24) and 1 Peter 1:10–12, which seems to indicate that prophets frequently weren't certain of the messages they had.

Sometimes we don't get what is being said because we are missing the context, or because the phrase is strange and only occurs once in someone's writings, or simply because we don't know. And while that can be scary for some people, remember: just because you can't "prove" a point or answer a question doesn't prove you are wrong.

It just means you've proven you don't have the answer—not that there isn't an answer.

Did she steal stuff?

A popular subject with Ellen's writings is the accusation that she ripped off stuff from other authors (also known as "plagiarism"). In the mind of the haters, no prophet should be borrowing work from other people—especially when they don't cite where they are getting their information.

Guess we can throw out all four Gospels then, since they all borrow extensively from each other without giving credit—particularly Matthew, Mark, and Luke, which are called the "synoptic" Gospels. Bummer. Those are my favorite books of the Bible. Shame for you as well, as they tell us the most about Jesus.

The issue, for contemporary scholars, is that we have modern laws that are very particular about how you use other people's stuff. For example, if I used a few words, putting them together in the same way another author did, without using quotation marks or giving them credit, I could be sued for stealing their material. It's pretty serious—especially in the scholarly world.

However, back in Ellen's day, they didn't always apply those rules the same way. For example, it would have been all good to copy and paste a Wikipedia article into your paper for school—it would be considered good research.

So, while keeping her own unique emphasis, Ellen searched for the best sources and compiled them to make her points. This wasn't unique to her, either. John Wesley (founder of the Methodist Church, great revivalist, and theologian) also liked to be, shall we say, "resourceful," when it came to using sources for his writings: "By modern definitions Wesley was guilty of plagiarism. Much of what was produced under his name was originally the work of others. But he should not be judged by twenty-first-century publishing standards. He was a man of his own times who worked within commonly accepted rules and practices of his own time."[6]

Sometimes, without meaning to, we have an underlying assumption that people in history should follow our modern rules—and when they don't, we judge them harshly.

In this case, we could complain that ancient Israel should never have killed witches because we don't accept that practice today, yet it was God Himself who gave Moses those laws (see Exodus 22:18). God meets people where they are and works with them within their own situation.

Again, Christianity 101.

ENDNOTES

1. E. G. White, *Manuscript Releases,* 20:23.

2. E. G. White, *Last Day Events,* 36.

3. W. C. White, letter to L. E. Froom, December 13, 1934; in E. G. White, *Selected Messages,* 3:462.

4. W. C. White, statement to W. W. Eastman, November 4, 1912; in E. G. White, *Selected Messages,* 3:447.

5. E. G. White, *Selected Messages,* 1:63; emphasis added. She would amend her position to view the "shut door" as the closing of the "first phase" of ministry in the Holy Place in the heavenly sanctuary where the door to the Most Holy Place was now open.

6. Daniel L. Burnett, *In the Shadow of Aldersgate* (Eugene, OR: Cascade Books, 2006), 61.

Chapter 8

What's the Difference Between Her Books and the Bible?

Ellen Whte did not write her own Bible. For that matter, she didn't even recommend a particular version of the Bible.[1] Her writings don't form a new book beyond the standard sixty-six in Scripture, either.

So, where do we place her writings then?

First of all, the Bible mentions several prophets who wrote books that are not included in the Bible. There is Nathan (1 Chronicles 29:29), Jasher (Joshua 10:13), and Iddo (2 Chronicles 12:15), to name a few. I don't have the books of Nathan, Jasher, or Iddo in my Bible. Maybe my Bible is defective, but I have a hunch those books aren't in yours either.

If your Bible does have one of these books, report it to a local university, my friend, because you have found an ancient relic that will make you a billionaire and able to buy thousands of copies of my book to hand out to all your new friends!

These books were written by what we call "noncanonical" prophets, that is, they don't appear in our canon (collection) of Scripture. Yet we know these books existed and that they were written by prophets mentioned in the Bible, so . . . what does that mean?

Noncanonical prophets were appointed at specific times to deal with people who had forgotten about what God wanted them to do. Remember how we talked about Nathan confronting David? David knew full well he wasn't supposed to kill or commit adultery; God had said so years earlier (see Exodus 20). David did it anyway, so God sent him a reminder, and David corrected his course.

A divine reminder

I have reminders on my iPhone. They pop up to remind me of what I am supposed to be doing. I also employ my wife, secretary, other associates, fireworks, dancing elephants, and various branches of the military to send me reminder texts as backup. Noncanonical prophets are God's reminders, sent to get people back on track.

Reflecting on her relationship to the Bible, Ellen wrote: "Little heed is given to the Bible, and the Lord has given a lesser light to lead men and women to the greater light."[2] Basically, if people had been following the Bible, she wouldn't have needed to come and function as a "reminder."

The *Ellen G. White Encyclopedia* puts it this way: "The primary role of Ellen White's writings was not to give new light, but to lead people back to the Bible and to help them apply Bible principles to their specific context."[3]

This doesn't mean that people haven't abused her writings, using them instead of, or even more than, the Bible. Hater D. M. Canright, in one of his disgruntled moods, wrote, "Any interpretation she puts on a text, or any statement she makes on any subject, settles it beyond dispute. It is what God says, and that ends it."[4] It appears this man had the unfortunate privilege of being bamboozled by one of those "buzzards" that drove Ellen White crazy.

The final word

Like playing the last card in a game of Uno, many people throw down a quote by Ellen White during a discussion and think they have won the game. They don't even offer an idea of what they think Ellen means, they just fling it out there and sit back satisfied.

People did this to her even when she was alive. One guy declared she was an infallible commentary on Scripture and that we should read Scripture through her writings.[5] Another story tells about the fight that broke out in some meetings in 1888 in which leaders demanded that Ellen White settle an issue. She flat out refused, saying that anything she may have written on the subject was now lost and that God wanted her writing on that point to be lost so people would have to study their Bibles for themselves.[6]

Ellen was careful to say that her words should never be put before the Bible,[7] and that people who did so were confusing others.[8] In serious debates she would not agree to have her writings settle the matter.[9] She consistently viewed her role as pointing people back to the Bible.[10]

Her husband, James, had her back when he wrote that no one is "at liberty to turn from them [the Scriptures] to learn his duty through any of the gifts [Ellen's writings]. We say that the very moment he does, he places the gifts in a wrong place, and takes an extremely dangerous position."[11] God gives great gifts, such as prophecy to the church, to help people understand His Word—not take over for it.

Ellen's writings are a great source of inspiration to help us understand the Bible and how it applies to God's people living in the days just before Jesus comes again. Her voice calls us in a unique way to find our identity and mission in the pages of Scripture—the final word for any of life's issues.

Do I need to believe in Ellen to be saved?

Back in 1856, Ellen's husband addressed the question of whether belief in her as a prophet was necessary for a saving relationship with Jesus. He said, "It is well known that we have been charged with testing all men by the visions, and of making them *the* rule of our faith. This is a bold untruth, of which those who uttered it were not ignorant. This I have denied, and deny it still."[12]

See how easy it is to bury very clear-cut expressions under years of misunderstandings? Because people used her in the wrong way, they gave the impression, even over a hundred years ago, that Ellen provided the key to being a good Christian. She is a great aid in pointing us to the Bible and to Jesus, but she never intended to take the place of either.

One hundred years after James wrote that statement, people addressed the same issue in a book called *Questions on Doctrine,* stating that God called Ellen "to do a special work at this time, among this people. They do not, however, make belief in this work a test of Christian fellowship."[13] Seems like belief in her writings isn't even required to be a good Christian.

However, it's important not to lose sight of the idea of living out what we know to be true. Asking if we need Ellen White for salvation is like asking if we need the Bible to be saved—in the sense that both are tools chosen by God to lead us to Him. If I believe the Bible is true, but don't read it, practice what it teaches, or give it any weight in my life, I am not being honest with myself. Likewise, if I choose to disregard what Ellen has to say, after having spent the time reading about her and becoming convinced that she had a prophetic gift, I am endangering myself.

Everyone is called to live out, albeit imperfectly at times, what they know to be true. When I deny what I believe to be truth, I am closing my ears to the Holy Spirit—and that does have consequences for my salvation. Ellen's writings are recognized, more than other books, to be a special source of inspiration for God's church. When we become convinced of that, it is important to live honestly and listen to God's voice through hers.

Conclusion

Prophets have a lot of problems.

Not only because they have their own human struggles like the rest of us, but because of their unique position, they are open to severe judgments and criticisms. They are some of the best figures to help us understand how to practice grace—not only in giving grace to them but in applying it to ourselves as we see how God uses broken people to do profound things.

Our disappointments in life are because of unmet expectations—yet often those expectations aren't reasonable or biblical. It's good to be aware of our culture, our faith, and our own personal baggage (hurts, joys, etc.) that lead us to put certain expectations on others, so we don't become as ungracious as we sometimes label others to be.

ENDNOTES

1. Arthur L. White, "The E. G. White Counsel on Versions of the Bible," The Ellen G. White Estate, http://www.whiteestate.org/issues/Versions.html.

2. Ellen G. White, *The Colporteur Evangelist* (Mountain View, CA: Pacific Press® Publishing Association, 1920), 37.

3. Fortin and Moon, *Ellen G. White Encyclopedia,* 648.

4. D. M. Canright, in Jud Lake, *Ellen White Under Fire* (Nampa, ID: Pacific Press® Publishing Association, 2010), 132.

5. A. T. Jones, "The Gifts: Their Presence and Object," *The Home Missionary,* Extra, December 1894.

6. E. G. White, *1888 Materials,* 1:153.

7. Ellen G. White, *Evangelism* (Washington, DC: Review and Herald® Publishing Association, 1946), 256.

8. E. G. White, *Testimonies for the Church,* 4:246.

9. E. G. White, *Selected Messages,* 1:164.

10. E. G. White, *Testimonies for the Church,* 5:663.

11. James White, "The Gifts of the Gospel Church," *Review and Herald,* April 21, 1851.

12. James White, "Note," *Review and Herald,* February 14, 1856.

13. *Seventh-day Adventists Answer Questions on Doctrine* (Washington, DC: Review and Herald® Publishing Association, 1957), 97.

Section II: Throwing Stones—Ellen's Childhood (1827–1844)

The biographical information in this section and those following draws heavily from Arthur White's six-volume biography, *Ellen G. White: A Biography,* and the historical sketches written by Ellen herself in *Testimonies for the Church.* I will include these books in the recommended reading. Where you see quotation marks citing historical details or dialogue, know that I am quoting from these sources. To pinpoint where I am quoting from, all the savvy reader has to do is perform a word search at http://text.egwwritings.org.

This way we will save a forest from a death by endnotes. Anything outside of the aforementioned sources I will cite as usual.

Chapter 9

The House of Harmon

Everyone is born into a family of varying size—and dysfunction. We arrive in a community of personalities that complement and conflict with each other in their own unique ways. A brief survey among your friends will yield a host of testimonies regarding the special weirdness everyone must participate in as a member of his or her family.

For example, in my family we frequently bypassed conventional games, such as baseball and football, for more avant-garde creations, such as "Shark." Shark was played in our family's above-ground pool—the object being to get from one side to the other without being pinched by the person in the middle designated as the "shark." And by "pinched" I don't mean it in a metaphorical way—I mean literally pinched.

My siblings and I also loved the music of Ray Stevens. Whenever our family went on vacation, during the long drives to various destinations, songs such as "Mississippi Squirrel Revival" (about a squirrel getting loose in church) and "The Streak" (about a man running in public places sans clothing) would be played at top volume—for hours.

In previous books, I have shared stories of attacking my father with a booby trap made from toys because we didn't want to go to bed; assaulting my siblings with croquet mallets in a game of, you guessed it, croquet that went awry; and the multiple times we crafted our own "peace pipes" from sticks in the campfire. (Note to self: inhaling campfire smoke really, really, really stings.)

Your oddball family has its own quirks too, just in case you forgot for a moment and were judging me. Remember the time your dad did that thing? Or your aunt made that comment at a certain place in front of those people? Neither do I, because you haven't told me, or anyone, because you are too embarrassed. You shouldn't be. Everyone's family is a little off, and the sooner you can embrace that for what it is, the sooner you can live a seminormal life like I do.

Now, when we come to Ellen's childhood in the Harmon household, it is weird in how normal it was. I mean, wouldn't you suspect that any family that produces a prolific prophetic figure would have some crazy superpowers or something? Maybe Ellen's dad had dreams that predicted the future, and Ellen's mom could fly, and they lived on top of a mountain in the ancient Near East, where thunder and lightning erupted each day at noon, followed by the voice of the Lord with specific instructions on what to do and who to save that day!

While that would make great comic-book material, the truth, instead, is frighteningly normal.

The birth of Ellen

Ellen was born on November 26, 1827, in Gorham, Maine. No magic castles, no ancient temples on a mountaintop, and no lost underwater kingdoms. Just plain old Maine—which is beautiful in the fall, but sadly, has no intrinsic supernatural powers.

Ellen did have a twin sister named Lizzie, which is pretty cool, but neither of them showed any signs of superpowers. Neither did any of their two brothers or four other sisters (*eight kids?*).

You might suspect that Eunice Harmon, Ellen's mama, was gifted at giving birth—though being a "superbirther" doesn't sound flattering. Truth is, larger families were as normal back then as small ones are now. Ellen's mom was, however, a very quick thinker, disciplined, and deeply spiritual. Her influence can be seen in the fact that three of her six daughters married pastors. Eunice expected great things from her kids and was swift to respond to any attitude she didn't like.

Ellen would receive some kind of chore and then leave the room muttering some complaint about it under her breath. Mom would hear it, tell her to march back in the room, and repeat the complaint—an awkward position many of you have been in, I'm sure. After Ellen repeated her sass, Eunice would remind her young daughter that she "was a part of the family, a part of the firm; and that it was as much [her] duty to carry [her] part of the responsibility as it was her parents' duty" to take care of children. Ellen would later say no hint of disobedience was tolerated in her mom's house.

Lectures, chores, and expectations? Sounds like a regular mom to me. Maybe Ellen got her prophetic genes from her daddy.

Robert Harmon was a farmer and a hatmaker.

Not a mad scientist, not a detective, not even a pastor.

Some people have suggested that the special glue used in nineteenth-century hatmaking was the cause of Ellen's visions and ministry. Seriously? You want to suggest her father was a "mad hatter," and by sniffing the special glue, she suddenly had visions, wrote voluminously, and had a following of millions?

That sounds as plausible as someone being bitten by a radioactive spider and suddenly having the ability to climb walls. And if all it takes to get a following and a legacy as massive as Ellen's is sniffing a little glue, then maybe they should start marketing that stuff as a health supplement.

Stupid.

A few years after the twin girls were born, the family moved from their farm to Portland, where the Harmon family was very active in a large Methodist Episcopal church. In the 1800s, Methodism was the largest denomination in the United States.

Ellen's personality

With such fervent parents, little Ellen said she felt the need to have her sins forgiven from an early age. Her folks, particularly her mother, prayed intensely for the conversion of each of the children. All this is as would be expected in the religious home of a future prophet—except that Ellen pretended not to be affected.

Once, Ellen overheard her mother praying out loud for her "unconverted children." Like any other Christian parent, Eunice sincerely desired her kids to be in heaven and cried out, "O! Will they wade through so many prayers to destruction and misery?" Eunice felt her prayers were bouncing off her kids like rubber balls and was distraught about it.

You'd expect little Ellen to come to her mother's side and assure her that she wanted to give her sweet heart to Jesus. Nope. Not a chance. Ellen didn't want to look as though she was troubled or concerned by her sins, so she would do her best to appear indifferent in front of her parents. She refused to tell her mom or dad what she was feeling, even though, she later admitted, her heart ached every night, because she was scared she would die in her sleep with unconfessed sins.[1]

Kind of a strange picture, isn't it? You have a spiritually troubled little girl who doesn't want to tell her religious parents that she is scared about dying in her sleep with sin still in her heart. It's sad—and even a little disturbing. Not the perfect little angel you might expect Ellen to be, and yet she wasn't trying to be mean. She just had her own insecurities, fears, and issues like every other kid.

School

Most of us started first grade when we were seven.

Ellen began school two months before she was six.

Sometime in the fall of 1833, Ellen enrolled in the Brackett Street School, located only a few blocks from her house. Brackett was full of all the wonderful discomforts a nineteenth-century learning institution had to offer. Hard wooden desks to numb your bum, bad lighting to strain your eyeballs, poor heat to freeze your fingers, weak ventilation to prevent any unnecessary breathing, extra-long days for your learning pleasure, and a curriculum nearly devoid of recess, because, after all, how much energy could a five-year-old possibly need to burn off?

They could also beat you with a ruler.

Ah, the good old days, when sassy students got slapped with measuring sticks! What a magical time for education among the young people of our great nation. The motivation to learn would be so much more vivid with the promise of a swift strike to the keister with a hickory stick.

One day, some kid sitting next to Ellen was disrupting class when the teacher unleashed the fury of yardstick justice—only to miss and crack Ellen on the head instead. Before we continue, I have to wonder if this poor teacher had any formal training in "measuring" out discipline. How do you miss a kid sitting so close? Not that teachers should be smacking their students, but still, no wonder they had no recess. A guy can't teach physical education with poor hand-eye coordination like that. In any case, Ellen got up and exited the room.

The abysmally uncoordinated teacher trailed after her apologetically, begging forgiveness for his mistake. Ellen, showing signs of perceptivity even at a young age, looked at him, forgave him, but then pointed out, "It is a mistake that you should hit anybody. I would just as soon have this gash in my forehead as to have another injured."

Awesome.

Ellen excelled at academics (in addition to shaming ill-tempered instructors) and soon became a favorite reader to all the younger kids. Years later, Ellen was traveling on a train when a woman approached her and asked if she were Ellen Harmon. When Ellen confirmed her identity, the woman said, "You used to come and read our lessons to us." The woman had been one of the little ones Ellen had read to at the Brackett Street School—signifying the power of her voice even as a girl.

What Ellen read

I freely admit to being a bibliophile—someone addicted to books. The thought of the knowledge, the epic story, the spine-tingling, brain-busting mystery that might be locked in the pages of a book is intoxicating to me. Bookstores are dangerous places—especially used bookstores. My wife demands I make a budget—for both money and time—before entering the halls of book purveyors.

Otherwise, she has to send in a search party and I get in trouble.

Nineteenth-century schools required everyone to have a copy of the New Testament. If you attend a Christian school, they may still require you to bring your own Scriptures to class—but back then every school made it as necessary as paper and pen. In addition to the pages of the Bible, the large Methodist church contained a huge library with children's books.

Alas, they didn't have incredible books like *The Day the School Blew Up* or *Camporee of Doom,* by authors such as Seth J. Pierce . . . sorry, that was shameless. What they had were books containing characters that made Ellen feel like spiritual garbage. She says, "I despaired of ever attaining to the perfection of the youthful characters in those stories who lived the lives of saints and were free from all the doubts, and sins, and weaknesses under which I staggered. . . . I can never be a Christian. I can never hope to be like those children."[2] Which, incidentally, is why I write about the plucky, imperfect characters I do in my children's books—despite a few objections from people who would much prefer the perfect offspring of people who could never exist.

Perhaps the most influential reading material Ellen discovered was a scrap of paper in 1836. The writing featured a man in England preaching that Jesus was going to show up very soon. Startled and fascinated, she shared this information with her family. However, her thrill turned to chill, "great terror" in her words, because she had always been taught there would be a thousand years of peace before Jesus came. With her ideas about what the Bible taught blown to bits and Jesus' imminent return a reality in around thirty years, Ellen "could scarcely sleep for several nights, and prayed continually to be ready" for His coming.[3]

The sad normalcy of her experience is striking. How many people who desperately love Jesus are terrified of His return? Even though the Bible says Jesus loves us (John 3:16), gave His life for sinners (Romans 5:8), and will come again and remove all pain and suffering (Revelation 21:1–4). Why have we made this so scary? Part of the answer is that we have made it about us—our holiness, our good works, our righteous, our "readiness."

The truth is, it is Jesus who makes us ready when we respond positively—by His grace—and ask Him for salvation and healing. Poor Ellen! Like a lot of us, she looked at herself and felt unsavable—and she didn't want anyone to know.

In the evenings, Ellen would go to her room and scour her Bible for more details about Jesus' return, but when she heard her parents coming, she would hide it. Most kids hide comic books or novels or any number of potential contraband under their pillow and quickly pull out their Bible when parents come to call. Ellen did the complete opposite. Some people think maybe she wanted to avoid parental attention to her spiritual feelings.

After all, her mother's epic prayers for her salvation bouncing off the walls may have convinced Ellen that telling her mom she struggled would only make things worse.[4]

So she hid her feelings along with her Bible.

And she was miserable because of it.

ENDNOTES

1. Ellen G. White, "Communications," *The Youth's Instructor,* December 1, 1852.

2. Ellen G. White, "Mrs. Ellen G. White—Her Life, Christian Experience, and Labors," *Signs of the Times,* February 3, 1876.

3. James and Ellen White, *Life Sketches,* 137.

4. E. G. White, "Communications."

Chapter 10

Between a Rock and a Hard Place

Shortly after I married my wife in 2003, I was injured in a flag football game. Yeah, I know, you aren't supposed to get hurt in a flag football game—that's why we have flag football in the first place. Let me remind you that people have hurt themselves walking up stairs, eating hamburgers, and falling in love. You can mess yourself up doing just about anything, so stop judging me and let me continue to regale you with my story of woe—and blood.

A church member and I, both locked on to the quarterback, were running full sprint across the field and collided with each other. My friend connected with his shoulder; I connected with my jaw.

An awful "popping" sound echoed around the field that morning.

The left side of my face went numb as I picked myself up on all fours and watched a deep-raspberry colored liquid ooze onto the fresh green grass. I immediately noticed I couldn't close the left side of my mouth. A quick look from my teammates told me I needed to call it a day and make my way home and then to the ER.

Initially, my wife didn't believe in the seriousness of the situation. But after waiting hours in the ER to be X-rayed, only to be told that I had "compound fractured" my jaw and would need surgery right away, I laughed at her doubtful spirit—right before they slammed a needle of penicillin into my rear end to prevent infection.

I didn't laugh about that.

For the next six weeks my patient new bride had to help her husband—whose mouth was wired shut. I had to communicate through gritted teeth and dine through a syringe filled with soup or refried beans. I would have rather broken an arm or a leg—or an arm *and* a leg—than deal with a busted jaw. It was misery and affected every aspect of life for almost two months. For crying out loud, I was a preacher—and I couldn't open my mouth!

After my time of trial was over, I was called in to have the hardware removed. The process was more painful than the break. They gave me eight shots of novocaine—some on the roof of mouth—before getting the wire cutters and snipping away. Then a pair of pliers latched on to a frayed end of wire and pulled and pulled and pulled until it twisted its way out of my bleeding gums.

I was told to spit into the sink, and I watched a host of grotesque colors splash into the metal basin. I felt light headed, and my heart raced as I recovered from pain I never knew conceivable. To this day I have a titanium plate with four screws in my chin, and at the time of writing this chapter I have new braces to correct the crowding done to my bottom teeth because of the break.

Good times.

We all have good "war stories" about the scars we have received from living our lives. My wife is very empathetic, so she hates it when I tell them. That's why I write about them in my books, where she won't have to shudder at my gory descriptions. Many of you reading this book have some incredibly painful traumas you like to bring out at social gatherings to gross people out. Kudos to you for being willing to create awkward moments about the afflictions your body has sustained.

Ellen also suffered a significant wound, when she was only nine. However, instead of a speedy recovery in a couple months, the damage she took from that bloody incident would change the rest of her life.

The incident

Ellen recalls that shortly after school one day, "in company with my twin sister and one of our schoolmates, I was crossing a common in the city of Portland, when a girl about thirteen years of age, becoming angry at some trifle, followed us, threatening to strike us. Our parents taught us never to contend with anyone, but if we were in danger of being abused or injured, to hasten home at once." We are never told what the "trifle" (a "small matter," not to be confused with "truffle," a "small chocolate treat") was. It may have been a mix-up at school or even jealousy over a better grade on a homework assignment. Whatever the case, things escalated quickly.

Ellen and her sister began to run from the older girl as fast as they could. Out of frustration, and apparently equipped with a good throwing arm, the bully grabbed a stone and hurled it after the nine-year-old Harmon sisters. At that moment, Ellen turned and peeked over her shoulder; the rock was there to greet her with all its screaming fury.

The crushing impact of the rock dropped Ellen on the spot.

Barely conscious, bleeding from a broken nose, and looking through bruised and bleary eyes, Ellen was helped to a nearby store by her sister and her friend. No mention is made of the girl who threw the rock; perhaps she panicked and ran from the scene. Sometimes we do things in an emotional moment that we regret immediately afterward.

Ellen "woke up" in the merchant's store, where she saw that her clothes were covered with the blood that was "pouring from my nose and streaming over the floor." She was offered a ride home, but refused for fear of getting blood all over the carriage. She did her best to stumble on home before falling into a stupor for three weeks. While modern medicine would have probably diagnosed her and treated her for a concussion—back in the olden days people began speculating about her inevitable death.

A "kind" neighbor even volunteered to buy her a burial robe. What do you say to that? "Wow, thank you"? "Next time, just get me a get-well card"?

Even though Ellen's mom was a source of encouragement, believing Ellen would make it, the little girl had to overhear family friends say things like, "What a pity!" "She's ruined." And "I don't recognize her." As a father of three little girls, I know that girls care about the way they look. These words stung Ellen, and she made the decision to ask for a mirror to see her reflection.

What she saw shocked her.

Bruises and the shattered bones in her nose seemed to change every feature of her face. She could barely process the face looking back at her—and she didn't want to live. Anyone who has been forced to work with an appearance that doesn't quite match that of their friends, rock stars, or celebrities knows how devastating it can be. Sadly, people put themselves through all manner of pluckings, waxings, reshapings, and even cuttings in order to bring their appearance in line with what they think it should be.

One of Ellen's doctors suggested running a silver wire up her nose to straighten it out, adding the comment that even if it worked, she would probably live only a short time. Great suggestion! Nothing like cramming a sharp, thin, metal object up a broken nose without novocaine—and then having the promise of premature death—to increase a person's feeling of personal well-being.

"Um, no thanks, Doc."

Ellen wanted to die, but at the same time she was far too scared to seriously contemplate ending her life. She was still terrified of her own sinfulness and the image of a God who delighted in torching sinners. After all, between a broken face and eternal torment, a broken face is the lesser of the two evils.

She overheard friends encouraging her mom to have a frank discussion with her about death. By this time, it should be apparent that folks in the nineteenth century had as much to learn about bedside manner as the Frankenstein-like doctors did about medicine. Ellen "began to pray the Lord to prepare me for death." And, thankfully, her prayers helped her feel peace and love. She felt she "loved everyone" and that "all should have their sins forgiven and love Jesus as I did." Her family's friends, however, did not feel love toward everyone.

Seeing the agony she was in, friends suggested prosecuting the bully's father. After all, it's always satisfying when the villain gets her comeuppance—when Batman finally punches the Joker in the face, when the police arrest the armed burglar, when the class cheater is caught and suspended. People pay millions to read books and see movies that feature dramatic justice served on those who hurt the innocent.

However, Eunice Harmon's reply made more sense than seeking retribution for her damaged daughter. She said she "was for peace" and that if prosecution could restore Ellen's health then it would be worth it, but since it could not, it would only add more conflict into an already sad situation. Ellen was losing weight and was almost "reduced to a skeleton."

It was this little, fractured, skeletal figure that greeted Robert Harmon when he returned from a trip to Georgia. Robert had no idea what had befallen his youngest daughter. Upon his arrival home, all the Harmon kids raced into his arms—except Ellen. Robert looked around the room and asked where his daughter was.

In that moment, Ellen "was forced to learn the bitter lesson that our personal appearance often makes a difference in the treatment we receive from our companions." Robert's wife pointed to a little person timidly shrinking back from what should have been a joyful reunion. He said something like, "Is . . . is that my little Ellen?"

Her own father failed to recognize her!

The lack of recognition broke her heart. Fighting tears, she tried to appear cheerful. Whatever strands of self-worth remained were eviscerated, even though her father still loved her very much. To have your appearance so altered that your parents can't recognize you is far worse than having no "likes" on your Facebook profile pic featuring your new/awful hairdo.

Everyone wrestles with messages that we are not good enough. A lot of it is due to the media and our own lack of perspective. As we grapple with our self-image and self-worth, we learn to discard the personal slams from people who may not like us or understand us. But, at that awful moment, Ellen had objective proof that she looked terrible. That's painful for anyone to deal with, but it's something much more devastating to a sensitive nine-year-old girl.

Ellen writes that she continued to feel deeply hurt, and because of her unusually sensitive nature, she was in a particularly dark place. Her pride was wounded, her self-image obliterated. She frequently went off alone to be with her sadness. Lizzie, her twin, was a crier—there's one in every group. People who burst into tears over sad music, picked flowers, or burnt dinners. Ellen wished she could weep—to have rivers of tears carry away the sadness locked in her mind, but she couldn't. The tears wouldn't fall.

Sometimes sympathy from her friends would momentarily drive away her gloominess, but she still felt isolated by her appearance and poor health. Her faith in Jesus helped in those moments; she sought Him and felt that He, at least, loved her. As she got some of her strength back, Ellen attempted to return to school and face the girl who had thrown the stone.

Back to school fail

In fifth grade, I once punched a kid in the face for making fun of my "moon boots" on a class skiing trip. While my fist didn't contain the power of the rock that hit Ellen, it did cause a nosebleed . . . as well as several awkward months of waiting for this kid to exact revenge on me. The whole incident is regrettable and demonstrates how in a fight everyone loses.

Ellen's return to school would place her in the path of the girl who had violently ruined her life. In a beautiful plot twist, however, the rock thrower became her tutor. Not only that, but Ellen said, "She always seemed sincerely sorry for the great injury she had done me, although I was careful not to remind her of it. She was tender and patient with me, and seemed sad and thoughtful as she saw me laboring under serious disadvantages to get an education." Not everyone who starts out an enemy remains an enemy. Yet, even with the girl's sincere help, school was not meant to be for Ellen.

Ellen writes that her "health seemed to be hopelessly impaired" and that she could not even breathe through her nose for two years. Her hands trembled when she wrote; her vision blurred, making all the letters on the page run together; drops of sweat would bead on her brow; and then she would be taken by dizzy spells. Coughing fits would rob her concentration, and her "whole system seemed debilitated."

Her school attendance became inconsistent, and finally her teachers asked her to leave school until her health improved. She had tried so hard—like many of you may have in school. Yet no matter how much she tried to bend her mind to the tasks before her, her body would not respond. Years later, she wrote, "It was the hardest struggle of my young life to yield to my feebleness and decide that I must leave my studies and give up the hope of gaining an education." Even three years later, when she tried school again, her health "rapidly failed." It became obvious that if she tried to resume school, "it would be at the expense of my life." So at twelve years of age, she was forced to leave school forever.

One of Ellen's greatest ambitions was to become a scholar, but now broken dreams accompanied a broken body in hammering away at her heart. She was left with the thought of being completely useless the rest of her life, and she muttered against God for allowing something like this to happen to her.

At some point, we all have to deal with the horrors of life and how a good God can allow bad things to happen to us or someone we love. It's called *theodicy*—the question of God's justice and where He might be in a world that contains so much evil. Had Ellen been willing to share the despair in her heart with her mother, she might have found some help and comfort. Depression is a crippling illness that traps its victims inside a world of darkness and shame.

Even robust comedians, such as Robin Williams, have lost their lives to it.

Ellen held her sadness inside out of fear of being judged. The "happy confidence in my Saviour's love" that she had enjoyed during her initial recovery "was gone." Thankfully, Ellen's life would not succumb to the clutches of despondency.

But for the moment, this twelve-year-old girl concluded that "heaven seemed closed against me."

Chapter 11

Rock Bottom
(1837–1842)

When someone says, "Jesus is coming soon," how do you feel?

Excited? Like when a loving set of grandparents comes to visit, bringing loads of gifts and candy, and permission to do whatever you want and frowns at your parents when they think of punishing you?

What about *indifferent?* Like the ancient fable of the boy who cried wolf, you might have heard people use this phrase so many times, without defining what "soon" means, that you feel nothing when you hear it.

How about *annoyed?* After all, maybe you were hoping to get married before Jesus comes—or at least have a first date, a driver's license, and job that doesn't involve the preparation of french fries.

There are a lot of emotions people have when they think about Jesus' return, but, sadly, the most common is fear.

What if I'm not good enough? What if Jesus is mad at me? What if I'll be engulfed by fire instead of embraced by nail-scarred hands? For Ellen, the flames of eternal torment crackled around her every thought as she wrestled with what she heard from a man named William Miller.

Miller's meetings

In March 1840, a Baptist farmer, turned preacher, was giving a series of lectures on Jesus' soon return. The presentations were the equivalent of a summer blockbuster, with people coming from all over the countryside, bringing lunch baskets and staying from morning until night.

Ellen went with some friends, like you might go to a concert, only the concert would be a preacher. She "listened to the startling announcement that Christ was coming in 1843, only a few short years in the future." As might be expected, the thought of

Jesus Christ coming back in less than four years created widespread terror throughout the Portland, Maine, area. Special meetings were held where "sinners" could seek salvation before Judgment Day rained down flames on all the evil people who weren't ready.

Ellen felt she was a part of the crowd seeking Jesus in order to be saved from her sins. However, in her heart she had "a feeling that I could never become worthy to be called a child of God." This is the same girl who, as an older woman, would straight up call out people's sins in front of hundreds of people in church meetings.

But we will look at that in another chapter.

For now, know that Ellen as a twelve-year-old had abysmally low self-confidence. She felt dumb asking friends for help, so she "wandered needlessly in darkness and despair," all while her friends thought she was just fine.

Sleepless

One evening, Ellen and her brother Robert were returning from an extra powerfully packed lecture about Jesus' epic return to earth. The speaker gave a call for everyone to prepare for the oncoming judgment, and Ellen was so freaked out she later said, "So deep was the sense of conviction in my heart, that I feared the Lord would not spare me to reach home."

Yikes!

What kind of person do you think Ellen pictures Jesus as? Some ill-tempered deity who enjoys smiting poor twelve-year-old girls with low self-esteem while they try to walk home from church? That's messed up, but that's how bad Ellen felt about herself—combined with a twisted view of God.

It gets worse.

As she went home, the words, "The great day of the Lord is at hand! Who shall be able to stand when He appeareth!" rang in her ears. Finally she broke down and, for the first time, told someone how terrified she was. She looked to her big brother Robert and attempted to explain what she felt, saying that she "dared not rest nor sleep until I knew that God had pardoned my sins." Feeling the weight lifted off her heart a little, she awaited Robert's reply.

Silence.

Then weeping.

Robert was just as scared as she was.

Encouraged by this, she continued to dump all her toxic feelings of despair out in the open. She told him that in the past she had had moments when she "coveted death," but now she was afraid to die, because she might be lost forever. Imagine their conversation.

"Do you think God will spare me if I spend all night in prayer?" she asked her brother.

"Yes," replied Robert, wiping away tears. "I think He might—if you ask Him with faith. I'll pray too . . . for both of us."

Ellen spent the dark night hours weeping and praying—again plunging herself into the lonely struggle for hope. Later, she reflected that she concealed her feelings from people because she feared hearing "a word of discouragement." Her hope and faith were so feeble that if someone should confirm her low opinion of herself, she would never be able to crawl out of her misery.

After all, her dad—who genuinely loved her—had once confirmed that her physical appearance was less than normal, so what was to keep her friends from certifying her spiritual shortcomings?

Little Ellen desperately wanted someone to assure her: "Tell me what I should do to be saved, what steps to take to meet my Saviour and give myself entirely up to the Lord." Just as many kids think it would be a great thing to be a superhero like Spider-man or Wonder Woman, for Ellen, she thought it a great thing to be a Christian.

However, Ellen thought she needed to do extra powerful or special things in order to be considered a part of God's family. She felt this way for months.

If I perish . . .

Most summer vacation destinations usually involve beaches, tents, and a lot of bug spray. The Harmon family opted for none of the typical spots that summer. They loaded up the wagon and took the kids down to the Methodist camp meeting sixteen miles away in Buxton. While normally this kind of family vacation pales in comparison with Disney World or backpacking in the Canadian Rockies—for the spiritually drowning Ellen, this was exactly what she needed.

During a sermon on the book of Esther (where the queen approaches the king without permission, hoping to see the scepter of approval), Ellen connected with the text, "I will go to the king, though it is against the law, and if I perish, I perish" (Esther 4:16). The speaker used these words to encourage confidence in those scared to approach Jesus.

Ellen also heard him say that waiting to make yourself a better person before coming to Jesus was a "fatal mistake." None of us can make ourselves good enough; only Jesus heals us from our sins. The pastor even called out the mistaken idea that you had to make "some wonderful effort" in order to receive God's forgiveness.

Ellen wrote, "These words comforted me and gave me a view of what I must do to be saved."

The beauty of salvation

I remember, a long time ago, trying to play an old video game on my computer. The game was something I grew up with, so it was not only a fun waste of valuable time but also a chance to relive my childhood. For weeks I fought with my lame PC (I now use Mac exclusively—#snob), trying to find certain files, plug-ins, fixes, and so on in order to get the dumb thing to work. All I would get was a black screen.

I tried off and on for months.

Then one day, thanks to a YouTube tutorial, I arranged the files—and the bright opening screen of the game appeared on my monitor.

It was so beautiful I cried.

OK, so I didn't cry. But I was overjoyed. I played that old game for hours with an incredible feeling of victory and hope. I had done it; no longer did a dark, blank screen fill me with despair. The digital world was filled with color and action and light.

While it may offend you that I have chosen to make an analogy between video games and Ellen White's salvation, I assure you it works. She had been living months and months in darkness. No amount of praying or sharing could bring her any light from the terrible spiritual blankness she experienced. But as the words of Esther settled into her heart, she "began to see [her] way more clearly, and the darkness began to pass away."

The only thing that hindered Ellen's view of God from erupting with sparkling colors of grace and love was the popular idea of a "second blessing" that Methodism taught. This idea taught that people had to have some electrifying spiritual rush after they gave their heart to God and that this meant they had been "sanctified"—or made perfect. A lot of people, even if they aren't Methodists, feel that way. They believe that if they don't have this fiery conversion experience, they must not be that connected with God.

Without such an experience, Ellen didn't dare think her Savior had accepted her. The simplicity of just giving your heart to Jesus eluded her, yet she went forward with others during the camp meeting with Esther's words becoming her own prayer. As she did, she felt her troubles vanish. This scared her, and she tried to pick them back up again.

Some people don't feel they are spiritual unless they are serious, solemn, and "burdened." Ellen went so far as to think she had no right to feel joy and happiness. Even today, there are kids who attend church who feel that being joyful and happy isn't the norm for people who are serious about Jesus (a rereading of Nehemiah 8:10 would be helpful).

Jesus seemed very near to Ellen in that moment. Suddenly, she realized that instead of withholding her sadness, confusion, and troubles from Jesus, she could hand them all over to Him, and He would take them. She felt sure Jesus understood and sympathized with her heartaches. Finally, she felt assured of His love toward people who don't feel so good about how their life has been going.

One of the ladies at the meeting saw Ellen praying and asked her if she had found

Jesus. Before she could answer, the woman said, "Indeed you have, His peace is with you, I see it in your face!" That moment was a tremendous act of grace from Jesus. Ellen's father had not recognized her face after the rock incident; now her face was recognized as shining with the love of her heavenly Father. All her worry about others confirming she wasn't worthy was blown away by someone confirming that Christ was in her heart.

Suddenly, everything was beautiful. She wrote, "Everything in nature seemed changed." Her feelings had matched the gloomy Portland weather—rainy and dreary—when camp meeting started. But now the sun shone as bright as the hope in her heart. The green of the trees was richer, the blue sky deeper, and the grass fresher.

"The earth seemed to smile under the peace of God."

Total immersion

Baptism is a major milestone in every Christian tradition, and Ellen was very interested in going through with the ancient ritual. Even at twelve, her reading of the Bible told her that immersion—going all the way under the water—was the baptismal practice portrayed in the Bible. However, some of her Methodist "sisters" thought that a sprinkling was good enough. They tried to get Ms. Harmon to see that a splash was better than submergence, but Ellen wasn't convinced. Thankfully, the local minster agreed to dunk the aspiring disciple.

I, like many of you, was baptized in a church in a nice tank full of warm water. But Ellen's baptismal service was outdoors on a windy day. She and eleven others made their way to the frigid sea waters, fearless in the face of high waves that began dashing onto the shore. The minister said a blessing, then taking the young Ellen, eased her back down into the briny deep.

Upon resurfacing, Ellen recalled, "When I arose from the water, my strength was nearly gone, for the power of the Lord rested upon me. I felt that henceforth I was not of this world, but had risen from the watery grave into a newness of life."

She was received into full Methodist Church membership. Her mind was happy and at peace until she noticed the person next to her. Glittering gold rings dripped from the woman's fingers, and shiny earrings hung from her ears. Her bonnet had artificial flowers accompanied with expensive ribbons tied in elaborate ways. Gazing upon what she perceived to be an outward display of vanity in a sacred moment that was about humility, Ellen wrote, "My joy was dampened."

She was also dismayed that the minister didn't say anything about this woman's "showy apparel," that he considered it acceptable for church membership. In her words, "We both received the right hand of fellowship. The hand decorated with jewels was clasped by the representative of Christ, and both our names were registered upon the church book."

This confused Ellen, especially as she reflected on Peter's words cautioning against overdoing your outward appearance (1 Peter 3:3). In her mind, this person was openly disregarding the Bible at the moment of her baptism. What made it worse, Ellen saw many people who were older and more experienced than her adorning themselves similarly.

Of course, it's also probably not a great thing to do at your baptism to be judging someone's worthiness to walk with Jesus. I don't think Ellen meant to be judgmental; she had just come out of deep spiritual darkness and was very earnest. She was ready to give up everything in light of her budding understanding of Jesus' sacrifice on the cross. However, this illustrates something important about Ellen and baptism.

Ellen still needed Jesus—even after her baptism.

On a broader scale, it is important to note that baptism isn't a declaration that you are perfect. On the contrary, it is declaring your need of a Savior and His grace. A lot of people put off being baptized because they are scared that they aren't worthy or that they will sin afterwards.

They completely miss the point.

Baptism isn't for perfect people, and it doesn't make perfect people, as is evidenced by what happened next in Ellen's life.

Chapter 12

Return to Darkness
(1842–1844)

I once took a class in historical research methods from a professor who wrote papers on the topic "The Comma." *I know, right?*

Pages and pages on this thing—",".

Every time I handed in my homework, Professor Pollack found something wrong with my grammar (much like my book editors do). For one assignment, I employed the use of no less than three professional editors. I felt confident in my work and handed it in without any angst whatsoever.

He *still* found errors.

After having my corrected assignment handed back, I half-jokingly asked, "Dr. Pollack, is there any hope?"

"No," he replied with a smirk. "Just keeping trying."

Eventually, I got an A in the class, but my hopes would rise and fall with each assignment. It took the entire stinking semester before my soul (and my grade) were at peace. For Ellen, even though she had finally found some rest and a blessing in her baptism, peace still seeped out of her heart and left her in distress.

When Ellen turned fourteen, she went to another set of lectures by William Miller. With the Lord preparing to descend from the heavens in T-minus-two years, things were getting a little crazy. Many churches, including Ellen's, shut their doors to Miller and forbade members to listen to someone they saw as a fanatic. They liked him initially, because he scared people into the church pews—but now, as the "end was nigh," churches became more skeptical.

"Thanks for the church growth, William, . . . now go away."

Despite being made fun of, Miller was a caring and gentle soul. He would stop midsermon if he saw an elderly person looking over the crowd in order to find a seat. Miller would step down, take that person's arm, and help them find a place to sit before returning to his presentation—earning him the nickname "Father Miller." Ellen hung on his every word, and her old feelings of not being good enough resurfaced with demonic force.

Back at the Methodist church, she watched friends around her weep, pass out, and then awaken to be pronounced: "sanctified!" Her friends would shout wildly at her with such phrases as "Believe in Jesus—NOW!" or "Believe He accepts you—NOW!"

As if the word "NOW," combined with an exclamation point, could make people holy or instantly grant people faith. Imagine yelling the next time you run into a crabby person: "Be happy—NOW!" They will probably get slaphappy on the side of your face or upside of your head.

Ellen worried that she had a "hard heart" and just couldn't understand the big theological words "justification"[1] and "sanctification"[2] that everyone kept using. She began to worry that attending Miller's meetings caused God to prevent her from being blessed like those around her.

But why would her Christian friends be angry about someone preaching Jesus' soon return? Shouldn't they want Him to come soon? It was a muddled mess in her mind, and she felt scared and condemned every night when she went to bed—crying out a single question to God: What must I do to be saved?

Like many people then, and even now, Ellen had been taught that on God's cosmic scales His justice was far heavier than His mercy. Some preachers actually suggested God delighted in torturing sinners. One famous preacher, a hundred years before Ellen lived, suggested: "The God that holds you over the pit of hell, much as one holds a spider, or some loathsome insect, over the fire, abhors you, and is dreadfully provoked; his wrath towards you burns like fire; he looks upon you as worthy of nothing else, but to be cast into the fire; he is of purer eyes than to bear to have you in his sight; you are ten thousand times more abominable in his eyes, as the most hateful venomous serpent is in ours."[3]

Charming message. This was the kind of heavenly Father Ellen saw in charge of her salvation. For her, God was an angry deity who would delight in sending waves of lava to drown her in a sea of fire—in less than two years. He was, in her words, a "tyrant."

Later she reflected that maybe her "sympathies were more easily excited by suffering because I myself had been the victim of thoughtless cruelty, resulting in the injury that had darkened my childhood." Ellen understood what it meant to be hurt, and the thought of a Creator doing those same things to His creation sickened her. "A wall of darkness seemed to separate me from Him," she recalled.

Losing her grip

"I have since thought," wrote Ellen years later, "that many inmates of insane asylums were brought there by experiences similar to my own." The images of hell "seemed to curdle the very blood in their veins, and burned an impression upon the tablets of their memory." Ellen reasoned that the horrors of imagining hell might have removed reason and trapped them in a terrible dream. She also had strong words for those who teach such a wretched doctrine.

I once went to a church that hosted what they called "Hell House" around Halloween each year. Their version of a haunted house involved a skit in which kids got into some horrible accident—with some going to heaven and others (including the audience) going to hell. The magical smell of burnt hair, the sound of screaming actors being poked by ferocious demons wearing rubber masks, and terrified members of various youth groups made for an unforgettably awful evening. Hell House was a nightmare meant to convert the kids to a greater nightmare—namely, trusting in a God who would embrace eternal suffering.

We should have just stayed home and ordered pizza.

Ellen began attending church "social meetings." No, there was no laser tag, movies, or charades . . . not even bingo. Socials back in the day were more like Bible studies or prayer meetings—and as she attended she felt impressed to pray. However, she "dared not" pray for fear of becoming confused and not saying the right words. I still run into adults who are scared to pray in public. Ellen's failure to pray only further clouded her heart and "despair overwhelmed [her]" for almost a month.

The "horror of the night"

Ellen went entire nights without closing her eyes from fear. After her twin sister would doze off, Ellen crept onto the floor to kneel in prayer. She prayed "with a dumb agony that cannot be described. The horrors of an eternally burning hell," she wrote, "were ever before me."

Instead of experiencing the peace that "surpasses all understanding" described by Paul in Phillipians 4:7, Ellen had the "hopelessness that passes all description." Sadly, she continued to lock her anguish deep in her heart so no one would know. And soon the tendrils of darkness entwined themselves around her even in her dreams. In one dream she saw a temple, a butchered lamb—ripped apart and bloody—and masses of people pushing past each other trying to enter the temple to find forgiveness. She remembered, "Even after I had entered the building, a fear came over me, and a sense of shame that I must humble myself before these people. But I seemed compelled to move forward. . . . An awful brightness illuminated the building, then all was intense darkness. The happy people had all disappeared with the brightness, and I was left alone in the silent horror of night."

Upon awaking, she was filled with dread. "It seemed to me that my doom was fixed, that the Spirit of the Lord had left me, never to return."

Dream residue

My wife calls it "dream residue"—after the filmy residue soap sometimes leaves behind in the shower. "Dream residue" refers to the shards of intense dreams that remain stuck in your mind's eye when you wake up. Sometimes they are great—like the time I dreamed I could fly by grabbing the bottom of my T-shirt and pulling it out in front of me. I know, weird, but you know deep down you would pay anything for a T-shirt that would allow you to fly, so don't judge me.

Other times the residue isn't so sweet—like when you die in your dreams, or someone you love dies, or you have visions of evil creatures hovering over you while you sleep (how's that for creepy?). Thankfully, bad dreams end and make room for good ones. After the horrors of the night, Ellen was given a famous dream that filled her with hope.

The green cord dream[4]

The dream happened shortly after her nightmare. She encountered the loving Savior:

> He drew near with a smile, and, laying His hand upon my head, said: "Fear not." . . . The loving eyes of Jesus were still upon me, and His smile filled my soul with gladness. His presence filled me with a holy reverence and an inexpressible love.
>
> My guide . . . handed me a green cord coiled up closely. This he directed me to place next my heart, and when I wished to see Jesus, take it from my bosom and stretch it to the utmost. He cautioned me not to let it remain coiled for any length of time, lest it should become knotted and difficult to straighten. I placed the cord near my heart and joyfully descended the narrow stairs, praising the Lord and telling all whom I met where they could find Jesus. This dream gave me hope. The green cord represented faith to my mind, and the beauty and simplicity of trusting in God began to dawn upon my soul.

At long last, hope began to stick, as Ellen realized that Jesus loved her and that she could place her trust in Him. Being saved wasn't about performing great feats of strength, going on daring missionary escapades, or praying elaborate public prayers; it was simply trusting Jesus and keeping the focus on Him.

Telling mom . . . and a minister

At last Ellen confided all her sad and confused feelings to her mom—and she found the sympathy and encouragement she had been starving for. Sometimes we think our parents will be disappointed in us when we tell them our struggles. But as a parent, I can tell you there is nothing we want to know more—so we can help you get where you want to go. Holding in scary feelings does nothing except make you feel bad about yourself and cause nightmares. Trust Jesus and trust those adults who take care of you.

Mrs. Harmon advised Ellen to share her feelings with Elder Stockman—a man who lived in Portland and who preached the same message William Miller did. Ellen agreed since she viewed him as a great servant of Jesus. She poured out all her feelings to the minister and then waited to hear what he would say. Gently, he placed a hand on her head, and she saw tears in his eyes.

"Ellen, you are only a child," he began. "Yours is a most singular experience for one of your tender age. Jesus must be preparing you for some special work." None of them had any idea just how special. He went on to tell her that even if she were an adult, he would tell her the same thing: there was hope through the love of Jesus.

Elder Stockman sympathized with her injury and encouraged her by saying that the Spirit of God had not been withdrawn from her. He spoke words of life into her heart and said that in time she would realize the incredible plans Jesus had for her. But for now, she should be patient and trust Jesus.

"Go free, Ellen," he said, smiling; "return to your home trusting in Jesus, for He will not withhold His love from any true seeker." Stockman prayed with her and released her to fulfill the next chapter of her walk with Jesus.

An opportunity to express her new faith occurred shortly thereafter, during a prayer meeting. She willingly prayed publicly,

> I lifted up my voice in prayer before I was aware of it. The promises of God appeared to me like so many precious pearls that were to be received only for the asking. As I prayed, . . . the blessing of the Lord descended upon me like the gentle dew. I praised God from the depths of my heart. Everything seemed shut out from me but Jesus and His glory, and I lost consciousness of what was passing around me.
>
> The Spirit of God rested upon me with such power that I was unable to go home that night. When I did return, on the following day, a great change had taken place in my mind. It seemed to me that I could hardly be the same person that left my father's house the previous evening. This passage was continually in my thoughts: "The Lord is my shepherd; I shall not want." My heart was full of happiness as I softly repeated these words.

Whoa! That's some serious praying. Have you ever lost consciousness in prayer? (Sleeping doesn't count.) Imagine calling home and telling your parents, or better yet having your pastor tell your parents, "I'm sorry Mr. and Mrs. Johnson, but Timmy won't be coming home tonight, he seems to have passed out in prayer. We'll send him home when the Lord wakes him up." Sounds like an epic prayer meeting—way more interesting than the ones that happen now.

Changed

Early in my career, I took a bunch of kids to Worlds of Fun in Kansas City. My goal, for many of them, was to place them on their first roller-coaster ride. As we arrived at the amusement park, we saw the great Mamba looming over two hundred feet in the air—zipping riders along at seventy-five mile per hour. Some of the children were genuinely terrified.

But I convinced some to ride.

I sat next to a girl who had never been on a roller coaster. She was shaking with fear, and as the great coaster began to climb the first hill, with the signature *clack-clack-clack* noise, she began to shed tears and have a mild freak-out session. Naturally, being the nurturing youth pastor that I was, I grinned and enjoyed describing the inevitable doom that awaited us.

As the coaster went over the edge—plummeting two hundred feet straight down faster than most cars drive on the highway—she screamed. Then laughed. As we pulled out of the drop and ascended the following hills, twists, and turns, she declared this to be "the best ever!" She spent the rest of the day enjoying the presence of Mamba—as well as the other "thrill" rides.

Ellen's view of God the Father was similar to that girl's initial view of roller coasters. She could see others apparently enjoying His presence, but she viewed Him as dangerous and terrifying. However, once she understood Him, her "views of the Father were changed." She saw Him as loving parent, and her heart warmed toward Him. She even said she "felt the assurance of an indwelling Saviour"—a statement many people can't say, and even have been taught not to say.

There are a lot of people who don't have "assurance"—the "knowing" that God loves them. Yet that is the most important thing you can know as a follower of Jesus. It gave Ellen incredible comfort: "It seemed to me as if I had been rescued from hell and transported to heaven."

Ellen speaks

The evening following her conversation with Elder Stockman, Ellen found herself at an "advent meeting"—gatherings dedicated to the belief that Jesus was coming in just a couple years. One of the features of these meetings was to go around the room and ask people to say something about Jesus.

Statistically, research suggests public speaking, for many people, is the most frightening thing in the world next to death; and some people prefer death. How much more impressed are you with the brave pastors who speak in front of people every week?

I know—we're amazing.

When the time came for Ellen to speak, she couldn't remain silent. She spoke "the simple story of Jesus' love" with complete freedom. She was so filled with happiness that she lost sight of the people around her to the point that it seemed only she and God were in the room. Tears of thankfulness fell from her cheeks as she testified to the love in her heart.

Ironically, Elder Stockman was present—and feeling discouraged. When he heard Ellen speak, he wept tears of joy—praising God for all to hear. There is an incredible power in the stories we tell about our experiences with Jesus; they can change people's moods as well as their lives. Never be scared to talk about how Jesus has blessed your life.

Shortly thereafter, Ellen attended a conference at another church. She was invited to share her story again, and the same power followed her words. With freedom and joy she spoke in a way that made those in attendance weep, and she noticed the "melting" power of God softening people's hearts. People—adult people—came forward for prayer in order to give their hearts to Jesus.

Remember, she was only fifteen.

A deep sense of responsibility rested on her as she thought about all her friends who might not know Jesus—especially since she knew what it was like to feel so sad and then to be filled with joy. Like a lot of people who meet Jesus, she became very excited and went about trying to convert her friends. They didn't respond well at first, and some not at all. But Ellen wrote about her determination:

> Several entire nights were spent by me in earnest prayer for those whom I had sought out and brought together for the purpose of laboring and praying with them.
>
> Some of these had met with us from curiosity to hear what I had to say; others thought me beside myself to be so persistent in my efforts, especially when they manifested no concern on their own part. But at every one of our little meetings I continued to exhort and pray for each one separately, until every one had yielded to Jesus, acknowledging the merits of His pardoning love.

Have you ever done anything like that? I have—although it wasn't as thoughtful or prayerful as what Ellen did. I experienced Jesus in a powerful way in the tenth grade (I even wrote a book about it called *Pride and Seek*). Afterward, the task fell upon me (or rather I pulled it on top of myself) to convert my friends. I would call up whomever of my friends I felt was the worst sinner and invite them to "take a walk."

I cringe now when I think about it.

The walk was a series of incredibly personal questions about their faith—in the hope of convincing them to say a prayer, asking Jesus into their hearts. I wasn't tactful, and to be honest, Ellen started with people who were at least attending church or who found church culturally acceptable. I was doing it from scratch, out of left field, without warning.

Thankfully, they were merciful to me—and one did start attending church again.

As for Ellen's experience talking to her friends—young and old—she writes, "Every one was converted to God."

Visions of the call

Instead of the old nightmares convincing Ellen she was doomed to an eternal barbecue, images of her "laboring for souls" filled her mind. Faces of people in need of Jesus flitted past her in the night, and upon waking up she would pray for them intensely. "In every instance but one these persons yielded themselves to the Lord."

Naturally, some people didn't appreciate her bold efforts—saying she was "too zealous" for the conversion of souls. Keep in mind that many believed Jesus was coming in less than two years. If now wasn't the time to be aggressive, then when would be? What would you do if you believed the Lord was soon going to rip the sky open and remake the world?

I'd be calling everybody in my smartphone for starters, followed by random door knockings, incessant tweeting, and maybe making a scene on street corners. For Ellen, "time seemed so short" that she needed to tell the world—even if "those older in experience than [herself] endeavored to hold [her] back." Ellen was no longer afraid of the fires of judgment, because she burned with the Spirit. And she refused to be cooled off by tepid old-timers who had lost their zeal. While we must always respect everyone, youth must especially be on guard against churches that would strip them of their spiritual fire (see 1 Timothy 4:12). Ellen stayed focused despite people's best efforts to discourage her.

"I went on my way with a joyful spirit," she wrote.

ENDNOTES

1. This word refers to God declaring someone to be in a right relationship with Him.
2. As well as meaning "to be like Christ," this word also means "to be set aside for God's special use."
3. Jonathan Edwards, "Sinners in the Hands of an Angry God," sermon, July 8, 1741.
4. You can find the whole dream in *Life Sketches of James and Ellen White,* 156, 157.

Chapter 13

Origin Story
(1844–1846)

Origin stories of great heroes have been popular for years. Everyone wants to know how dynamic characters, committed to fighting the darkness in the world, came to be. We want to know that they were once vulnerable like we are, so we can find some common ground and identify our experience with theirs—helping us to believe that there can be something better out there for us than the pain we might be going through.

All great heroes and heroines have this vulnerability:

Batman lost his parents to a gunman in an alleyway when he was a boy.

Captain America was a scrawny wannabe military recruit who received repeated rejections to serve his country in World War II.

Wonder Woman begins life as a girl named Diana who, in order to save a stranded pilot, has to leave her secluded existence among the Amazons on the isle of Themyscira.

Not a superhero fan? Consider the following:

Anne of Green Gables starts out as an unwanted orphan who finds family in Prince Edward Island.

Another famous Annie was an unwanted orphan in New York under the rule of the awful, alcoholic Miss Hannigan.

Oh, you only like Bible characters?

Moses was nearly killed as an infant, then had to flee for his life when he prevented the death of a fellow Israelite.

Queen Esther, a.k.a. Hadassah, an orphan being raised by her cousin, nearly had her people killed by a genocidal maniac.

Sarah spent the vast majority of her life unable to have a baby.

Jacob began as a thief and was duped into marrying the wrong woman after seven years hard labor.

Whether war, deep loss, being abandoned, or having to abandon what is

69

familiar—most great heroes begin with some kind of tragedy or challenge. Ellen's story is no different. The future prophet, along with her family, was kicked out of church.

Kicked out of church

One evening at the Methodist church the Harmon family had been involved with for years, Ellen's brother Robert shared his thoughts on how important it was to be ready to meet Jesus—who, incidentally, was coming in just over a year. Ellen said it was a powerful presentation and soon followed it up with her own testimony. She had no doubt that her Methodist friends would appreciate her words.

But something was wrong.

Several women groaned, shuffled their chairs noisily, and actually turned their backs on Ellen. Real mature, ladies. Ellen was baffled as to what would have offended them so much. What happened next went something like this. Elder B., the elder chosen to preside over the meeting that had suddenly turned a bit chilly, turned to Ellen and asked, "Would it not be more pleasant to live a long life of usefulness, doing others good, than to have Jesus come speedily and destroy poor sinners?"

Ellen replied, "I long for the coming of Jesus. Then sin would have an end, and we would enjoy sanctification [being like Jesus] forever, with no devil to tempt and lead us astray!"

Unfazed, the crusty elder countered, "Would you not rather die peacefully upon your bed than to pass through the pain of being changed, while living, from mortality to immortality?" In other words, in the mind of this elder, being made like Jesus at His return would be like having wisdom teeth extracted or a leg amputated.

"I am willing to live or die as God wills," replied Ellen confidently. "I wish for Jesus to come and take His children. I can easily endure whatever pain there might be in that moment we are transformed." Those in the meeting were upset at these words—even as Ellen continued to share how much Jesus' love meant to her and how His soon coming had fired her up to strive to be more like Him.

"You become like Jesus through Methodism—Methodism!" interrupted another class leader. "Not through some goofy theory that Jesus is coming soon" (my paraphrase). Ellen argued back, but to no avail. At the end of the class, she and her brother were convinced they would never return to these meetings.

Around the same time, the Harmon family had been studying the Scriptures and coming to the realization that people don't go to heaven or hell when they die. They came across a belief, rooted deeply in Scripture and becoming more popular today, that when individuals die, they simply "rest" or "sleep" until Jesus comes and resurrects them. This belief, called "conditional immortality" and joined together with "annihilationism," sees that God is the sole source of eternal life and gives it when He returns—not before. The wicked are destroyed instead of tortured forever.

You can read more about it in my book *What We Believe for Teens.*

In addition to the belief that Jesus was coming soon—the doctrine of conditional immortality did not mix well with Methodism. As the Harmons embraced this new truth, which helped remove the picture of a tyrannical torturer God, they shared it with their friends. Ellen says they didn't push it in people's face, but casually talked about what they were learning.

Their newfound joy alerted the local Methodist minister to give them a special little visit. He showed up and informed the Harmons that this newfangled belief didn't fly in his church. He wasn't interested in how they came to believe it—just that they stopped. The minister didn't even offer any Bible texts to show them they were wrong—just a simple, "Stop it."

Ellen's dad, an important member of the Methodist Church, opened his Bible and showed their pastor a few of the texts that had led them to believe God didn't torment people eternally. The pastor didn't argue; he just excused himself as not having enough time to engage the issue. But not before he told Mr. Harmon and his wayward family that they should quietly withdraw from church unless they wanted a public trial.

Public trial? At church?

Ellen knew that many others who believed Jesus was coming soon were facing the same kind of treatment. It baffled her, since they had asked for Bible texts proving them wrong, but no one would offer them. The only answer anyone ever got was that they had "walked contrary to the rules of the church." But aren't church rules supposed to be based on the Bible?

The Harmons loved their church, but they loved Jesus and His Word more. They demanded to know where they had gone wrong. No answer was given, so they held on to the truth they had been given. Not too long after their meddlesome minister had visited, Ellen's family received a summons to a special meeting in the church.

It wasn't a potluck.

As the family entered the church vestry—a small room attached to the sanctuary—they were greeted by a handful of people. The dimly lit room was the site of the "public trial." However, due to Ellen's dad being an important figure in the church, many church members were too cowardly to face him themselves. The Harmons were accused of not following church rules and asked to fall back in line.

Ellen stood by her family as they refused to be bullied into giving up what they knew to be true. They left the meeting feeling a sense of peace and freedom. The following Sunday, sometime in September 1863, during Communion no less, all of the Harmons' names were read, and it was announced they had been "discontinued" (a fancy word for "kicked out") from the Methodist Church.

As Ellen processed what had happened, she clung to the words of Jesus, "Your brethren that hated you, that cast you out for My name's sake, said, Let the Lord be glorified: but He shall appear to your joy, and they shall be ashamed."

Insanity and despair

The date for Jesus' return had been set: October 22, 1844.

Many people had been removed from their churches; scholars estimate that anywhere from fifty thousand to one million people prepared to meet their Savior. People sold their businesses and farms in order to spread the word—because who would need that kind of stuff in heaven?

The group, known as Millerites (named after William Miller), was a great source of mockery when Jesus didn't return on the announced date. William Miller even received a letter from Noah Webster (of dictionary fame), calling his message "a great annoyance" that drives people to "insanity" and "despair."[1]

Millerites also endured taunts such as, "You haven't gone to heaven yet? Well, when do you expect to go?" It's never easy to have your beliefs ridiculed by others—whatever those beliefs may be. Despite the rudeness of so many, Ellen stayed strong and even enjoyed this time. She describes the twelve months prior to the advent date as "the happiest year of my life."

Ellen witnessed a new community forming, made up of those who didn't fit in the mainstream churches. They encouraged each other, shared what they had, and did everything they could to be more like Jesus and to be ready when He came. Ellen, at sixteen years old, would go about visiting and praying with people who felt trapped by the same darkness she once had felt.

Sadly, she struggled during this time with illness. Her particular challenge was tuberculosis—a sickness that spreads from person to person via the coughing and sneezing expressways. Tuberculosis attacks the lungs and causes chest pain, fatigue, fever, and severe coughing . . . sometimes with blood.

Ick.

Ellen describes experiences during this time when she felt the presence of the Spirit so powerfully that her weakened body could barely endure it. She seemed to "breathe in the atmosphere of heaven" and continued, despite poor health, to feel incredible joy at the thought of Jesus coming to take her to be with Him.

However, as presumably you realize by now, Jesus didn't come on October 22, 1844. That is why you still have to go to school, eat brussels sprouts, get a flu shot each year, and clean up the "gifts" your dog leaves in the backyard. For all those staring up at the sky on that awful day, expecting to see Jesus, the reality was devastating. It choked the hope and tears out of grown men.

Washington Morse, a follower of Miller who watched the skies intently that day, wrote, "My feelings were almost uncontrollable. I left the place of meeting and wept like a child."[2]

Another man, Hiram Edson, simply said, "We wept till the day dawn."[3]

William Miller retreated to his farm and remained publicly silent on the matter for a month. One scholar described the experience perfectly when he said: "For Miller and many of his followers, the world did indeed come to an end on October 22, 1844, not melted in divine fire but dissolved in bitter tears."[4] "Bitter" would be a common description by those who lived through that day—including Ellen White.

Imagine being notified that your family is the winner of the Eighty Billion Dollar Sweepstakes—with the promise of a bank transfer for the full amount in a year. For a whole year you imagine what life will be like in your new house, driving new cars, and traveling around the world without a care, well, in the world.

And then the day of the bank transfer you are told, "Just kidding; it's a hoax." What would you do? Ellen said, "It was hard to take up the cares of life that we thought had been laid down forever." In addition to being a great source of all kinds of cruel jokes in newspapers and conversations around the horse trough—people had to figure out what they were going to do now that they had sold farms and businesses.

The words of Noah Webster haunted the discouraged believers. Some gave up their faith entirely, while others sheepishly returned to their smug churches that did their best not to say, "I told you so." Stranger still were a group of people who, to use Webster's words, went "insane" and believed they were actually in heaven.

Seriously—and they did some *straaaaaaange* stuff that Ellen would eventually have to fight against.

While the fallout was massive, there remained a few faithful souls convinced that while they had gotten the event wrong, the prophetic time line Miller used (based on Daniel 8) was correct. In their thinking, something else significant must have happened on that date. Ellen was a part of this group, and she declared they were "disappointed, but not disheartened."

Death and scandal

The 1800s saw the epic rise and demise of many religious movements; the life of the Millerite movement wasn't the only casualty in this period. A new American religion, Mormonism, was officially born in 1830. Its leader, the prophet Joseph Smith, had written a new Bible that had created a sincere following.

And severe opposition.

In 1844, while the Millerites were preaching Bible prophecy in the northeastern United States, another prophetic voice was being silenced in Nauvoo, Illinois. Due to a combination of misunderstandings, practices, and personalities involved in the new religious movement, Mormons came into bloody conflicts with the communities around them.

On Thursday, June 27, 1844, Prophet Joseph and some of his buddies were handed over to the Carthage Greys—Nauvoo's local militia. They kept Joseph and his homies locked in a bedroom. Late that same afternoon some gunmen rushed the building firing shots. Joseph and his crew braced themselves against the door battered by the assailants.

Bullets tore through the wooden barrier—burying themselves in the face of one Mormon and in the leg of another.

Joseph, apparently packing heat of his own, fired a few shots at his attackers before racing to escape through the window. As he began the leap, several bullets ripped into his back, sending him crashing through the panes. He was then fired upon from several gunmen from the outside. He landed near a well, tried to sit up, but expired on the road in a pool of blood.[5]

This was headline news in Ellen's day. People weren't warm to the subject of new prophets, they were skeptical of "fanaticism" (wild behavior in the name of faith) and, as has been seen, could protest against prophetic voices with extreme prejudice. It was a terrible time to be a prophet—and a woman.

What women didn't do in the 1800s

While women enjoy a variety of rights and opportunities today, back in Ellen's day it wasn't always so great.

If you were a woman living in the early to mid-nineteenth century, you couldn't vote—and why would you need to? You weren't a person; you were a piece of property belonging to your husband or father. They would be the ones you gave your wages to and asked to sign contracts too complicated for your pretty little head. Sound like fun? You could specialize in kitchen work, housework, and birthing babies—just like Mrs. Harmon! As for hobbies, tea drinking and gossiping in the parlor were always popular, and if a social situation became too intense, you had the option of fainting.

It took a massive effort by dedicated women to overhaul this kind of life. In many ways, we still have ground to cover in the area of equal rights for women in terms of respect, wages, leadership, and . . . well . . . lots of stuff. The point is that Ellen, now a seventeen-year-old girl trying to pick up the pieces of her shattered faith and identity, was not in a great place to start receiving visions.

As a matter of fact, sending visions to a young woman in 1844 has to be about the worst timing possible. But often what appears bad timing to us is perfect timing for God.

ENDNOTES

1. Herman Bauman, *I Am Saved and, Yes, I Am Perfect* (Bloomington, IN: Xlibris, 2011), 184.

2. Washington Morse, "Remembrance of Former Days," *Review and Herald*, May 7, 1901.

3. Ronald L. Numbers and Jonathan M. Butler, *The Disappointed: Millerism and Millenarianism in the Nineteenth Century* (Knoxville, TN: University of Tennessee Press, 1993), 215.

4. David L. Rowe, *God's Strange Work: William Miller and the End of the World* (Grand Rapids, MI: Wm. B. Eerdmans Publishing, 2008), 192.

5. Matthew Bowman, *The Mormon People* (New York: Random House, 2012), 89, 90.

Chapter 14

Teen Prophet

I have walked a few narrow paths before—mostly during backpacking trips where exhaustion ejected my common sense. Once, I found myself clinging to the face of a mountain, my feet and hands embedded in patch of snow—500 feet up—because I was too tired to find a way around the snow blocking the trail.

Really, really bad idea.

I clung to that snow having some very important time with Jesus before continuing to punch and kick my way through the snow to conclude my shortcut.

I've walked over two-foot wide paths with breathtaking drop-offs into rocky gorges, traversed slippery rock pummeled by waterfalls that cascaded down to certain death, and mucked through muddy patches that threatened to give way and dump me off to an early demise.

Many times my body protested that giving up would be so much easier—after all, my calves were screaming along with my back from walking up steep inclines with a forty-five-pound backpack. My feet hurt, my clothes stuck to me with sweat, and the sun beat down in my eyes. Why keep going? What was the motivation? What was wrong with me?

Destination, my friends.

At the end of every well-planned backpacking trip is raw beauty. Pitching a tent in untouched nature in all its majesty is a phenomenal experience. To see what only other adventurers see, to drink from streams so pure they don't need to be filtered, to be able to dig your own toilet—well, no, that part isn't so special. But to experience the secret places of the world in perfect serenity is indescribable—and worth whatever it takes to get there.

A couple months after the Millerites' journey died in disappointment, Ellen received a vivid answer to prayer letting her know that the path she had been on still existed—and people still needed to walk it. She had been at a friend's house with four other women having prayer, when in the middle of her prayer something strange happened.

While kneeling among her friends, she felt "the power of God" fill her like she had never felt it before. Suddenly, she found herself surrounded by light and rising higher and higher until she was above the earth. That ever happened to you? Me neither. But there's more. Ellen's eyes were directed to a narrow path towering above the world.

The path led to the city of God, and behind the path was a great light that illuminated the footsteps of all the people who walked it. The light reflected the experience and study that had been a part of the Millerite movement. Up ahead, Jesus walked in front of the people, and as long as they kept their eyes locked on Him, they were OK—which is a good general rule no matter what path you are on.

As Ellen watched the walkers, she noticed some became worn out and discouraged. In these moments, Jesus would raise His right hand, wave it, and shower the people with light for their journey along the slender celestial walkway. At this, Jesus' followers would shout, "Alleluia!" and continue forward.

But some fell.

Ellen heard some of those on the journey deny that their time waiting for Jesus to return had meant anything at all. These people had the light go out behind them—and stumbled off the edge of the path into darkness, never to be seen again.

Eventually, Ellen heard the thundering voice of God announcing the arrival of Jesus' long-awaited second coming, and the Spirit of God filled people so full that their faces glowed with glory. In the next scene, the wicked, enraged by what they saw, tried to rush the followers of Jesus. Then in a move almost akin to a Jedi knight, the believers stretched out their hands "in the name of the Lord," and the wicked fell "helpless to the ground."

Slick.

The vision then focused on the appearing of Jesus with countless thousands of angels. So powerful was their arrival that even the followers of Jesus experienced a momentary fear that they weren't good enough to be saved. Jesus comforted them with the words, "My grace is sufficient for you," and then all was well. Ellen saw the dead raised to life, and all who believed, including Ellen herself, were taken to heaven, where they saw amazing things.[1]

When the vision came to a close, Ellen felt nearly as sad as she did when Jesus failed to come on October 22. She commented, "It was a sad and bitter change to wake up to the realities of mortal life." Yet, the vision relieved some major stress she and her fellow believers had been wrestling with.

It reassured them that God had been leading them as they looked for Jesus to return—that was huge.

The question as to why God had allowed them to misunderstand prophecy would be answered later through Bible study. For now, the fact that they had not been abandoned would be a rallying message that would give strength for a new movement to take form. However, although the revelation of God's leading was a comfort, the reality that she would be the one delivering that revelation to others made Ellen feel a little sick.

Groups of people had been meeting at her home in the evening to pray and study together, and she knew she would be called upon to relate what she had seen. So, taking a cue from the ancient prophet Jonah, she ran. Not as far as Tarshish maybe, but she did take a sleigh four miles to her friend's house in order to hide from the church meeting at her parent's house.

The only problem was that a man named Joseph Turner, one of the leaders of the Millerite movement as well as an editor for their printed materials, was chilling at her friend's house too. Upon seeing Ms. Harmon dash into the house, he asked how she was doing and if she was doing all she knew God wanted her to do.

She responded by running upstairs to one of the bedrooms and shutting the door.

True, she didn't actually tell him "No," but when teenage girls run upstairs and hide in a bedroom, it's a safe bet that not all is "happy happy gumdrops" in their world. Eventually, Joseph made his way upstairs to check on the distraught young lady. The encounter must have gone something like this.

"Will you be going to the meeting tonight Ellen?" he asked gently from the doorway.

"No," replied Ellen.

"People have heard about your vision, and it is your duty to share it with them," insisted Mr. Turner, doing his best to remind Ellen of her responsibility.

Ellen answered with the same amount of depth she had before, "No."

Turner left her alone and made his way to the meeting, leaving Ellen to her anxiety. Lying in that room, she began to ruminate on what the consequences would be if she didn't share the message God had given her. Suddenly, she felt forsaken—as if the Spirit had been taken from her. In a panic, she left her friend's house and raced home, hoping to arrive at the meeting in time.

She didn't.

And the Spirit left her, and she fell into obscurity—teaching us the importance of never ever skipping church. The End.

Not really. God is gracious to us when we are scared, and while Ellen did not arrive in time to tell others what she had seen, she did purpose to share at the very next meeting—which she did. In front of sixty people, Ellen shared the vision God had given her, and the people accepted it gratefully.

If only all her messages would be so well received.

Second vision

Ellen's second vision occurred shortly after her first—this one not as heavenly.

The images that erupted in Ellen's eyes involved the challenges, opposition, and enemies that would try to prevent her from doing what God wanted her to do. She was shown that her heart would be broken, as criticisms and wild characters would batter her on all sides. God had called her as His special messenger, and her duty was to fulfill this role faithfully. His grace would hold her close if only she obeyed the words echoing from the angel in her dreams: "Make known to others what I have revealed to you."

It's an epic vision—but a scary one too. Sometimes people think it would be a great job to have God call them as a prophet, but as we have seen earlier in this book, and as you will see as you continue to study, the job of a prophet is fraught with perilous paths that most of us would be content to avoid.

Compounding the vision challenging Ellen to embrace prophethood was her poor health—partially due to the tuberculosis. She lamented that her body constantly hurt and that some days she looked as though she had only a couple of days to live. She described herself as "small and frail, unused to society, and naturally . . . timid." She also said that it was physically painful for her to meet new people.

Not exactly the best qualifications to put on a resume—for any job. She prayed for God to find someone better qualified.

Other thoughts plagued her—such as who would go with her to tell people God's messages? Her father had a family to support, and her brother, Robert, was even more "feeble in health" and timid than she was. Great, no help there! However, her dad told her that if this were God's will, He would make a way.

Ellen, meanwhile, was in a panic; she even had days when she wanted to die. (See? Even back then people freaked out about public speaking.) A seventeen-year-old female prophet in the nineteenth century? She couldn't vote, but she was going to tell people, even grown men, what they were doing wrong and what God wanted them to do?

She was going to be *really* popular.

Give the job to someone else—please.

Eventually, she was prevailed upon to share her message again at another home meeting, and this time the supernatural nature of her experience was visible to a man named Father Pearson. Pearson had previously demonstrated a tepid view of God displaying His power in miraculous ways—yet as the people prayed in this meeting, Ellen saw light erupting around her, the fears tormenting her melted away, and an angel spoke the words, "Make known to others what I have revealed to you."

When Ellen came out of vision, she realized that she was not the only one who had seen something unusual. Father Pearson, shaking, declared, "I have seen a sight such as I never expected to see. A ball of fire came down from heaven, and struck Sister Ellen Harmon right on the heart. *I saw it! I saw it!* I can never forget it. It has changed my whole being. Sister Ellen, have courage in the Lord. After this night I will never doubt again."

Fireballs in prayer meeting? They had all the cool stuff back then.

Pearson's proclamation gave tremendous street cred to Ellen's experience, and soon the pieces came together for her to begin traveling to share her gift with others—accompanied by a young man named James White, who will become very important in our story later on for obvious reasons.

ENDNOTE
___

1. You can find the complete description of the vision in *Testimonies for the Church,* 1:58–61.

Chapter 15

Hazen Foss

In January 1845, Ellen's brother-in-law stayed at her house while on a business trip to Portland. While he stayed with the Harmon family, he told Ellen that her sister, Mary, would love to have her visit them in Poland (Maine, not eastern Europe), thirty miles away. She agreed, and bundling up in a blanket made of buffalo hide (seriously), she made the trip in the bitter cold via sleigh.

When they arrived, Mary embraced her warmly and told her that they would be holding a meeting in a small chapel not far from the house. She went on to ask Ellen if she would share her vision, and despite being numb and feeling a little ill from the frigid journey, she agreed. That night, when all the believers had been assembled, they looked to Ellen to bust out some amazing revelations.

She could only whisper.

The variety of medicines we enjoy had not been invented yet, and the ones that had would probably kill you, so no one expected her voice to improve any time soon. The group had some tense moments as Ellen tried to power through her talk. Then, after about five minutes, her voice began to clear up and stayed strong for two hours. That's some epic-long talking. I think the longest I have ever spoken was an hour—but I had cool PowerPoint slides.

Ellen held their attention simply using the voice God had given her, and when she was done, the whisper returned. The "power of the Lord" would free her vocal cords each time she needed to speak to the group—and then each time, the whisper would become her mode of speech until she recovered from her illness.

The following morning, a man named Hazen Foss—which, even back then, may or may not have been a cool name—visited Ellen at her sister's home. Mr. Foss needed to talk with Ellen after hearing her speak at the meeting the night before. Her vision had unnerved and saddened him. As they sat in the living room, he began to unfold his sad tale of disobedience and the terrible consequences that now haunted his every thought.

Before Ellen had been given her vision in December, Hazen told her, he had been shown the very same thing. He had seen the narrow path above the earth, the believers walking behind Jesus, the light going out—all of it. He had been told to share the message, just as Ellen had. However, while Ellen embraced the truth of the vision and wrestled through her fears and presented it to others—he had not.

Instead, he refused to believe that the 1844 movement had value, and he didn't want to put up with people who might not like what he had to say.

The Spirit of God had spoken to Hazen again, he said, telling him that if he refused to share the message, it would be taken from him and given to someone else—someone who was "the weakest of the the weak." Foss just couldn't bring himself to accept the task; he told God that he didn't have the stomach for vision sharing. Upon speaking these words a "very strange feeling" overtook him.

A voice spoke, "You have grieved away the Spirit of the Lord."

Uh-oh!

Horror gripped Hazen as he pleaded with God to give him back the vision and the Spirit. He even called a meeting of the believers and tried to share what he had seen—but he couldn't remember it. Only when the feeble seventeen-year-old girl spoke of her vision could he remember. He had heard every word, standing outside the door of the little chapel, and now he pleaded with Ellen not to follow his footsteps in words like these.

"I was proud," he told her with tears in his eyes, "so the visions have been taken from me and given to you. Don't refuse to obey God, Ellen. It will cost you your soul! I am a lost man. The crown I might have had now belongs to you."

Well, that's a bit intense.

As you might expect, Ellen was deeply affected by Hazen's story. Rejecting the voice of the Spirit, when it is so clearly spoken to you, is eternally dangerous. The broken man in front of her vividly portrayed what would happen if she failed to accept her prophetic path. She steeled herself and accepted the will of the Spirit. Just in time too. The malevolent forces of opposition, revealed to her during the second vision, now broke loose in order to destroy her.

Chapter 16

Rise of the Fanatics

Nobody likes people full of information who are also full of themselves. Even if what they say is helpful, their arrogant attitude makes you want to reject what they are saying just to spite them.

"So what if this *is* hot sauce and not butterscotch? I'm going to put it on my ice cream, anyway!"

Ellen's great fear in embracing the role of a prophet was developing prophetic pride. Through a vision, Jesus assured her that He would watch out for her and save her from falling into the primal sin of pride—and, ironically, one of the ways that Ellen was preserved from pride was the fact that not everyone appreciated what she had to share.

Enter the fanatics—the very first haters.

Fanaticism can be described as "excessive enthusiasm." I have known excessively enthusiastic people—and they can put on quite a show. I have watched grown men scream and cry at football games, friends forget to sleep so they can finish a video game, and high school girls throw temper tantrums, kicking and screaming on the floor, when they don't get their way (that's awkward and a little awesome at the same time).

In a religious setting, fanatical enthusiasm isn't so entertaining. When spiritual fanatics throw temper tantrums, they blow themselves up or cut off someone's head.

The particular flavor of fanaticism that confronted Ellen grew out of the disappointment of October 22. Groups of people began teaching that Jesus had come on that date—spiritually—and that now all His followers were in a spiritual heaven. Since they were now in "heaven," one of the practices they enjoyed was pretending to be like little kids—after all, Jesus said we need to be like children to enter heaven (Matthew 18:3). So they would crawl on all fours, like babies, into town and into shops, pretending to be babies; sort of tops the weird scale, doesn't it?

Grosser than this, however, was the idea that in order to practice "loving your neighbor" husbands could switch wives back and forth. This was OK, they maintained, because they were in "heaven," and there is no sin in heaven—right? Other practices, and ideas, as crazy as these, were claimed by people who said they had found them in the Bible or heard God tell them straight up.

Ellen described these fanatics as "ones [who] seemed to think that religion consisted in great excitement and noise." They spoke in ways that annoyed unbelievers, made people hate them, and made even the truths they did follow seem crazy to people. The presence of these wild people among the sincere followers of Jesus made the latter seem guilty of the same erratic behavior and shady beliefs. To Ellen it was obvious that "Satan loved to have it so."

Ms. Harmon began losing friends to the fanatics. The fanatics pressed hard on Ellen's friends and turned them "to the dark side of the force" (to use a modern phrase)—even some of Ellen's family fell to fanaticism. Making matters worse, as Ellen shared her visions, someone with the initials "JT" started smack talking about her. JT slandered, lied, and criticized the seventeen-year-old girl. Probably because God gave her a vision exposing JT's beliefs as cray-cray, which she shared with all who might have the unfortunate experience of hearing his nonsense.

Even though she knew to expect opposition and knew that God loved her, the lies hurt. She had never been spoken of so poorly, and it made her physically sick. Prophets aren't above feeling pain, and for two weeks Ellen lay in bed feeling as if she wouldn't survive. Thankfully, the friends she still had rallied and had special prayer for her. The power of darkness was broken, and she felt released from her sickness—and immediately had a vision.

She was shown that if she ever felt attacked by other people, she had only to go to God in prayer and "an angel would be sent to [her] rescue." She said that she had one angel guard continually, but that in the heat of spiritual battle, the Lord would send others to back her up.

Ellen rolled with a heavenly entourage—and nothing would stop her from completing her mission.

Naked church

Throughout her role as messenger, Ellen would come into contact with unsavory characters seeking to sabotage her work. I offer a few colorful examples, from when she was still a teenager, to give you an idea.

When Ellen returned from visiting her sis in Poland, she soon left again—traveling thirty miles north to Topsham to visit the Howlands. The Howland family had held some church meetings in their house, and they had experienced miraculous healings. Frances Howland had rheumatic fever—the epic illness that occurs when you don't get the right medicine for strep throat (think antibiotics, not popsicles). Some people prayed, and the fever vanished. Shortly after that, William Hyde was miraculously cured of dysentery—bloody diarrhea. I think that's the grossest thing I have ever written. Glad you could witness it—and glad Mr. Hyde was healed.

However, as amazing as the healings were, the fanatics had a flare up. Slipping into these special moments of prayer, they began teaching that they (the fanatics) were completely perfect and could help themselves to each others' wives, which may be grosser than the dysentery. Some of these fools even declared that it was impossible for them to sin—and to prove it, a few of these special people attended prayer meeting in the nude. You heard me—naked church.

That's awkward.

The stories get much worse, and naturally Ellen was extremely disgusted by these nightmarish meetings. When she returned home, she found out that these disturbed people had extended their influence and were now back in her hometown of Portland. Heartbreaking. She did her best to expose the, uh, . . . "exposed" individuals, but few people seemed to listen. They actually responded by being jealous and competing with her.

Just stop and catch your breath for a moment. Imagine showing up to a friend's house out of town, only to discover they were having "nay-nay" (my three-year-old's term) church. Grossed out, you return home to find out that everyone at your church thought "nay-nay" church was the best thing ever. And when you point out the obviousness absurdity of what is happening, it just makes people mad.

Nay-nay church is a living nightmare.

Even people Ellen trusted in earlier now had a variation of "spring fever" that revolted her beyond description—one of the worst being a man named Joseph Turner (of aforementioned "JT" fame). He had been a member of her faith community in the aftermath of the Great Disappointment, but now he had joined the fanatical group known as "the spiritualizers."[1]

Creeper

Joseph Turner was a creeper. In late spring of 1845, Ellen had a vision showing her that she needed to encourage the people of New Hampshire. Naturally, she would need a ride—and who do you think should present himself as a reliable mode of transportation? You guessed it—a founding member of nay-nay church.

"I'll take you wherever you want to go," Turner told Ellen, driving up to her house in a beautiful buggy.

"No, sir," said Ellen, "you cannot do that." The creeper continued by using one of the most deplorable, überlame tactics of desperate men everywhere throughout history.

"But, Ellen," continued the shyster, "the Lord has told me that I must."

God told you to? You are going to claim a false vision to persuade a prophet? Check out the story in 1 Kings 13; doesn't end so well, does it?

What a piece of work—and Ellen knew it.

She was not about to be taken for a "ride" by this creepiest of creepers. "No," she replied firmly, "He has not." Ellen knew this man wanted to gain some kind of power over her, but instead she straight up called out his manipulative dishonesty.

She went on to tell him that God had already provided a ride for her, someone known through a mutual friend—someone named James White. God had shared with Ellen in some visions, way before Creepy Turner made his offer, that men would offer their services to her—but she should trust only James.

Naturally, she did not travel alone with James before they were married—often having a good friend, such as Louise Foss, go with them to prevent the already hyperactive rumor mills of the nineteenth century from spewing out more lies. And marriage wasn't on her mind yet anyway. They all believed Jesus would come soon, so there would be no point.

Washington Morse

While Ellen at times wrestled with her fears and even skipped out on a few sessions she knew she should have attended (see? No perfect prophet here)—there were some great victories. One win involved a man named Washington Morse. Ellen's caravan stopped at his house while she dealt with some health issues.

While the group offered prayer for Ellen's recovery, another vision erupted around her. She saw that Mr. Morse wrestled with depression stemming from the Great Disappointment. At one time he had been solid in his belief, but when Jesus didn't return, Morse's faith was so shattered he didn't have the strength to encourage others around him. He, and those he had the potential to help, were left like "sheep without a shepherd."

And wolves in no clothing were prowling around to prey on them.

The vision continued to unfold, showing Ellen the story of Jonah and how he had expected God to do certain things and was disappointed when He didn't. Mr. Morse felt that everyone thought he was an idiot and made fun of him behind his back. Ellen saw that while the failure of Jesus to return had disappointed many, it still served God's purpose and that more light would be revealed in the future as to what had actually happened.

Coming out of vision, Ellen relayed what she had seen. This was not the time for "selfish sorrow," she said, but the time to follow the light that God was giving through visions. Morse accepted what he heard, shed his sadness, and "became a strong minister in the developing church."[2] One more soldier in the fight against the fanatics boosted Ellen's spirits as she went on to grapple with a new accusation leveled against her.

ENDNOTES

1. The name comes from the belief that Jesus had come "spiritually" in 1844 and that now people were in "spiritual" heaven.
2. Arthur White, *Ellen G. White,* 1:86.

Chapter 17

Mesmerism

Ellen finally arrived in New Hampshire—without help from Creeper Turner. There, she recalled later, she had to deal with "spiritual magnetism of a similar character with mesmerism." Mesmerism was a unique brand of medical quackery developed by the Frenchman Franz Anton Mesmer (hence "mesmerism"). Treatments involved a combination of hypnotism and such cutting-edge procedures as sitting with your feet in a fountain of "magnetized" water while holding cables connected to "magnetized" trees.

Some of Mesmer's patients in Paris reacted with prolonged sleeping, convulsing, and dancing. There are people who still use this kind of crazy treatment with devices called "ionic foot cleansing." They swear it works as they put electrical pulses through their feet in a basin of water—turning the water a variety of colors based on the impurities in their body. I'm not lying to you. Google it.

Ellen didn't have to deal with the foot cleansers but with the idea of hypnosis. "It was our first experience of this kind," she wrote. But it wouldn't be her last. In the city of Claremont, Ellen encountered a group of people professing to hold on to the faith they had inherited from William Miller. Initially this was happy news—until she met their leaders, Elders Bennett and Bellings.

Sounds like a law firm. "Have you been injured in a terrible accident? Call Bennett and Bellings, attorneys at law . . ."

Actually, don't call them.

These two told Ellen that they "were above the possibility of sin." They wore lovely finery and smelled fresh and clean. This would have been impressive had not a "little boy about eight years old entered, literally clad in dirty rags."

"We were surprised to find that this little specimen of neglect was the son of Elder Bennett," wrote Ellen.

The mother looked ashamed at the state of her little specimen of neglect, while dear old Dad was completely unconcerned and continued bragging to Ellen about how spiritual he was—not even glancing at his poor little one. Bennett spent his life in prayer and meditation, casting off all earthly responsibility. As he continued to wax eloquent about his spiritual accomplishments, Ellen's eyes narrowed.

"His sanctification had suddenly lost its charm in my eyes."

She went on to observe that although Bennett claimed that acquiring "true holiness carried the mind above all earthly thoughts," he sure enjoyed sitting down at the table and eating "temporal food." Making the whole situation worse, Bennett trashed talked his wife—sharing with the young prophet that the missus "allowed worldly things to draw her mind from religious subjects."

What a class act.

Now pause for just a moment and ask yourself what you would say to this man, if you were a prophet. Would you be gentle? Would you shrug your shoulders and say, "Well, it's not my place to judge"? Or would you call Child Protective Services and maybe dropkick Dad in the chest?

If sometimes Ellen's writings seem harsh when you read them, just remember the situations she was often addressing. She often faced individuals, such as Elder Bennett, who practiced unbelievable cruelty to marginalized women and children—and did so in the name of Jesus. Cut her some slack and let her prophetic words seek and destroy the delusions held on to by professed followers of God.

While Ellen didn't dropkick Bennett in the chest, she did make it known that his holiness failed to impress her. A few days later, she received a vision letting her know that Jesus didn't look favorably on Bennett's absurd spirituality. Ellen said she saw that many, like Bennett, lived their lives in direct opposition to what they claimed to be and believe. The vision informed her that these people practiced "the worst sins" and deceived God's people.

This vision fueled Ellen's righteous anger toward sin and convinced her that she was needed more than ever—even if she had to encounter incredibly sad situations.

Creeper Turner gets called out

One night not too long after this, the Holy Spirit impressed Ellen that fanaticism had broken out in her hometown of Portland. When she made her way back, everything there was saturated in the typical fanatical ideas about Jesus' "spiritual" return and being "perfect" despite obnoxious evidence to the contrary. When Ellen attended her first meeting back home, during prayer, her mind's eye blazed with a brand-new vision starring Creeper Turner—who was attending the meeting.

This time, in a unique twist, Ellen narrated what she saw in vision while she was seeing it. What a deliciously awkward moment this created as Ellen informed the group that Creeper Turner's work "led to corruption, instead of purity and holiness." Needless to say, this was not a vision that led to a lot of smiles for Creeper.

"She's under the wrong influence!" he cried out, and disregarded her words.

It was difficult for those present to believe him, however, because Ellen also mentioned some specific sins Turner was committing that his wife confirmed to Ellen in a later conversation. Oh snap! Ellen's parents became so disgusted as the details emerged that they shut down their house in Portland for a while and moved to Poland, Maine, to live with their other daughters.

Creeper's brand of fanaticism, in addition to all kinds of rampant sinfulness, promoted meetings full of wild excitement and noise. The fanaticism became so rooted in Portland that little could be done but walk away for a season. Just like Jesus told His disciples—sometimes you have to shake the dust off your sandals and leave (Matthew 10:14).

Especially heartbreaking, as Ellen's family moved away, was Creeper's success in turning some of Ellen's friends—and even some relatives—against her. He was so upset at being called out that he tried to hurt Ellen in any way he could—going so far as to lie about her character and spread gossip about her all over the community.

But Ellen still had enough spiritual fire to fight against him.

Don't mess with the messenger

Not too long after her first battle with Turner, they met again at another meeting. This time Ellen's nemesis declared that he could "mesmerize" her, thus preventing her from either seeing visions or relating them to anyone. The Creeper's powers were formidable, but Ellen's powers came from God, and nothing could stop her.

"I arose in the congregation," remembered Ellen. "My visions came up fresh before me, and I commenced relating them." At this the Creeper began to work his magic—using words and gestures to break Ellen's concentration. She could feel it.

"I felt a human influence being exerted against me," she recalled. "I then turned to this man and related what the Lord had shown me in Portland." The epic battle between magician and prophet took place at a prayer meeting—one using mesmerism, and the other infused with the Spirit of God.

They were locked in mortal, spiritual combat. Ellen, unflinchingly, focused directly on her opponent and raising her hands to heaven, cried out, "Another angel, Father! Another angel!" Instantly a surge of power blasted away Creeper's influence, and Ellen felt completely shielded by the Spirit.

Untouchable now, Ellen finished eviscerating Turner's lies with her straight testimony. Those in attendance felt comforted and openly rejoiced in the Lord. Some turned to the defeated mesmerizer and asked him why he hadn't stopped her from relating the vision.

"Uh, well, because some of you wanted her to talk," he lied unconvincingly.

Undaunted, and no doubt encouraged by her victory, Ellen felt impressed by the Spirit to make her way to Paris, Maine, to deal with a man named Elder Stevens.

Death of a deceiver

Elder Stevens had called a gathering in Paris, Maine, and all believers were encouraged to attend. Ellen and her escorts arrived the next morning at the appointed time, but when Elder Stevens entered and saw them, he seemed troubled. The meeting opened with prayer as it usually did, and as Ellen "tried to pray" she sensed the powerful presence of the Spirit and was "taken off in vision."

Elder Stevens was outraged.

He said something like, "I will not listen to anything but the Bible!" to the group trying to pray. But Ellen, deep in the rhythms of the Spirit, saw the ideas that Stevens held—and how they directly contradicted the clear teaching of God's Word. Not only that, but Stevens was spreading his lies to honest, sincere people who were stumbling and falling over his teachings.

What, exactly, was Elder Stevens teaching?

That it was a sin to work.

Really, you can't make this stuff up! Stevens said that if you did any kind of work, you were sinning. Take two minutes and imagine what kind of nonsense this world would descend into if nobody worked.

You wouldn't be enjoying this book, because I wouldn't have written it.

You couldn't read, anyway, because you wouldn't have bothered to learn.

Not that anyone would have gone about teaching you in the first place.

No learning, no medical advances, no cooking, no exercise, no . . . well, no nothing! For crying out loud, Stevens, at least set it up so *other* people have to work and you can live a lazy life based on their slave labor—that's Cult Creation 101. Even when the world was perfect in the Garden of Eden, God placed humanity inside it to "work it" (Genesis 2:15).

What kind of dumb world doesn't do any work? Ellen didn't want to find out. Someone had to stop the powerful influence of this elder whose ideas, ironically, seemed to be "working." Ellen said, "The Lord gave me a reproof for him"—and she wasn't afraid to use it.

If Stevens had been troubled before, he was in for it now. With the same intensity she had shown in dealing with Creeper, Ellen turned her message on Stevens in front of the group. She systematically dismantled his unscriptural stupidity. Reeling from her rebuke, Stevens rejected everything she said and refused to change—no matter how much people pleaded with him.

The results were tragic.

Elder Stevens followed his "impressions" and went on long, weary journeys. He would walk great distances, and when people rejected his no-work ethic (sometimes abusively), he claimed he was "suffering for Christ." He eventually abandoned all reason and judgment—going so far as to say Ellen's visions were from Satan. Later, Ellen penned the sad conclusion of Stevens's story: "His friends at length were obliged to confine him, where he made a rope of some of his bed clothing with which he hung himself."

House of friends

Eventually, Ellen came to the town of Roxbury, Massachusetts, where a good-sized group of believers assembled in a private home. In this place Ellen discovered a very rare, and much appreciated, warm welcome. As she spoke about her initial vision, a woman who had previously opposed Ellen stood and interrupted her.

Grabbing Ellen's hand, she basically said, "I used to say the devil had sent you, but I can doubt no longer. You are a child of God, and He has brought you here." I can imagine Ellen sighing with relief as she looked into the woman's smiling face—and into all the loving faces present in the meeting. Every so often, young Ellen's constant struggle against wild personalities would find moments of acceptance and peace. As tough as she was learning to be, she was still a teenager and needed moments of affirmation—as we all do.

These moments didn't last long enough, however. And even though everyone, including the leader of the group at Roxbury, had been so happy with Ellen, an old enemy began unsettling them. You guessed it—Creeper Turner. His view that Jesus had returned "spiritually" infiltrated the hearts of many people, and Ellen, again, found herself fighting battles against fanaticism.

A kind man, named Otis Nichols, invited Ellen and her friends to stay with his family in their home. Ellen and her sister Sarah would stay there again in September 1845 for eight months—or until April 1846. The Nicholses' home became her base of operations in the war against Turner.

"We had to be on our guard," said Ellen. She had to immerse herself in Scripture and prayer and boldly preach that Jesus would return someday—literally and personally. Staying in a house of friends helped Ellen through the bad days when people met her messages with icy stares and unkind words. Her friends prayed for her and encouraged her until she felt "the light of heaven" cheering her on. There was no end to the Nicholses' kindness, and they walked alongside her whenever they could.

Chapter 18

Sargent and Robbins

In Boston and the surrounding vicinity, a "company of fanatical persons" began embracing the lethal lie, taught by Stevens, that work was a sin. Their main message asked people to sell everything they had and give it to the poor. They claimed they were living in the biblical "jubilee"—an Old Testament idea that involved freeing everyone from debt and giving farm land a rest (see Leviticus 25). However, they had taken this beautiful concept and twisted it to support their own laziness.

Two men, Sargent and Robbins, told everyone to dump their hard-earned money into the hands of the poor without any expectation of them working for it. Moreover, they denounced Ellen as "of the devil"—mostly because she had been showing how ridiculous their ideas were. If anyone did not believe as they did, "they were severe" upon them.

Charming people, don't you think?

They made a visit to the Nicholses' house to have a little chat and prayer time—no doubt wanting to convert the family to their wacky, no-working world. Otis welcomed them, despite their destructive ideas, and even expressed interest in discussing matters of theology. However, when they learned that Ellen made her residence at the Nicholses' home, Sargent and Robbins made some nervous excuses and left straightaway, saying something like: "Her visions are from Satan, and I feel blessed every time I say it."

"We judge the visions by their fruits," replied Otis, unfazed by the rather strange comment. "Her visions seem in accordance with the Bible—and all who believe them are led to a more holy and devoted life." He went on to affirm the experience the Millerites had gone through and their hope of a literal Second Coming—and he praised Ellen's Christian character. "The only reason people like Turner turn against her is because she sees right through their hypocrisy," he declared.

Bazinga!

At the conclusion of Otis's epic burn on his hastily departing guests, he informed them that Ellen wanted to attend one of their meetings in Boston and asked whether they had any objections to her coming.

"None at all," said Sargent. "Let her come."

Arrangements were made for Nichols to bring Ellen and her sister Sarah to Boston the next weekend, where they would meet with the believers there. But before they left for Boston, the Spirit gave Ellen's eyes supernatural sight. God told her that they needed to go to Randolph instead—thirteen miles south of Boston. The vision instructed Ellen to meet the believers at this new location and deliver her message. Those there who honestly desired to know the truth would be convinced.

So the following morning, instead of making their way to Boston, Ellen and her party veered south to Randolph, where Sargent and Robbins were conducting the meeting. These two liars discovered that changing the location of a meeting at the last minute, even before Google Maps had been invented, was a rather poor plan for deceiving a prophet.

The moment must have been gratifying. To stand outside the meeting place, hearing the people who had tried so hard to trick you carrying on with their nonsense—completely oblivious that in a few seconds you would walk in and shatter their sad deceptions. Making the entrance more striking was the fact that it was held in a large room in a home belonging to the Thayer family.

"As we entered," Ellen wrote, "Robbins and Sargent looked at each other in surprise and began to groan." Surprise! The stunning arrival of the young prophet caused Sargent to close the morning service early and have a "short intermission." Who would have thought that Ellen could cancel church services simply by attending?

During the "intermission" critics muttered amongst themselves, and the ridiculous Robbins, speaking to Ellen's sister, said something like, "Ellen cannot have a vision in my presence!" However, when the meeting resumed at one o'clock, with several believers earnestly praying, Ellen did indeed have another vision—with dazzling manifestations of power. The vision began, and Ellen started speaking in an unusually shrill voice—crystal clear—that could be understood by everyone in the room.

Sargent and Robbins were extremely annoyed. "It's the devil!" they cried out while she spoke. Well, THAT'S annoying. They did everything they could think of to influence everyone against her. They tried singing as loud as they could to drown Ellen out. Next they tried alternating between talking and reading the Bible at top volume so Ellen's words wouldn't be heard. They did this until their hands trembled with exhaustion and they could read no more.

But you can't out preach a prophet.

Many in the meeting, even their own friends, told them to put a sock in it, so they could hear what Ellen was trying to say. "But," protested Robbins, "you are worshiping a golden calf!" The listeners—including Mr. Thayer, the owner of the house—ignored this and pressed in to receive the message Ellen had for them.

Thayer was not convinced Ellen's incredible gift was of the devil and wanted to test it somehow. Somewhere he had heard the powers of evil could be stopped by opening a Bible and placing it on the person under demonic influence. Quickly, he grabbed the large family Bible on a table nearby. Ellen was leaning against the wall in the corner of the room, and Thayer opened the massive Bible and laid it on her chest.

Something happened, but not what the haters had expected.

As soon as the Bible touched her, Ellen stood to her feet and made her way to the middle of the room. She held the great family Bible—probably weighing nearly twenty pounds—in one hand, as high as possible. Her eyes gazed upward, and she announced in a serious tone, "The inspired testimony of God." Then, she spoke for a very long time—all the while holding the heavy Bible aloft in one hand and turning to certain passages with the other, reciting them perfectly.

Those present stood up, peered over the cover of the family Bible to check the accuracy of her readings—because the whole time her eyes were looking upward and not at the pages. Yet she was accurately quoting the texts. What were the passages she was citing? They ranged from texts about judgments against the wicked to instructions for those doing their best to follow Jesus. As she spoke, her enemies became silent, troubled, and shut their eyes—like children waiting to receive a tetanus shot, a tetanus shot of truth! (Sorry, couldn't resist that alliteration—every preacher's weakness.)

Ellen recalled that in this vision she saw the "errors of these wicked men [Sargent and Robbins] and others united with them." She also saw that they would not succeed, even though they would cause some to lose their faith before the truth finally broke loose and brought them down. The men perpetrating these crazy ideas were not honest, and Ellen saw that in the future they would only drift further and further away from the light—eventually leaving them in total darkness. And, in the end, everyone would see them for what they were. Before the vision came to a close, Ellen was given a "chain" of Scriptures to combat their dangerous deceptions.

When she felt released from her vision, she noticed candles burning. Ellen inquired as to the time and realized she had been in vision for "nearly four hours"— unconscious of her surroundings the entire time and holding that big, old family Bible longer than the strongest man in the room could have ever held it.[1]

A few weeks later, Ellen returned to Randolph to check on this group of believers before whom she had received this vision. The key members of the group continued to marginalize her, mock her visions, and reject the light she gave to them. Her reply was basically, "The curse of God will follow your course." Her words found swift fulfillment.

One by one, the leaders of this little group of fanatics were led to openly confess "some of the most shameful acts of their lives," which busted up the meetings in

Randolph. Sickened by the true colors of these people, good, honest people abandoned their group and came into harmony with the truth. Only twenty people remained with Robbins and Sargent as they took their traveling "no-work" circus back to Boston—cursing Ellen all the way.

What eventually happened is recorded by Ellen's pen, "They continued together in this state of feeling some time, a year or more, when they made a wreck of all their faith in the doctrines taught in the Bible and then broke up and scattered." Even in the midst of devious enemies—people who curse you, lie about you, and seek your destruction—God has a way of vindicating His followers who walk in the light, even when they are surrounded by the dark.

ENDNOTE

1. Eighteen to twenty pounds may not seem like much, but go get *any* book and try to hold it as high as you can for ten minutes—and see how you do.

Chapter 19

The End of Adolescence

Believe me when I tell you the stories I have shared barely scratch the surface of all Ellen went through as a teenager. Plenty of stories involving amazing victories, devastating defeats, and nefarious characters seeking her downfall exist in other places—for example, a popular villain named Israel Damman, who operated between 1845 and 1875.

A lone court document that managed to survive the passing of time describes Damman as "a vagrant and idle person, . . . going about . . . town . . . begging: . . . a common railer, or brawler, neglecting his calling, or employment, misspending his earnings, and . . . not provid[ing] for the support of himself [or] his family."[1]

What a beautiful soul. Want to know more about this archenemy who attacked Ellen for thirty years? Or about the friends who helped her through bouts of illness? Or a bunch of other things about her life they never tell you when you are a kid?

Check the list of further recommended reading at the back of this book—more stories await you.

For now, know that Ellen wrestled with all the self-conscious awkwardness we all do as teenagers—except she had to be a prophet at the same time. Her teenage years brought her in contact with some pretty intensely ugly things. She watched families fall apart and children being neglected, and she found herself persecuted whenever she tried to speak out against these things.

At seventeen years old, Ellen received rejection from people professing to follow Jesus. Grown men mocked her, lied about her, cursed her, and said she was possessed by the devil—all while she battled poor health and tried to be the messenger God called her to be.

It's often cathartic to read about people going through the same pain you are experiencing—or worse. To know you are not alone in your suffering. To know you aren't the only one meeting resistance as you try to do what you believe is right. To know you aren't the only one to be rejected by "Christians" while trying to follow Jesus.

Ellen knew what it was like to feel the way you feel in those dark moments. Her writings are full of raw honesty. Maybe that's why we so easily dismiss them as "angry" or "crabby." Very few people are as real in their struggles as she was. We like it when people pander to us, minimizing the ugly things that we all wrestle with—Ellen doesn't do that. She can't. Her role is to speak the things that need to be heard even if people don't want to hear them—even if they call her the devil because of it.

I respect Ellen for doing what she knew to be right in the face of extreme opposition. I respect her for dealing with being the underdog, for standing up to abusive fathers, cruel husbands—and worse—when she was only a teenage girl. She spoke what God put in her mind. She had her heart broken as she lost friends and family who didn't understand her or who chose to do things that led them to their own destruction.

When you feel rejected, cursed, and unloved, Ellen's writings can let you know you aren't alone. She went through circles of hell created by those who should have held her up in prayer and loving support—and yet, she made it with God's help.

You can too.

ENDNOTE

1. Quoted in James R. Nix, "Another Look at Israel Damman," http://www.whiteestate.org/issues/Israel_damman.html#_ftn17.

Section III: Ellen, Wife . . . and Mother (1846–1881)

Chapter 20

Ellen, Wife

Most little girls dream about their wedding day.

I don't know this from personal experience. I'm a boy. I dreamt of driving the Batmobile and punching bad guys in the face, flying and punching bad guys in the face, or carrying out secret missions for the United States government, which included punching bad guys in the face.

I do have three little girls, however, and already one of them is dazzled by anything bridal. On a recent picnic at the park, a wedding party—including a bride with the usual trimmings—walked by. Instantly, my daughter was enthralled, waved at the lovely wife-to-be in her white dress, and even tried to get in the picture to give her a hug.

We stopped her.

Weddings speak to the inner princess in many girls. They hoard magazines with fashion ideas, stationery concepts, and all kinds of frilly things that terrify most grown men—and anyone with a budget. The average American wedding costs between $10,000 and $20,000—traditionally paid for by the father of the bride.

Which is why I have insisted that, along with her dreams of marriage, my daughter also dreams of a well-paying job.

Even as we get older, most people hold out hope for a "significant other" to journey through life with. Especially in our teens, we hope for the chance to experience marriage before Jesus comes. In the traditional Christian worldview, marriage is where we should have our first experiences with sexual intercourse, having children, and building a home. We don't want to miss out on those things—particularly the sex, if we are being honest.

Ellen didn't have the typical view of weddings you might expect—and she certainly didn't have any bridal magazines. Matter of fact, Ellen, and a lot of the people she knew, thought weddings were a dumb thing to do. No, she didn't despise love and affection. And no, it wasn't because she couldn't find a boyfriend that she disdained holy matrimony.

Those who had been hanging out with William Miller still believed Jesus was on His way very soon—even if He hadn't shown up when they expected Him to. If you live in a community of folk who are convinced that Jesus, and heaven, and the new earth are all going to happen in a few years—what kind of statement are you making by talking about marriage? What are you suggesting by actually going through with the vows?

Exactly. *"We have plenty of time to chill on earth, enjoy romance, have children, and set up homes, because Jesus is decades away from showing up."* For people who had sold all they had, endured ridicule, and were barely clinging to hope in Jesus' coming—a prophet getting hitched was about as holy as a haunted hayride.

White wedding

After working together throughout 1845, it became apparent to James White and Ellen Harmon that they could enhance each other's writing and speaking ministries if they became husband and wife. James thought that she could "be of great help to me" and that with all her responsibilities, Ellen needed a "lawful protector."

Romantic stuff, right?

They both prayed and felt that God was leading them to take the marital plunge—a good thing for any couple to do, really. Several of their associates, however, saw their decision to wed as nothing less than a "denial of the faith." Like Romeo and Juliet, James and Ellen did not find support for their relationship. Thankfully, unlike the young Shakespearian lovers, James and Ellen did not drink poison and commit suicide.

Oops—spoiler alert!

However, as reality sunk in for friends and family, they realized that this arrangement needed to happen. Ellen was an eighteen-year-old who weighed eighty pounds and battled "consumption"—another term for tuberculosis (that gross stuff we talked about earlier). She fainted at random and would "remain breathless for minutes."

James, believing in her role as a prophet, made the point that, as the situation presently was, she needed multiple attendants to help her. Her "aged father" didn't possess the strength to help her, nor did her "feeble brother." That sounds like smack talk—after all, Ellen's dad was only sixty years old. But life spans were shorter then, and Ellen's bro suffered from illness too.

Compounding the challenges she faced were the potential accusations that could fly if James and Ellen traveled alone all the time. Remember, this is the nineteenth century we're talking about here—handholding could be considered disgraceful in the right setting. An unmarried man and a woman traveling across the country, alone, would be downright scandalous—and damage Ellen's street cred as a prophet.

Marriage seemed a practical solution, so the date was set for August 30, 1846. Even though their engagement may seem lacking in the "warm fuzzies" department, we know that love did blossom in their home. A letter from James to his friend, Brother Collins, a few days before the wedding suggests he was excited: "I have a chance to get to Fairhaven tonight by sailboat, and shall take the cars [the train] tomorrow morning for Boston, and the express train of cars for Portland at four-thirty. Shall be in Portland tomorrow night at six o'clock. . . . Sister Ellen says that the way is made plain. We are published; we shall be married perhaps Monday."

James sailed and took a train to get to his Ellen in time for the wedding. Even though they weren't registered at Target or Bed, Bath, and Beyond—they did get an announcement in the paper.

Ah, yes—when Sunday rolled around there was love in the courtroom.

What? You expected a prophet to get married in a church? Flower bouquet? Awkward wedding toasts with sparkly (nonalcoholic) drinks?

Nope. Sorry to disappoint, wedding fans, but James and Ellen's nuptials involved no groomsmen, bridesmaids, tuxedos, or rice throwing. And as for a shimmering white dress for Ellen? Sadly, the only white thing present was her new last name.

Justice of the Peace Charles Harding pronounced eighteen-year-old Ellen and twenty-five-year-old James a newlywed couple and handed the happy pair their marriage certificate—just a small wisp of paper with a tiny bit of writing and Charles's signature. But if we are real, weddings aren't about rings, flowers, or fancy clothes (fun as they may be). Weddings are about two people committing to living a life of love, together, in the presence of God. In this, Ellen and James succeeded—in some ways maybe more so than those who dump tens of thousands of dollars into ceremonies that really have no bearing on whether or not a couple will stay together.

Their simple service before a justice of the peace produced a marriage that lasted thirty-five years, fought through difficulties, and continually dedicated itself to the cause of God. I don't care how good your wedding cake is or how many tiers it has—it takes something deeper than gourmet sweets to hold on to love when life is unlovely.

And life for the newlywed Whites proved to be unlovely.

"We entered upon this work penniless," wrote James, "with few friends, and broken in health." James, who had been the model of health, was also the poster child for overworking and had worn himself down into a "dyspeptic" state—another way of saying chronically crabby.

"In this condition," he continued, "without means, with very few who sympathized with us in our views, without a paper, and without books, we entered upon our work." They had no church or tent to meet in—sticking mostly to private homes—and it "was seldom that any came into our meetings, excepting Adventists, unless they were attracted by curiosity to hear a woman speak."

Starting a family . . . and a movement

Their "work" involved starting both a family and a movement. During their thirty-five-year marriage, James and Ellen would put everything into spreading fresh truths from God's Word to believers all over the world. As they studied deeply into their experience with William Miller and the visions given to Ellen, biblical truths began to surface. Truths such as the following:

- The importance of the seventh-day Sabbath
- Jesus' ministry in the heavenly sanctuary—fulfilling the misunderstood prophecy of Daniel 8 that Miller thought pointed to Jesus' return in 1844
- The understanding that when you die you don't go directly to hell or heaven, but await new life at the resurrection when Jesus comes
- The fact that hell destroys the wicked instead of burning them in an eternal BBQ
- Various prophecies pointing to world events indicating that humanity is living in the "time of the end"
- An explanation of Ellen's unique gifts and how they were to be used in relation to the Bible
- The need for church organization and a system of handling donations so the church could send missionaries everywhere from Missouri to Mozambique
- The need to create magazines, books, and publishing houses to scatter printed materials "like the leaves of autumn"

All of these glorious truths can be explored in my other books: *What We Believe for Teens, Prophecies of Daniel for Teens,* and *Prophecies of Revelation for Teens.*

See how smoothly I slipped that in there?

In the following pages it will be impossible to ignore the fledgling Seventh-day Adventist movement growing up around the White family. A host of characters, including Ellen's own family, have their own amazing stories drift in and out of Sister White's life. Yet, we will do our best to focus on Ellen more than everyone and everything else—and there is a lot to see.

Thirty-five years' worth—and, sadly, we can't see it all.

My fingers would fall off typing it all, but what I have chosen to show you I think you'll find intriguing. So, let's take a peek inside the home of the newly minted Mrs. White.

Chapter 21

White House

Their first home was in Gorham, Maine—with Ellen's parents.

Yeah, I know—no honeymoon in Cancun, Europe, or even Motel 6. The last place newlyweds want to be is with their parents or in-laws. Again, not the typical "dream" wedding experience. And think of the parents—how much faith would they have to have to allow this? What would you say if your daughter claimed to have visions from the Lord, married someone with no money, and wanted to live in your house?

Not a great plan on paper, but the Harmons knew Ellen's experience was from God and did what they could to support the penniless pair. It's also important to note that one cannot remain still when trying to start a spiritual movement. James and Ellen had a beastly travel schedule that kicked in only a couple months after they married.

In November, they traveled to Topsham, Maine, to the home of "Brother Curtis." A man named Joseph Bates, who would bring the idea of the seventh-day Sabbath to the forefront and play a pivotal role in launching the church, attended the meeting at Brother Curtis's house. While in this meeting, Ellen White had her first vision as a married woman.

Of outer space.

She saw planets and asteroid belts and moons and many other heavenly bodies. As she described what she saw while in vision, Bates—a sea captain and someone interested in the stars—began to call out the technical names for what she was seeing. When the vision was done, Bates grilled her about her studies in astronomy. When he saw she had no previous experience in the subject, he was duly impressed and became a friend of the new couple.

As their friendship grew, Joseph Bates convinced James and Ellen of the importance of the Sabbath, and the Whites began to teach and defend it in the fall of 1846.

When they returned to Ellen's parents' house, she became ill. She had been warned in a vision she would. Her new husband watched as his wife agonized for three weeks—so much so that she asked people to stop praying, because she thought it was only prolonging her pain. "Every breath came with a groan." Poor James watched as Ellen's health diminished.

Was that it? One trip together? One vision, and it was over?

Ellen's old friend Otis Nichols sent his son Henry to join those praying for Ellen and give some comfort to the family. Ellen later described the effect of Henry's presence: "Brother Henry commenced praying, and seemed much burdened, and with the power of God resting upon him, rose from his knees, came across the room, and laid his hands upon my head, saying, 'Sister Ellen, Jesus Christ maketh thee whole,' and fell back prostrated by the power of God."

Wow! That doesn't happen when I pray for people. Ellen believed that Henry's prayer was of God—and the pain vanished. She felt at peace and ready for her next prophetic assignment. James had his bride back, and soon they took off for Boston by boat.

No, it wasn't a romantic cruise. The boat they took ran into troublesome weather and took a severe beating. It rocked back and forth violently; water dashed in through the windows; the chandelier crashed to the floor; and the tables set for breakfast lost their dishes with crash. Panic struck many of the people on board.

"We're all going to die!" is never a helpful thought or a comforting thing to say out loud, but Ellen found herself surrounded by people crying out to God for mercy, calling on the virgin Mary for help, and vowing to the Lord that they would devote their lives to His service if He would only let them escape this ship of terror.

Good times.

One lady, trying to sleep in the bed above Ellen in the ladies' quarters, was ejected from her top bunk onto the floor. Another looked at Ellen, noticed her calm expression, and asked, "Are you not terrified? I suppose it is a fact that we may never reach land." While it was true that death loomed near, Ellen had peace.

"Christ is my refuge," she basically replied, "and if my work is done, I might as well lie at the bottom of the ocean as anywhere else." Man, Ellen seems a little morbid— nice "bedside" manner! But I don't think her reply was meant to be dark or indifferent. I think that even at her young age Ellen had wrestled so much with criticism, illness, and a variety of other challenges, she had learned—through painful experience—that God, not she, was in control.

She also followed up her statement with, "But if my work [is] not done, all the waters of the ocean could not drown me." Now, there's the motivational phrase we're after. If God wanted her to continue her work, she would—and she did. God led the ship to shore, and Ellen lived to prophesy another day.

James and Ellen traveled throughout Boston, despite the boat's best attempt to drown them, and when they finally returned to the Harmons' home—seven weeks after they had left—they had a surprise with them.

Chapter 22

Expecting

Well, that certainly didn't take long.

Having been married less than half a year, Ellen was now expecting her first child. It would seem that, despite the unusual and practical nature of their courtship, a little romance made its way into the Whites' wedding after all. James felt pleased, and Ellen found herself in the best health she had had in the past six years.

That isn't to say all was well. Ellen's parents didn't yet appreciate the idea of the Sabbath, and this created a little tension amongst the family. James wrote a letter to his buddies, the Howlands, saying, "Here is not one soul that we can meet with or unite in serving the Lord." Ouch. At one point James went so far as to complain, "Oh, I am sick of our ungodly, hypocritical, dishonest, cheating neighbors. . . . What a deathly degrading thought, to think of spending a life in this horribly unchristian world and then lay down in the dust. But it won't be so. No! No! No!"[1]

Awesome.

I don't know that all this grumbling was directed at his in-laws, but no matter who was harassing James, it's refreshing to think that leaders sometimes get annoyed by people as much as we all do. Thankfully for the Whites, by April they were staying with the Howlands in their "well-constructed" home in Topsham, Maine.

Here, Ellen had a vision about the Sabbath, confirming its importance for God's people before Jesus returns. Bates assisted the Whites in creating a pamphlet on the topic and sending it out to those believing in the soon coming of Jesus. And while all this was going on, Ellen made the curious decision to get baptized.

Baptizing your wife the prophet

Wait, wasn't Ellen already baptized? Well, yes. But sometimes, when we have a deeper understanding of Jesus and His truth, and when we need to make a fresh commitment—being rebaptized is a very meaningful way to express our fresh experience. Ellen wanted to make a new commitment, and James, being a minster in a previous denomination, had the privilege of officiating in the ancient ritual that Jesus Himself participated in.

James wrote, "As I raised her [Ellen] up out of the water, immediately she was in vision."

James's statement is the only record of this experience, so it is hard to know exactly what she saw in this vision, what date she was baptized, or much else about this experience.

However, we do know that on April 21, 1847, Ellen wrote a letter to a man named Eli Curtis who had written articles for a Millerite periodical called *Day-Dawn*. In her letter, she outlined in tremendous detail what she believed the Bible taught about what will happen before Jesus comes—including her thoughts on two resurrections, the millennium, the significance of 1844, and many other things.

At the age of nineteen, Ellen already possessed a stunning grasp of eschatology (the study of last-day events). Also in April, James published his first work, *A Word to the Little Flock*. This booklet encouraged those who were looking for Jesus' coming, affirmed the Bible as more important than prophetic visions (unlike the position taken by Mormonism), and offered a few other encouraging items.

While *A Word to the Little Flock* proved helpful, it didn't become a *New York Times* bestseller. With very little money and the expense of trying to get a writing career off the ground, the Whites welcomed their first baby.

Baby on board

On August 26, 1847, Henry arrived.

Mama and baby were healthy, but family finances weren't—never a great element to introduce into a young family trying to launch their careers and a religious movement. Having friends such as the Howlands helped tremendously. They opened part of their home to the Whites and even loaned them furniture. Ellen was frank in her description of their life at this point: "We were poor, and saw close times."

Most new couples are poor, especially if they are still in school. Jokes abound about eating a steady diet of ramen noodles, rummaging through the trash for sustenance, and wearing clothes not quite old enough to be retro and not new enough to be socially acceptable—like skinny jeans, which should never be worn at all by anybody at any time, period.

Period.

My personal experience with babies is that they are beautiful, needy, and expensive. In other words—work. And James knew it. Straightaway, the budding author did what he had to do in order to generate income, namely hauling heavy stones away from railroad construction sites. Carrying huge rocks is a curse for anybody, and making it worse was that James had to get tough in order to extract his paycheck from the rock boss. From rock hauling, James worked a second job chopping wood in a nearby forest from early morning to late at night—earning an amazing fifty cents a day.

That's some serious man points.

James's sides ached at night, making it difficult to sleep, but he did what he had to do to provide for his wife and son. Meanwhile, Ellen worked hard at managing their meager monies. She could afford a pint of milk per day for her and Henry—though eventually she had to cut that out in order to afford a "bit of cloth for a simple garment for the baby." As this hand-to-mouth existence went on, Ellen finally despaired. "Have we come to this?" she asked. "Has the Lord left us?"

She broke down and wept for hours until she fainted.

Mommying is a difficult job under any circumstances—even when you have diapers, clothes, bottles, and plenty of milk to go around. Ellen had a mother's heart—a fierce thing full of love willing to die at a moment's notice to protect a child. But all Ellen's love felt powerless in the face of abject poverty. The ratio of love to her ability to provide ripped her apart, and she broke. Even prophets have breaking points.

For six months James and Ellen and their discouraging situation remained unchanged.

James, working hard and watching his little family hurt, said he "suffered more in mind and body than he could show with pen and paper." Good fathers who want to provide for their families but can't, hurt. No one likes feeling powerless when life gets hard.

Where *was* God here? Did He really call a young family into ministry and then just leave them when they had a little baby? What kind of God does that to His prophets? Ellen would find out in a vision that would lead her to make the most difficult decision of her life.

ENDNOTE
_____

1. James White, letter to S. Howland, March 14, 1847.

Chapter 23

Left Behind

In order to perform her prophetic role, Ellen would have to be tough—and understanding. If God simply eliminated all pain and suffering from the prophet's life and kept her in a plastic bubble, how on earth would she have any credibility speaking to the lives of people who were hurting? Moreover, she was still young in her profession, and she would face her worst moments of opposition as an adult from people in her own church. She needed to know how to be strong in the fires of suffering.

Just as Navy SEALS go through "hell week" in their training, prophets seem to have a testing period to prepare them for the challenges they will face. I mean, even John the Baptist wandered around the desert for decades, wearing a loincloth and eating bugs, before arriving in town to confront the hypocritical, and lethal, religious leaders.

Ellen was shown these things in vision (except the part about the Navy SEALS). She was also shown that God had been "stirring up our nest, lest we should settle down at ease." In other words, Ellen's domestic endeavors had the potential to eliminate her desire to fulfill the greater mission God had called her to.

There is no doubt that God loves children—the first commandment He ever gave humanity was to make babies (Genesis 1:28)—and when adults tried to shoo them away, Jesus welcomed children to His side (Matthew 19:13–15). The challenge was that God loves *all* children—not just Ellen's little Henry. Ellen's message of truth needed to go to all families, not stay locked within her own.

Henry soon became sick and "lapsed into unconsciousness." The Whites took it as a sign that if they used Henry as an excuse not to fulfill their mission, they might lose him. They prayed for healing and vowed that they would return to traveling if Henry should recover. From the moment of their promise, Henry began to recover.

Soon after Henry was well again, they received an invitation to travel to visit people keeping the Sabbath in Connecticut. They made the journey with seven-month-old Henry in their arms, depending on a few donations from friends. However, after seven more months of traveling, speaking, and relating visions (one vision let the Adventists know that Bible study came before Ellen's visions, and another told James to start his own magazine), it became obvious that the incessant travel wasn't healthy for Henry.

Ellen would have to leave Henry behind.

Mercifully, their friends, the Howlands, opened their wonderful home to the little guy and agreed to raise him until James and Ellen were in a better spot—which would turn out to be five years later. The Howlands cared for Henry as their own, providing everything from food to clothing, except for a garment Ellen brought him each year.

At first blush, this story seems outrageous. What kind of mom leaves her kid behind? However, think of all the military moms and dads who, because of their commitment to keeping the entire nation safe, have to be gone for months at a time. Ellen had been drafted into the "Lord's army," and sacrifice characterized her calling. She knew that she didn't have the means to care for her child properly, so as a loving mother, she made the decision to entrust her child to people who could. The sacrifice was excruciating. "It was hard parting with my child," she wrote. "His sad little face, as I left, was before me night and day."

Over the next five years the Whites helped develop several important ideas—among them, that Ellen's visions did not take the place of Bible study, the need for publishing work, and the importance of the Sabbath. As they traveled together, ministering to God's people, they soon found themselves expecting another blessing, even as they continued to expect the soon return of Jesus.

"July 28, 1849, my second child, James Edson White, was born," wrote Ellen. The Whites still had very little money and fought discouragement that their publishing work wasn't taking off faster.

James lamented their situation in a letter, stating: "Ellen is well. She would write if she could, but has not time. She has some writing of her visions to do, and the babe is teething, and is troublesome." In May 1850, the Whites decided to visit Vermont and Maine. Ellen had to leave behind in New York her second son, nine months old, with a friend named Sister Bonfoey.

As James and Ellen made the forty-mile trek in a bumpy stagecoach to Vermont, Ellen would stop and rest in hotels while the horses were changed. Her mind would drift to her children—far away in two different states—and she cried. Despair led her to cry out regarding her whole mission, "It won't pay! So much labor to accomplish so little!"

Their work continued to be met by too many haters and not enough subscribers for the work. James exhausted himself to produce little income and little praise. Was this what Ellen had given up her babies for? Surely, it wasn't worth it! Thankfully, God spoke into Ellen's darkened heart and gave her hope.

God gave Ellen a vision—just for her. An angel told her, "You have given to the Lord two beautiful flowers, the fragrance of which is as sweet incense before Him, and is more precious in His sight than gold or silver, for it is a heart gift. . . . The path will brighten before you." In other words, God knew what she had given up for Him, and He would work it all out in the end.

As James and Ellen continued their efforts, their publishing work began taking off; support came in; organization began taking shape; and in 1853 mother and children could finally be together again.

Chapter 24

Reunited

When James and Ellen arrived at their home in Rochester, New York, on June 21, 1853, their hearts were full. The young mother wrote, "We . . . found our family as well as usual and what was best of all, enjoying the sweet presence and blessing of God." James was excited too.

The Howlands returned Henry to his parents as a "well-trained, praying boy." James wrote, "We are not able to express the gratitude we owe that dear family, not only for their care and labor for our child, but for their labors of love to us in times past when the friends of the Sabbath were very few and the cause feeble."

The year was 1853, and the White family would only continue to grow. A third son, William Clarence, was born in Rochester, New York, August 29, 1854. And six years later, on September 20, 1860—just a few years before the Seventh-day Adventist Church received its official name—John Herbert White arrived. We might like to idealize the White children as perfect angels—what else would you expect from the offspring of a prophet?

However, Ellen would need the insight, foresight, and hindsight that all mothers do—especially with four boys.

Toddler trouble

Willie nearly drowned in a mop bucket.

No seriously, he did.

He was twenty months old and messing around with a tub of mop water in the kitchen. He held a stick that served as his boat, and swirled the water around, pretending it was a lake. Jennie Fraser, the young nanny, stepped out to get some woodchips for the fire. On her way out she playfully asked little Willie what he was doing.

No reply.

When she returned with the woodchips she saw "one little foot sticking out of the dirty water." Frantically, she pulled the limp body out of the water and ran to Ellen screaming—probably the same response you would have if a prophet's kid drowned on your watch.

"Was the water hot or cold?" asked Ellen, taking her child into her arms.

"Cold."

Ellen told Jennie to send for the doctor and get ahold of her husband. Snatching up the scissors, Ellen cut the wet clothes free of her baby's body. Next she set him on the lawn and rolled him back and forth on the grass as "the sudsy water gurgled from his nose and mouth." After a few moments of rolling, she would lift him up to look for signs of life, before going back to rolling him.

"Take that dead baby out of that woman's hands!" demanded a neighbor to James, who had arrived on the scene. James was not amused.

"No, it is her child, and no one shall take it away from her," he told the tactless bystander.

After a tense twenty minutes, Willie's eyes flickered, and his lips puckered. Ordering Jennie to warm up some blankets, Ellen took her child inside. Wrapped in warmth and tucked into his crib, he had been saved by his quick-thinking mom.

No doubt, too, his mom had quite a letdown after the adrenaline in her body subsided.

Every parent knows that toddlers do whatever they can to kill themselves. Whether it's putting things in their mouth, touching sharp things, locking themselves out—or in—places they aren't supposed to be, or playing in mop buckets with dirty water—they need constant supervision. I bet they would be more effective at sniffing out bombs in airports than German shepherds. If it's dangerous, they will locate it.

Even if their mom is a prophet.

Chapter 25

Letters From Your Mother

I am sure you have had some spectacular lectures from your mom. No doubt you have heard a variety of stimulating discourses beginning with phrases like:

"When I was your age . . ."

"Why can't you be more like . . . ?"

"What were you thinking . . . ?"

Maybe you have received text messages alerting you to your parents' displeasure at some behavior of yours—knowing that as soon as school is over you will be treated to an in-depth discussion of the dismal future you are marching toward unless you make some drastic changes.

As the rambunctious White boys grew up, they would receive a number of letters from their mother, and their father, too, full of exhortations to behave themselves. It may be disturbing to think about it, but Ellen lectured her kids like everyone else—not in an abusive way, but certainly in ways that every mother flustered by their kids' behavior can relate to.

Actually, we have a lot of letters Ellen wrote to her sons. Since Ma and Pa White had a rigorous travel itinerary to keep up, they had to parent long distance in the same way your grandma or babysitter might receive a phone call from your parents who are *trying* to have a date night but have been interrupted because of your shenanigans. Even worse for Ellen's offspring, however, would have been the long, agonizing anticipation of discipline to come—when their parents returned from a trip at last.

You know how you feel when you hear something like, "Just wait until your father gets home . . . ," and you have a couple of hours to ponder your fate before Dad comes home from work? Well, imagine living in the age of horse and buggy and getting a letter from your mom that said, "You are in a lot of trouble, Mister—when I get back in the fall . . ." The anticipation would be agony.

So what kind of character flaws could a prophet's kid possibly have?

In 1860, writing to six-year-old Willie from Iowa, his mama said,

I have just finished a letter to your brothers, and will write a few lines to you. I should so love to take you, my sweet Willie, in my arms this moment; but this cannot be. I hope we shall be returned home safely, that we can see you all again in our own happy home. Willie, you must be a good boy; you must overcome an impatient spirit. To be impatient, is not to be willing to wait, to want everything you desire in a moment. You must say to yourself, *I'll wait.* "He that is slow to anger, is better than the mighty; and he that ruleth his spirit, than he that taketh a city." Willie, if you would be happy, you must rule well your own spirit. Be obedient to Jennie, love your brothers, and be good all day. . . .

. . . When you go to your grandfather's, you must not act rough and boisterous, but gentle and mild. When the boys go to the office, you must try and not be lonesome. Make yourself contented and happy. Don't fret, but learn to be patient, my dear boy. We love you very much, and will now say good by for the present. Your affectionate Mother.[1]

Reading between the lines, it appears that Willie was impatient, demanding, quick tempered, and a bit rough in his playtime with Grandad. I know kids like that, and so do you. You can feel Ellen's frustration in certain places—like when she says "be good all day," "love your brothers," and quotes a Bible text to him about not being mad.

She also had a few words for Henry and Edson, who were moving into their teens. To them, Mom wrote,

Don't give way to fretful, unkind feelings; but remember that the Lord reads even the thoughts of the heart, and nothing is concealed from His all-seeing eye. Right acts, right thoughts, will be remembered in heaven, and every victory you gain when tempted to do wrong, every temptation manfully resisted, will be recorded in heaven. Don't forget, dear children, that evil deeds are faithfully recorded, and will bring their punishment unless repented of, and confessed, and washed away by the atoning blood of Jesus. It is easier to go in an evil way than to do right; for Satan and his angels are constantly tempting to do wrong.

But there is one who has promised to hear the needy when they cry. Go to God when tempted to speak or act wrong. Ask Him in faith for strength, and he will give it. He will say to his angels, There is a poor little boy trying to resist the power of Satan, and has come to me for help. I will aid him. Go stand by that child.[2]

Well, well, looks like we have some moody teenagers enjoying some "fretful" feelings. Typical. And notice how Mom so clearly reminds them that even when she can't see what they are doing, God can. Even moms with prophetic eyesight don't know all the trouble their children get into. Even prophet moms need help and strength from God. Maybe you should go give your parents a hug right now. I'll wait . . .

And if you happen to be an adult who sneaked a copy of this book past the cashier at the book store or the checkout online, claiming you bought it for your "youth group"—when in fact it was for yourself—Ellen had things to say to her kids after they became adults too.

Of all her kids, Edson was the most exasperating to her—though he turned out well in the end. As an adult, he mishandled finances, nearly bankrupted one of the publishing presses, wandered from the faith, dressed in "flamboyant" clothing, and did many other things that drive moms nuts.

When Ed was fifteen, Ellen wrote him a letter marked, "Read this alone, Private." The letter reads:

> My dear Son Edson,
> . . . When we went to Monterey last summer, for instance, you went into the river four times and not only disobeyed us yourself but led Willie to disobedience. A thorn has been planted in my heart from that time, when I became convinced that you could not be trusted. . . .
> . . . A gloom which I cannot express shrouds our minds in regard to your influence upon Willie. You lead him into habits of disobedience and concealment and prevarication. This influence, we have seen, has affected our noblehearted, truthful Willie. . . . You reason and talk and make things appear all smooth to him, when he cannot see through the matter. He adopts your view of it and he is in danger of losing his candor, his frankness. . . .
> . . . You had so little sense of the true value of character. You seemed as much pleased in the society of Marcus Ashley as with your own innocent brother Willie. You never prized him as he deserved to be prized. He is a treasure, beloved of God, but I fear your influence will ruin him.[3]

Ouch. Now Ellen is comparing her children—to her children. This literary tongue-lashing cut Edson deeply, and it might appall some people to think of a prophet treating her child this way. But remember, Ellen was a human being like all moms. And like all moms, she lost her patience from time to time—especially with her teenage son. She needed grace like all moms.

By 1869, things hadn't gotten any better. Now an adult, Edson received this little treat in the mail: "Father weeps over your case. But we are both at [a] loss to know what to say or do in your case. We view it just alike. You are at present not fitted to have a family, for in judgment you are a child, in self-control a child. You have no strength to resist temptation, although by yielding you would disgrace us and yourself and dishonor God. You would not bear the yoke in your youth. You love ease and to be free from care."[4]

That's a harsh letter—but moms never stop worrying over their children just because they grow up—well, grow up physically at least. Many adults have the mind of a child, and it gets them into trouble. James and Ellen were heartbroken and frustrated as they watched their adult son make poor choices. You know things are bad when you make your dad cry.

Sometime in 1899, when Ellen was seventy-one years old, she wrote to her son Willie about his brother, trying to work out why Edson had such a difficult nature. She wrote, "I . . . am more sympathetic for Edson than for you, because before his birth circumstances were peculiarly unfavorable in regard to his stamp of character. My association while carrying him, the peculiar experience I was forced to have, was most objectionable and severely trying. After his birth it was no less so for years. It was altogether different in your case."[5]

Looking back on all her hectic travels and health problems during pregnancy, she figured that all the stress had messed up Edson. You can sense the guilt in the letter—even though all children have to make their own choices, regardless of how stressed their mother may have been during pregnancy.

Eventually Edson did pull it together and became a dynamic missionary to the black people living in the South. Ellen had always felt strongly about taking the gospel across the color line, that salvation was for all and especially needed in the late nineteenth century after the ravages of the U.S. Civil War.

Edson would craft a boat known as the *Morning Star*—complete with its own library, photography lab, chapel, printing press, and staff quarters. He and his crew traveled up and down the Mississippi River taking the gospel to African Americans, making his parents proud . . . finally.

Willie went on to be known as "W. C." White (in case you are doing historical research) and became one of his mother's most important editors, defenders, and spokespersons. And while it would be nice to imagine that all Ellen's kids grew up to be spiritual superstars, not all would survive to make their appearance on the world stage.

ENDNOTES

1. E. G. White, letter to W. C. White, March 3, 1860; letter 2, 1865, quoted in Ellen G. White, *An Appeal to the Youth* (Battle Creek, MI: Seventh-day Adventist Publishing Association, 1864), 60, 61.

2. E. G. White, letter to Henry and Edson White, March 3, 1860; letter 1, 1865, quoted in E. G. White, *An Appeal to the Youth*, 58, 59.

3. E. G. White, letter to J. E. White, June 20, 1865; letter 4, 1865.

4. E. G. White, letter to J. E. White, June 10, 1869; letter 6, 1869.

5. E. G. White, letter to W. C. White, August 1899; letter 245, 1899.

Chapter 26

Of Life and Death

Some years are better than others.

Remember the year you learned to ride your bike, tie your shoes, and read? How about the year you made the basketball team, got your first smartphone, or passed driver's ed? And how could you forget the time you managed to stay up on the wakeboard, or cruise down a black diamond on a snowboard, or shoot the curls on a surfboard? The years that brought you your first kiss, a solid 4.0 GPA, or first prize at the talent show for your rendition of Beethoven's *Moonlight Sonata* on the spoons will remain etched in your heart forever, and so will the bad years.

You remember them too. The year your face exploded in acne on picture-taking day. The year your parents divorced. The year you broke your arm, needed glasses, or got dumped. The year you needed counseling and the year you failed gym class—in front of everybody. (Stupid Whiffle ball—who cares that you couldn't hit it . . . even off a stand?) Bad, bad years you want to forget, but they hurt you too deeply. They scabbed over and became scars called "memories."

For James and Ellen, 1859 was one of those bad years.

John and Mary Loughborough were BFFs with the Whites. Both young families had kids and had dedicated themselves to sharing the good news of Jesus' soon return. Think of the families that are closest to yours—the ones your parents invite over for movie night and game night and go camping with. Picture their kids, your friends, the ones you spend time with. Great people.

Now imagine one of them dying.

Early one morning, someone was sent to fetch James and Ellen and bring them to the Loughboroughs' house. The messenger told them that John and Mary thought their little Teresa was dying. Dressing as fast as they could, the Whites raced to the house to be with their friends. All would be well—right? After all, who better to have as a buddy than a prophet?

Ellen entered the house and saw her friends watching their child in agony. Quickly, everyone gathered for prayer—asking for strength for John and Mary. Prayers offered for Teresa centered around her salvation. The group pleaded for her name to be written in Jesus' book of names of those who will rise from the grave when He returns.

"We witness[ed] the dying struggle," recalled Ellen. "The little eyes . . . closed, no more to look on earthly things. . . . Her troubles are ended. Quietly will she rest until the Life-giver calls her from her dusty bed." Teresa was ten months old—and the Loughboroughs' only child.

The horror of losing a child is unmatched by any other grief known to humanity. Often the loss is so devastating that marriages fall apart, moms and dads need to be watched carefully so they don't hurt themselves, and a person never fully heals even in the best cases.

Reflecting on the loss of the little one and the anguish of her friend, Ellen commented, "This is a dark, dreary world."

And it would only get darker and drearier.

A death in the family

The Whites had welcomed their fourth (and last) son into the family on Thursday, September 20, 1860. He went nameless for three months. When the baby turned three weeks old, James felt that he (James) could travel west. Ellen relished the chance for some stay-at-home-mom action with her new baby—especially since recovering from this delivery took longer than usual.

James took off from Michigan, headed to Wisconsin, on October 9. When he arrived in Chicago, he penned a quick note letting his family know he was fine. Shortly thereafter, Ellen shot off a message saying she was doing well—though spending most of the day in bed and anticipating staying like that for another week, because she was "yet a cripple."

She also noted, "You may be assured I miss your little visits in my room, but the thought you are doing the will of God helps me to bear the loss of your company." Sweet stuff. As for the little nameless one, she reported that he "grows finely" and "he is well." Ellen told James she expected "a letter as often as once a week." For two weeks the couple wrote newsy letters back and forth.

"I am well," wrote James on October 11. "Tell dear Henry, Eddy, and Willie that I love them and pray for them. Hope Eddy will learn to be careful and good." Typical Edson.

Ellen replied with a letter on October 22, letting the doting daddy know that she was feeling better. In answer to James's prayers, she informed him that "the children are well and obedient" and that the "little nameless one is fat and rugged." Mary, their good friend who had lost her little girl, stopped by daily to help out.

All was well . . . until James had a strange premonition. Writing from Iowa, he told his wife, "Be careful of your health. Do not want for anything that money will buy. Remember me affectionately to Henry, Edson, Willie and —— without a name. Tell them that Father prays for them and loves them very much. . . . Yours in love, James White."

We also have a letter James wrote from Wisconsin in which he says he feels things aren't well at home—and that he has felt a sense of dread concerning "Nameless." James also said he had visions of the child "lying before him with face and head dreadfully swollen." Pretty scary experience for a young dad away from home—and a disturbing letter for a young mom to receive while her husband is away on business. Ellen read his words and felt confused as she looked at her perfectly healthy baby boy.

The next day, James's premonitions slipped out of the world of nightmares into living terror. The nameless boy contracted a severe case of "erysipelas" in his face and head. The name of the illness means "red skin"; it's also known by other names, such as "holy fire." Fever, shaking, chills, and vomiting appear within the first forty-eight hours, and then red lesions appear on the skin. Nasty stuff—especially for a child only a few weeks old.

The telegram informing James of his new baby's condition reached him in Illinois, and immediately he cut his travel plans short. He made it home within two days—the illness would last for twenty-four.

"My dear babe was a great sufferer," wrote Ellen. "We anxiously watched over him, using all the remedies we could for his recovery, and earnestly presenting his case to the Lord." She confessed, "At times I could not control my feelings," and "much of my time was spent in tears." During that time, they also gave the baby a name—John Herbert.

But no sooner had they chosen a name than they had to say goodbye.

On December 14, just before Christmas, Ellen was called into the baby's room. John was much worse. She remembered: "I listened to his labored breathing, and felt his pulseless wrist. I knew that he must die. That was an hour of anguish for me. The icy hand of death was already upon him. We watched his feeble, gasping breath, until it ceased, and we felt thankful that his sufferings were ended. When my child was dying, I could not weep."

Grief is a strange and very personal thing—often with mixed emotions. Watching her baby die ripped Ellen's heart in two, and yet she felt peace that her little one wasn't in such pain anymore. No doubt shock played a role in her lack of tears.

Ellen was not able to shed a tear at the funeral, either—though she did faint during the service. Her whole outlook on life, she recalled, was one of "despondency and gloom," not only because of the devastating loss, but because the infant Adventist Church appeared to be full of indifferent people who didn't take their faith seriously. She wrote, "The condition of God's cause and people nearly crushed us."

John's father also felt the effects of his child's death deeply. Ellen remembered James losing confidence in "almost everyone." One morning, on the way to church to preach, he lingered outside the sanctuary. Grief consumed him, and while everyone waited inside for him, he broke down and, in his wife's words, "wept aloud."

The death of the two children—Teresa Andrews and John White—helped create an incredible friendship between the two families—and the two grieving mothers. In a poignant letter to her friend Mary Loughborough, Ellen wrote, "I went up to Oak Hill Cemetery and fixed our babes' graves. . . . Fixed ours exactly alike. Put some pansies on the graves, and some myrtle, and at the foot of the stake put a bunch of tall moss. It looked very pretty. We shall go up again soon and see if the flowers are doing well."

History gives us a much different picture of a woman so many consider cruel, rigid, and even heartless. Ellen was a good friend, a good mother, and strong. She had to be in order to endure this kind of grief one more time.

Noble Henry

In 1863, Ellen received a vision about how people might change their health habits and lead more vibrant lives. This promising vision opened the door for an important discussion regarding diet, exercise, and mental health. As a result, the Seventh-day Adventists (their brand-new, official name) would become one of the healthiest people groups in the world. Which is what makes Henry White's death six months later so painful.

Pneumonia is an awful illness that some of you may have struggled with. It assaults the lungs, creates chills, snatches breath away, and saturates its victims in fever. Modern medicine can easily treat it, but even so, it takes up to three weeks to cure. Left untreated, pneumonia can be lethal. Henry lived in a time when medicine hadn't caught up with pneumonia's wicked abilities.

Even as a robust sixteen-year-old in pioneer times, Henry's body lacked the power to master the deadly sickness. His finest effort lasted only eight days—and he was gone. More ironic even than the timing of the health vision was an unopened set of books by Dr. James Jackson that James had ordered weeks earlier. They contained the latest methods of treatment that might have helped cure the Whites' teenage son. The books had sat untouched, still in their wrappers, for weeks. James and Ellen had been traveling so much they hadn't had time to explore their contents yet.

Despite calling the local doc who administered drugs, the Whites couldn't save Henry—even though ten months earlier, using natural remedies, they had successfully defeated at attack of diphtheria he had picked up (involving nose, throat, and lots of mucus).

When infant John died the same year that he was born, their "hearts did bleed" in a way that "none may know but those who have followed their little ones . . . to the grave." "Death," wrote Ellen with a broken heart, "stepped over our threshold, and broke the youngest branch of our family tree." Ellen went so far as to say that while certainly the rest of the family who lose their babies "feel the blow keenly," the "tenderest earthly tie is between the mother and her child." The mother feels the grief as the father cannot.

So be nice to your mother.

And your father, too, of course.

They love you in ways no one else can understand.

"But oh, when our noble Henry died . . . ," continued Ellen, reflecting on the loss of her teenage son, "when our sweet singer was borne to the grave, and we no more heard his early song, ours was a lonely home." I have had people tell me, after the loss of a child or a sibling at a young age, that the worst part is coming home—after the hospital, the funeral, and all the other events that accompany a death—and lying in their bed in a house devoid of the loved one's voice and presence.

Even though the snake of grief coiled around James, Ellen, and their remaining children, she testified, "God comforted us in our bereavements, and with faith and courage we pressed forward in the work He had given us, in bright hope of meeting our children who had been torn from us by death, in that world where sickness and death will not come."

They still had their hope that when Jesus comes again, their family would be as fresh and alive as the new earth—and that strengthened them to continue their work on this old earth.

Chapter 27

Marital Bliss . . . or Miss?

From time to time I have been acquainted with a couple of lovebirds who claim that when they get married all their problems will fade away. They recoil at the thought that there could ever be a disagreement, a fight, or a screaming match in their relationship. When having a conversation about their future nuptials, they cannot fathom the possibility that their home could ever contain a conflict of any kind.

Now, I don't enjoy people's pain, but I do enjoy watching them learn, and there have been times when I've encountered these same couples—the ones with the crazy idea that different people, living in the same house, could never be a recipe for arguments—after they have gone through with marriage.

It doesn't take long. I remember walking into a recently married friend's living room when the usual singsong voices and happy greetings were nowhere to be found.

Matter of fact, I couldn't even find my friends. They were in opposite parts of the house. I grinned. *Well, well—looks like we finally have a real marriage.* This probably sounds quite cynical to you, and I assure you I love romance and "happily ever after" as much as anybody else, but those things require good, hard, tear-stained efforts.

Even in fairy tales there is usually a dragon to slay before the knight can rescue the princess. Sometimes that dragon is the pride and ridiculous expectations that both the knight and princess have to get over before they can live a life together. And being good, old-fashioned, 100 percent human beings, James and Ellen had themselves a few dragons to slay in their relationship.

Privacy

In an 1877 letter, Ellen wrote about buying a farm in northern California, saying: "We must have a place of retirement where we can step out of doors without being seen by our neighbors." At first blush, this looks a little crabby, a little crotchety, and a lot reclusive. However, one of the challenges the Whites had was their complete lack of privacy.

Just as celebrities cannot live their lives without some member of the paparazzi capturing every moment, the Whites, because of Ellen's prophetic gift and James's leadership in the new Seventh-day Adventist Church, couldn't escape the attentions of the faithful. Everyone wanted a word from Ellen, or to test her gift to see if it was real, or to ask James a question.

Then you have to factor in those traveling Adventists needing a place to stay—and what better place than Casa de White? Not only did their house usually contain any number of sojourners, but the Whites' personal health, travels, messages, and family tragedies all found their way into the new *Review and Herald* magazine that James edited.

All of this created a public arena for marital fights, separations, and frustrations. I can tell you from personal experience, having a fight with your spouse, covertly when company has left, isn't an ideal environment to resolve conflicts. The Whites' house, because of their hospitality and sense of duty, constantly contained a flood of guests.

Personality

I tell people interested in marriage that everybody is crazy—you just have to pick the kind of crazy you want to live with the rest of your life. Regardless of how functional we think we are, we all have quirks, eccentricities, and annoying habits that will drive another person nuts when in constant contact for prolonged periods of time. James and Ellen had their own special ways of testing each other's patience.

First of all, Ellen's health made her timid and feeble . . . at least in the beginning. While this calls to the heart of a husband to become a protector and caregiver, it can also be frustrating when you have to worry about whether or not she is going to faint. All the time. Ellen fainted at funerals, during prayer, when she was sick, while she slept, and when she was stressed . . . which was a lot of fainting.

Eventually, she developed incredible boldness, and James occasionally received a word from the Lord during arguments. It can't have been easy having a disagreement with your spouse, who happens to be a prophet, when suddenly in the heat of disagreement the Lord speaks—in your spouse's favor! Reportedly, in a letter to a friend, James laments, "Somebody has turned this woman against me."

James was no picnic, either.

Starting a business, much less a religious movement with nationally distributed periodicals, requires incredible strength of character, work ethic, and a strong personality. At times, Ellen said James did the work of "two men" and other times "three men." His incessant drive led him to chronic workaholism—and woe to you if you got in his way.

When the Adventist Church was hotly debating the virtues of becoming an organization, with many individuals believing organization to be evil, James fired off a sassy article in the *Review and Herald*: "We are aware that these suggestions, will not meet the minds of all. Bro. Over-cautious will be frightened, and will be ready to warn his brethren to be careful and not venture out too far; while Bro. Confusion will cry out,

'O, this looks just like Babylon! Following the fallen church!' Bro. Do-little will say, 'The cause is the Lord's, and we had better leave it in his hands, he will take care of it.' 'Amen,' says Love-this-world, Slothful, Selfish, and Stingy."[1]

Vintage Adventist sarcasm—awesome.

James's personality gradually became a double-edged sword. While he needed the drive to power through opposition, most wives don't appreciate that same approach when they have concerns about their own family and ministry. For example, calling your wife "Bro. Do-little" will probably cause a severe lack of affection in your life.

Not that James did that, of course, but he did become increasingly difficult because of some health challenges he faced as a direct result of his inability to rest. I am the first one to encourage people to work hard to achieve their dreams, but I also, in my house and from my pulpit, plead with people to take care of themselves.

As I write this chapter, I am in a family suite at Great Wolf Lodge. A very generous gift allowed our family to spend some time at this extravagant lodge, complete with water park, restaurants, children's spa, and so much more. So I am taking a break with my family to rest and recuperate before going back to work tomorrow.

So, why am I writing? Shouldn't I be traveling down a waterslide right now?

In a minute—the kids are still getting ready for their day. The point is that all of us need to separate from work and school from time to time to just have fun, to let our minds and bodies rest, and to remember that despite the sinfulness of this world there are still beautiful experiences to be a part of.

James couldn't do that—and between 1865 and 1881 he had a series of five strokes. To put this in perspective, the average age of a modern American having a stroke is sixty-five. James was forty-four when he had his first one. That's pretty bad. Despite Ellen begging him to slow down, James's health deteriorated. He set himself up for paralytic strokes—and they can change a person forever.

Known as a "brain attack," strokes are created by blood clots in the brain, causing cell death, with many functions of the brain at risk of permanent damage. While James managed to fight his way back from his first massive stroke, his personality and manner were altered forever—creating a very difficult time in his and Ellen's marriage.

What follows is the account of James's first stroke, which in my humble opinion, offers us a powerful glimpse into the dynamics of Ellen's marriage and her role as wife. However, before we go there, I have to go to a water park with some excited children. So if you'll excuse me, I'm going to fetch my swimsuit and take a break.

ENDNOTE

1. James White, "Yearly Meetings," *Review and Herald,* July 21, 1859.

Chapter 28

Stricken

OK, I'm back and, oddly enough in light of my discussion in the previous chapter of Ellen's fainting spells, my wife just threw out her back and fainted from the pain while at the water park. I'm writing the day after, and my wife is resting and recovering at home now—thank you for your concern.

It was pretty scary.

In another strange coincidence, James and Ellen were checking out a new medical facility in 1864—the one James would spend time recovering in after his first stroke. Located in Dansville, New York, and operated by a Dr. Jackson, "Our Home on the Hillside" had all the latest medical advances of that time.

James and Ellen spent three weeks there in September to check out the goings on in order to give a proper review to friends. The facility could care for three hundred patients, and the Whites gave great reviews on the staff, the water therapy treatments, and the food—James calling it a "luxury" for the patients. Duly impressed, the Whites left ready to recommend this place to others. James little suspected that he would be experiencing the facility's "luxury" for himself about a year later.

The Whites embarked on an ambitious year of travel—lecturing on health of all things. James never allowed himself the luxury of rest. Our bodies need rest. Not just sleep, but downtime to live in the moment—to actually live life instead of racing to the end of it. If we don't stop to rest, our bodies have ways of making us stop.

On August 16, James's body made its move—forcing him to rest for nearly two years.

While on a walk with his wife in a cornfield, admiring the beautiful ears, James snatched one off the stalk and peeled back the husk. Ellen, who had been at his side, heard him make an unfamiliar noise—and it wasn't the sound of devouring an ear of sweet corn.

She looked at him and saw that his face had gone bright red, and his right arm was dangling helplessly by his side. She saw him try to raise his arm, but the strength wasn't there. Instead of walking, he staggered. Nothing in his body responded like it should. As quickly as she could, Ellen helped him to a nearby friend's house, with James barely managing to utter a single word: "Pray."

Ellen later wrote, "We dropped to our knees and cried to God, who had ever been to us a present help in time of trouble. He [James] soon uttered words of praise and gratitude to God, that he could use his arm. His hand was partially restored, but not fully."

The docs were called but had little help to give. True to form, as seemed the case with all the White health scares, the doctors offered little encouragement—suggesting James probably wouldn't survive.

"Thanks for being a part of our 'get-well' team, Doc!"

A couple of days later an announcement in the *Review and Herald* informed the faithful of James's "dangerous attack." Thankfully, James could now move the stricken hand and fingers to some extent, as well as speak and think clearly. But he had a long way to go. Ellen cared for him for five weeks, along with help from some friends. But there is only so much a family can do, and Ellen believed the next best move for her husband was Our Home on the Hillside.

The program there would use hydrotherapy and avoid the ridiculous drugs (a.k.a. "poison") of the day. The journey would be taxing. The Whites lived in Michigan at the time, and there wouldn't be any direct flights to New York for almost a hundred years. But as exhausted as she was, Ellen loved her husband and was committed to finding a way to get him there. One of the local physicians working at Our Home on the Hillside, Dr. H. S. Lay, agreed to take James and Ellen with him as he returned to the institution.

Upon their arrival, Dr. Jackson, the lead doctor, greeted them and gave James a proper examination the following day. Jackson broke it down for James, telling him that it was a good thing he had been stopped by the stroke when he was. Otherwise, had he continued with his workaholism, something worse might have occurred.

Jackson made something else very clear. James was not allowed to do any work for the next six to eight months. That was like telling a teenager not to text. This wasn't going to be easy. Recovery would be slow, but Ellen determined to stay with her man. They found a nice little apartment upstairs in a cottage close to the facility and readied themselves for the healing process.

When some believers found out that James was at Our Home on the Hillside (which I will refer to from now on as OHOH . . . not to be confused with UH-OH), they started accusing the Whites of giving up on their faith in prayer as a means of healing. Wow! Thanks, guys. In the midst of caring for her sick husband, Ellen had to fire off a letter for the peering eyes of the uninformed public.

"Not so," she said, referring to the accusation. "We did not feel like despising the means God had placed in our reach for the recovery of health. . . . We believed that God would bless the efforts we were making in the direction of health." In other words, God has given us tools and common sense to use in helping us feel better. She continued, "We did not doubt that God could work a miracle, and in a moment restore to health and vigor." But she said that if God had healed James in this way, they wouldn't have made the healthy choices needed to prevent this kind of thing from happening again.

God doesn't reward stupidity—or cheer us on with supernatural healing when we persist in doing dumb things to ourselves. Ellen told the ignorant masses that God has given us natural laws to work with, and in addition to faith in His power, these will give us a happy life if followed.

This isn't to say that everything at OHOH met with Ellen's approval.

Some of the ways the docs kept the patients' minds off their illnesses involved dancing, playing cards, and going to the theater. Theaters in Ellen's day were not like your local Cineplex 16. Drinking, smoking, and prostitution were common around the local theaters. Card playing had a strong link to gambling—an addiction that has cost many their life's savings; and while some forms of dancing have to do with tradition—and even worship— the kind practiced at OHOH stimulated other things besides devotion to the Lord. Not to mention it exhausted the patients' already feeble faculties.

While Ellen was in the ladies' bathroom at OHOH, someone asked her for money to help hire a fiddler for an upcoming dance. She responded, "I am a follower of Jesus. . . . This dancing is thought essential to keep up the spirits of the patients, but have you not marked that the very ones who engage in this exercise are languid for a day or two afterward, and some are unable to rise from their beds?"

It's not that Ellen hated fun—but she grew irritated that the study of how to stay well, including religious philosophies of health, took a backseat to simply keeping patients entertained. They wore patients out with entertainment and then put forward the idea that people were too tired to study health or religion.

Imagine attending a meeting to help homeless children find homes—only to have the chair of the meeting entertain attendees with funny cat videos on YouTube. Hilarious? Yes. But no children are finding homes. Or imagine stopping someone on the way to physical therapy and playing a few rounds of tennis with them. Fun? No doubt. But now they lack the energy to do the physical therapy needed to return the range of motion to their shoulder needed for a wicked backhand.

Also think about how tired Mrs. White was. She was already exhausted from the usual cares of her public, prophet life. Her husband had a paralytic stroke, and she cared for him for over a month. In the midst of having to help her husband as one would a child or an elderly person, she had to put up with streams of letters offering unsolicited advice—and even questioning her belief in prayer. And at the apex of all these draining tasks she made the massive trip from Michigan to New York with her debilitated husband, because she expected him to undergo therapy, lifestyle changes, and reeducation—*not* learn how to play blackjack!

At OHOH Ellen even ran into the idea that the study of religion made people invalids. "Do you ever see me gloomy?" she asked in response. "I have a faith that forbids this. It is a misconception of the true ideal of Christian character and Christian service that leads to these conclusions. It is the want of genuine religion that produces gloom, despondency, and sadness." In other words, a true relationship with Jesus is a source of truth and joy—not crabby crotchetiness. In Ellen's words, "A hearty, willing service to Jesus produces a sunny religion."

As treatment continued, James had good days and bad days. In October, an article by Dr. Lay told *Review and Herald* readers, "Though he [James] has made marked progress toward recovery since coming to this place, yet he is far from being well; and in order for him to fully recover, it seems indispensably necessary that he should devote at least several months to that special object."

He also noted Ellen's constant love and care for her husband. As time went by, however, Ellen felt impressed by God that the care at OHOH focused too much on entertaining and not enough on keeping people active.

As the months rolled by, Ellen described her view of her husband's situation at OHOH:

My husband could obtain but little rest or sleep nights. He suffered with the most extreme nervousness. I could not sew or knit in his room, or converse but very little, as he was easily agitated, and his brain confused almost beyond endurance.

Many nights when my husband was suffering with pain, unable to rest or sleep, have I left my bed at midnight and bowed before God and earnestly prayed for Him to grant us this token of His love and care—that my husband might realize the soothing influence of His Holy Spirit, and find rest in sleep. . . . We had the evidence that God heard us pray, and my husband would drop into a quiet sleep.

By December, Ellen knew that the tight quarters they were staying in would not be adequate. James's recovery was moving as fast as a snail swimming in peanut butter, and depression clawed at him. Ellen wondered if the time hadn't come to go home to Battle Creek, Michigan.

The White house had "high and airy rooms," a "large reservoir of hot water," an "immense cistern of soft water," a "filter in the cellar," and "various bathing pans." Ellen looked around their tiny quarters at OHOH and figured that James would move faster down the road to recovery by being at home and among good friends of similar faith.

After spending time in prayer, she approached Dr. Lay and told him that it was time to move James. He said No—figuring James would drop dead on the way. However, after consultation with Doc Jackson, they agreed to try the journey in phases. In early December, they packed up their things and left during a drizzly, rainy morning.

Even though the Whites had some differences with the people at OHOH about what patients did to get their groove back, Ellen did write a note of appreciation for everyone at the institution: "I shall ever remember with gratitude the kind attention and respect we received, not only from physicians at 'Our Home,' but also from the helpers. The attendants in the bath rooms and waiters at the table were as attentive to our wants as we could wish. They seemed desirous to make our stay with them as pleasant and happy as it was in their power to do."

Four months of caring for James without much results. What would happen when Ellen got him home? A vision gave Ellen the answer.

Vision of recovery

"God will be glorified in the restoration of His servant to health," an angel revealed to Ellen in vision. The vision also showed her that "God has heard the prayers of His servants. His arms are beneath His afflicted servant." Encouraged to have faith, regardless of how desperate the situation seemed, Ellen continued to care for her husband, but she also reminded him to maintain an "active" faith.

Sometimes we use prayer as a stalling tactic, instead of doing what we know we should. We tell someone in pain, "Hey man, sorry you don't have money for food this month. I'll pray for you," making sure we stay "in prayer" until somebody else gives him grocery money. Lame.

Regarding her husband, Ellen wrote, "If he should wait for the power of God to come upon his body, to feel that he was made whole before he made efforts in accordance with his faith, saying, When the Lord heals me I will believe and do this or that, he might continue to wait and would realize no change."

Faith is like a dead body—if you aren't working alongside it (see James 2:17). James needed to work at it but trying to inspire him to do so would work Ellen's nerves.

The last part of her vision warned her that James wouldn't appreciate her pushing him to action. She had it on good authority that he would "shrink" from his duties and that current fears and anxieties would make him "timid." In her words, as she gazed upon her beloved, "He looks at appearances, at disagreeable feelings of the body." For James, if he felt bad, that meant his condition *was* bad—and he couldn't be bothered to exert himself.

After all, who likes being told to do stuff when you have sore muscles—or when you are dizzy from watching Netflix in bed all day? But the angel was clear: "Feeling is not faith. Faith is simply to take God at His word." The word had been given, and Ellen was going to motivate her ailing husband starting in the late summer of 1866.

Chapter 29

Field Trips

Field trips are the best.

My favorite was to the Old Dutch potato chip factory in Roseville, Minnesota . . . back in the early '90s. Yeah, I know—the age of slap bracelets, pogs, and Hammer pants. (Check Wikipedia.) Imagine, if you will, being ten years old (unless you are ten years old, then skip this part) and touring the building where they make salty, greasy chips. All throughout the tour you are treated to samples—and at the end you get to stand in front of conveyer belts plucking freshly fried chips off the assembly line.

Hot, crispy, glistening chips, tasting like cheddar, sour cream and onion, dill pickle, and happiness, filled our mouths with glorious cholesterol.

My other field trip highlights included Amtrak train rides, exploring the Metrodome (now torn down in the hopes of building a new stadium that will inspire the Vikings football team to actually win a game), and skiing. I don't think I remember ever having a bad field trip. Who would object to being removed from school and the boring daily routine of life in order to play for the day?

James White might.

"I always took my husband with me when I went out driving," wrote Ellen. I assume she was a safe driver (James never had any accidents or fell out of the carriage). Ellen also dragged him to all her preaching appointments. She tried to get him to sit on the platform beside the pulpit while she preached—maybe even to say a little something. He chose to warm a pew and remain silent instead. The man who had done the work of many, the man who had edited the church magazine—now embraced lumpitude.

This laziness went on for months, until Ellen finally said, "Now, my husband, you are going into the desk (the pulpit) today." James made it clear that he was not excited about getting his preach on, but Ellen "would not yield." She hauled him up with her, and she writes, "that day he spoke to the people." Don't mess with Ellen Wife.

She watched her husband break free from his illness for thirty minutes and deliver a message to several people who hadn't yet embraced the Adventist message. After countless months of frustratingly slow progress, Ellen saw James beginning to recover, and even though she faced a large group of people she didn't know, she "could not refrain from weeping" from a heart "overflowing with joy and gratitude."

James still hadn't recovered his full power, but Ellen knew that the time had come to go back on the road again with her testimony. Friends and family rained on her fiery excitement, suggesting that by going on tour with James she was shouldering a burden that risked her life and the well-being of her kiddos. Her life mattered, they said, and sacrificing it for an invalid husband didn't seem like a smart thing to do.

"In this matter," penned Ellen Wife, "I was obliged to move contrary to the judgment of my brethren and sisters." In other words, a prophet is gonna do what a prophet is gonna do—even if it upsets her in-laws.

Chapter 30

In-Laws

When Grandma and Grandpa White found out about Ellen's plans, they "remonstrated" with her with tears in their eyes. That's a fancy way of saying they gave Ellen a passionate lecture on how she was ruining people's lives with this crazy idea of going back on the road. Most married couples do their best to avoid upsetting their spouse's parents. Ellen not only cared for her ailing husband, looked after her kids, and dealt with criticisms from the local church—now she had her in-laws upset with her.

Nobody seemed to care what God had shown her about James's health. They thought she was nuts for attempting an extended preaching tour with him. Even doctors told her that her expectations for this trip fell just shy of ridiculous. They had never seen someone recover from such a severe stroke.

Ellen's reply?

"God will raise him up."

Their response went something like this. "Ellen! You have done all in your power to help our son—don't attempt the impossible. Your life is too precious for that! Think about your boys!" Ma and Pa White loved Ellen, and they didn't want to see her health vanish as their son's had—and they certainly didn't want the boys to lose their mother.

"As long as life is left in him and me," replied Ellen, "I will make every exertion for him. That brain, that noble, masterly mind, shall not be left in ruins." Dramatic stuff, isn't it?

She insisted, through tears, that God would care for them and that Satan's quest to destroy them would fail. "You will yet see us standing side by side in the sacred [pulpit] speaking the words of truth."

Couples usually ride off into the sunset together on a horse that conveniently happens to be there at the end of the movie; Ellen's idea of riding off into the sunset involved tag-team preaching. She left Battle Creek, Michigan, on her journey "carrying . . . the sympathies of many and losing the sympathies of many, because [she] would follow [her] own judgment, not theirs." So, December 19, in the dead cold of winter, Ellen headed ninety miles north, to Wright, Michigan—with James in tow.

In-Laws

James "stood the long and severe journey" better than she anticipated, and when they finally arrived at their friend's home in Wright, he "seemed quite . . . well."

Chapter 31

Signs of Life

James and Ellen once slept in a bar while a party was going on.

James, dictating to his wife, reported an account of their journey north in the *Review and Herald:* "We drove forty-six miles that day, and were obliged to put up at a noisy rum-tavern. . . . The next morning we arose at five o'clock, and drove to Brother Hardy's, a distance of fifteen miles, against a keen north wind before taking our breakfast. . . . We then drove twenty-three miles to our old home at Brother Root's, where we have remained until this date [January 2], enjoying their sympathy and hospitality."

James and Ellen once stayed in a "rum-tavern." And a noisy one to boot! That's a fun fact that won't go unappreciated in Sabbath School class.

Would you have opted for the "noisy rum-tavern"? Or would you have toughed out the frigid weather in the carriage? Sometimes we aren't always dealt an ideal situation when we are working for Jesus. And it's good to remember that we are called to mingle with broken people, like us—not just spend time with perfect ones. In any case, it's fun to picture the pioneer couple trying to sleep in a tavern—maybe humming a hymn to drown out the chaos of the drinkers.

It should be noted that in James's account he did express gladness when they finally arrived at an "Advent home" (a house belonging to a fellow Adventist—free from rum-taverning).

As that first Sabbath in Wright rolled around, the Whites found the house of worship filled to the brim with believers. James gave a twenty-five-minute chat about the importance of donating money to help spread the Adventist message (early Adventist pastors were retiring from exhaustion in their twenties due to lack of support), and then Ellen took the pulpit for an hour on the subject of health.

"Here commenced our first effective labors since the sickness of my husband," wrote Ellen. She noted that James still felt weak, but that the work he had once done made its way back into his life. At Ellen's continual urging, James prepared reports for the *Review and Herald*—a huge step forward compared with his illness-induced complacency some months before.

"May God bless our scattered thoughts," wrote James in the *Review*, "and make them a blessing."

James created seven reports, reading like journal entries, and they held the attention of *Review* readers everywhere. Like following your favorite celeb on Twitter, the Adventists looked forward to the latest entry regarding the work, and James's recovery, in northern Michigan from January to March 1867.

This work fit James perfectly. The church in Wright had no regular minister, and when the Whites arrived, they found the members feeling disconnected from each other. The members were also getting on each other's nerves. Mercifully, Ellen and James arrived in the nick of time to bring encouragement. The believers gulped down the Whites' words like a bear at an all-you-can-eat buffet.

James and Ellen settled in for an extended stay at the weakened church, enjoying the hospitality of their friends, the Roots. Ellen recalled that their friends cared for her and James like "Christian parents" caring for "invalid children." Of course, this remark referred to the incredible hospitality of the Roots—not the condition Ellen allowed her sweet hubby to stay in.

Time to get to work, Jim.

Chapter 32

Fitness Time

Exercise.

The word makes me think of relay races, laps around the gym, sit-ups, push-ups, pull-ups, dry heaves leading to throw-ups, and nurses' notes to help me escape the Presidential Fitness test.

Don't judge me.

I'm all about playing sports, but the intentional building of muscle and stamina on weight machines, and running tracks, and aerobics classes means coping with a pile of painful experiences. I have frequently gotten back into shape—and while it is true that I feel better afterward, I feel worse before that. Aching muscles, stiff ligaments, and sweaty clothes that need to be removed with scissors accompany the reestablishment of healthy living—not to mention the frequent calls of nature because of increased water intake.

Ellen demanded that James exercise. The program started as two walks a day. Not too bad, right? James just needed a little nudge out the door, and soon the Whites were walking down the road to wellness, until snowmageddon launched a chilly attack on Ellen's exercise plan. The walking routine had a wet blanket thrown on it—a thick one too. But James didn't get a snow day.

"Brother Root," Ellen asked her host, "have you a spare pair of boots?"

I remember being caught in the great Halloween blizzard of 1991 (yes, still in the era of *Saved by the Bell* and *Animaniacs,* and yes, they can be found on Wikipedia). You can Google photos of the blizzard. It arrived without warning, so my dad and I had to use the snowmobile in order to get to Kmart to buy boots. The trip was epic—our snowmobile nearly sank in the snow twice.

Thankfully for Ellen, Mr. Root happened to have a spare pair of snow boots. Ellen grinned, "I should be glad to borrow them this morning." Pulling on the big boots, she "tracked a quarter of a mile in the deep snow." When she returned to the warm house, she honed in on her husband and surprised him with a conversation like this.

"Ready for your walk?"

"What?" James said surprised. "I can't go out in weather like that!"

"Oh, yes, you can," replied Ellen Wife. When James realized that his wife had already been outside walking in the winter wonderland, his male ego kicked in, and he quickly decided he had better walk or he would lose major man points. Carefully, because he was still in recovery mode, James placed his feet in the grooves Ellen had made with her boots, and James completed Ellen's exercise routine.

In addition to James's physical routine, Ellen set up some mental challenges for him. People often dropped by the Roots' house with spiritual questions nagging at their souls. Company made James run and hide in his room. Seriously, in his midforties he retreated to his man cave whenever members of the congregation came by! Ellen noticed—which is why she would escort visitors straight to his room.

"Husband," she said sweetly and probably with a knowing look, "here is a brother who has come to ask a question, and as you can answer it much better than I can, I have brought him to you." Clever, clever girl.

"Of course," wrote Ellen, "he could not help himself then. He had to remain in the room to answer the question." James's mind came online again—had it not, it may have remained in sleep mode forever. Ellen went on to say that she helped James "in this way, and in many other ways."

The physical, emotional, and spiritual challenge of helping her husband recuperate paid off. James returned to her side, and together they continued to spread the truth God gave them in ways that would take the message around the world. But James would go through four more strokes, and while he maintained a full and fruitful ministry, they would forever alter him in ways that would break Ellen's heart.

Chapter 33

The Lucinda Letters

My friend, and fellow author, Melanie Bockmann has given me permission to share a tragic story that happened to her in high school involving her diary. In exchange, I am supposed to tell you to go buy all her books (i.e., *Unrapped, In the Shadow of the Mob, Convicted, Just Plane Crazy*). I know you won't let her down, and I know this epic story won't let you down.

Many girls keep diaries, even as adults (btw, men don't keep diaries; we keep journals). Melanie had such a diary when she attended Auburn Adventist Academy, and her brother, Rod, knew all about it. As a budding entrepreneur, Rod saw financial gain was to be made from such a precious item. After acquiring the rare book from wherever Melanie attempted to hide it, he opened a museum in the boys' bathroom—charging a handsome fee of $1.00 for a peek at the pages containing his sister's intimate thoughts.

This happened back in the early nineties, so a buck was like thirty dollars today.

Melanie remembers: "That was back when I was still writing about my crushes in excruciating detail. Shortly after that, like *seconds* after that, I stopped." The reason she stopped grew out of a devastating incident in which the wrong person paid for a perusal through her literary confessions.

"It was bad," recalls Melanie. "I had a crush on a guy I was going to school with, but I also had a lingering crush on a guy from a previous church we had been at, and I wrote about the previous guy . . . and the new guy read it . . . and suddenly, all his passion for me withered and died."

Tragic, and not a little hilarious. Well played, brother Rod, well played.

Whose secrets would you like to read about? Your sister? Your dad? Maybe that person you like? You know who I'm talking about . . . of course, *I* don't know who I'm talking about. I have no idea who you like, and even if I did, I couldn't help you. Nope, I have no power to reveal the intimate thoughts of your family members, your teachers, your favorite football player, or your pastor.

But how about a prophet?

In 1973, scholars found a bunch of letters from Ellen written to one of her best friends, named Lucinda. In one letter, Ellen told Lucinda, "My precious Lucinda, you are dearer to me than any earthly sister I have living."[1] The "Lucinda Letters" provided a sneak peek into a few years when the Whites' wedding vows felt a little cold.

James had always possessed a strong personality and had led with great power, but after his multiple strokes, those same traits often morphed into something demanding and controlling. Case in point is an incident recorded in his autobiography about a man who said some harsh things to him.

Reflecting on the critical man, James called him "a coarse, hard-hearted man, possessing in his very nature but little more tenderness than a crocodile, and nearly as destitute of moral and religious training as a hyena."[2]

Well, that isn't very nice. You can get sent to the principal's office for talk like that.

James's personality, while helpful when trying to overcome all the obstacles of starting a religious movement, could be a bit of a liability in a relationship. Exacerbating the problem was the fact that his wife had visions "challenging" him from time to time. How can you argue with a spouse who gets directions straight from the Lord? It didn't matter that James launched magazines, crafted an organizational structure, and served as church president—if the missus had a vision, you needed to comply.

Even friends, such as G. I. Butler, had run-ins with James. Writing to J. N. Andrews, Butler said, "Our dear Brother White thought we were his enemies because we did not see things as he did. I have never laid up anything against that man of God, that noble pioneer who labored so hard for this cause. I attributed it all to disease and infirmity."[3]

What would you do if the personality of the one you loved changed due to illness—and not for the better?

Ellen confided in a friend—something we all need to do from time to time.

Before we look at a couple of Ellen's letters to her friend, you should know that, eventually, Ellen told Lucinda to burn them. That's a clue this is good stuff, but it also raises the question as to whether it is appropriate to read them. The short answer is that no one involved in these letters, or even their children, are alive to feel embarrassment. Secondly, when we read these, it isn't to find fault with the Whites; it is to normalize them (make them human) and to encourage other marriages that might be going through rough patches . . . which all of them do.

So, without further ado, I present one of the "Lucinda Letters"—highlighting in bold type what I feel are striking statements (although, keep in mind that this highlighting doesn't appear in the original letters).

Letter I: "Thoroughly Disgusted"

Dear Lucinda,

We received your letter last evening. We also received one from James.

Lucinda, I have no idea now of exchanging a certainty for an uncertainty. I can write more, and am free. **Should I come east, James' happiness might suddenly change to complaining and fretting. I am thoroughly disgusted with this state of things,** and do not mean to place myself where there is the least liability of its occurring. **The more I think of the matter the more settled and determined I am, unless God gives me light, to remain where I am.** I can never have an opportunity such as God has favored me with at the present. I must work as God should direct. I plead and entreat for light. If it is my duty to attend the camp meetings, I shall know it.

Mary is now secured. I may lose her if I should go east. Satan has hindered me for long years from doing my writing, and now I must not be drawn off. **I can but dread the liability of James' changeable moods, his strong feelings, his censures, his viewing me in the light he does, and has felt free to tell me his ideas of my being led by a wrong spirit, my restricting his liberty, et cetera.** All this is not easy to jump over and place myself voluntarily in a position where he will stand in my way and I in his.

No, Lucinda, no camp meetings shall I attend this season. **God in His providence has given us each our work, and we will do it separately, independently. He is happy; I am happy; but the happiness might be all changed should we meet, I fear.** Your judgment I prize, but I must be left free to do my work. I cannot endure the thought of marring the work and cause of God by **such depression as I have experienced** all unnecessarily. My work is at Oakland. I shall not move east one step unless the Lord says "Go." **Then, without one murmur, I will cheerfully go, not before.**

A great share of my life's usefulness has been lost. If James had made retraction, it would be different. **He has said we must not seek to control each other. I do not own to doing it, but he has, and much more.** I never felt as I do now in this matter. I cannot have confidence in James' judgment in reference to my duty. **He seems to want to dictate to me as though I was a child**—tells me not to go here, I must come east for fear of Sister Willis's influence, or fearing that I should go to Petaluma, et cetera. **I hope God has not left me to receive my duty through my husband.** He will teach me if I trust in Him.

I am cheerful and happy. **My nerves are getting calm.** My sleep is sweet. My health is good. **I hope I have not written anything wrong, but these are just my feelings, and no one but you knows anything about it.** May the Lord help me to do and feel just right. If things had been different, I might feel [it was my] duty to go to camp meetings. As they are, I have no duty. God blesses me in doing my work. If I can get light in [a] dream or in any way, I will cheerfully follow the light. God lives and reigns. I shall answer to His claims, and seek to do His will.

In love,

Ellen[4]

Notice Ellen's concern about saying something hurtful; her intent is not to trash her husband. Prophets have feelings, too, and sometimes they are overwhelming. Anyone who has had a relationship of any kind, for any length of time, will have frustrations that need to be aired—that's normal and OK.

However, as we find trustworthy people to share with, we need to be sufficiently aware of ourselves that we don't seek to destroy the other person. Processing our feelings is different than seeking someone else's destruction. Be open, honest, and raw—but always aware of your intent. Are you trying to find peace or tear someone to pieces?

Letter V: "Dear Husband"

Dear Husband,

It grieves me that I have said or written anything to grieve you. Forgive me and I will be cautious not to start any subject to annoy and distress you. We are living in a most solemn time and we cannot afford to have in our old age [Ellen was forty-eight; James fifty-four] differences to separate our feelings. I may not view all things as you do, but **I do not think it would be my place or duty to try to make you see as I see and feel as I feel.** Wherein I have done this, **I am sorry.**

I want a humble heart, a meek and quiet spirit. Wherein my feelings have been permitted to arise in any instance, it was wrong. Jesus has said, "Learn of Me; for I am meek and lowly in heart; and ye shall find rest unto your souls" [Matthew 11:29].

I wish that self should be hid in Jesus. I wish self to be crucified. **I do not claim infallibility, or even perfection of Christian character. I am not free from mistakes and errors in my life. Had I followed my Saviour more closely, I should not have to mourn so much my unlikeness to His dear image.**

Time is short, very short. Life is uncertain. We know not when our probation may close. If we walk humbly before God, He will let us end our labors with joy. No more shall a line be traced by me or expression made in my letter to distress you. **Again I say, forgive me every word or act that has grieved you.**

I have earnestly prayed for light in reference to going east and I have now decided my work is here, to write and do those things that the Spirit of God

141

shall dictate. I am seeking earnestly for the higher life. Mary and myself are at work as hard as we can. God in His providence has given me my work. I dare not leave it. **We will pray that God may sustain you, but I see no light for me east.**[5]

Closing thoughts

Ironically, despite Ellen's strong feelings about not joining James in the east, she changed her mind a couple of days later and spent the 1876 "campmeeting season" with him. They filled fourteen separate camp meeting engagements—working together as a team. They spoke, they wrote, and when it was all over they returned, together, to their home in California and continued to preach the message of Jesus' soon return.

Many modern marriages crumble at the slightest inconvenience or season of sadness. The Whites went through the deaths of children, four strokes that permanently altered James's personality, and extreme public pressures. Yet they stayed together. How do you foster that kind of commitment? Films make relationships and love look so easy. Yet most of the actors in those movies have "starred in" as many marriages as they have movies. The Whites' intact marriage is just one of the many miracles God performed throughout their ministry.

ENDNOTES

1. E. G. White, letter to Lucinda Hall, October 14, 1874; letter 71, 1874.

2. James White, *Life Incidents* (Battle Creek, MI: Seventh-day Adventist Publishing Association, 1868), 116.

3. G. I. Butler, letter to J. N. Andrews; quoted in Ellen G. White, *Daughters of God* (Washington, DC: Review and Herald® Publishing Association, 1998, 2005), 266.

4. E. G. White, letter to Lucinda Hall, May 10, 1876; letter 64, 1876.

5. E. G. White, letter to James White, May 16, 1876; letter 27, 1876, in *Manuscript Releases*, 20:23.

Chapter 34

Dynamic Duo

Complementary is a term used to describe two or more things blending together to enhance or affect the qualities of the others. For example, we have complementary angles in math. (I know, math, gross, but just hang in there, this illustration will be over soon.)

Complementary angles are created when two angles are combined to create a ninety-degree angle (also known as a "right angle"). Wow, life-changing right? Well, consider how ridiculous life would be if the doors in your house were at thirty-five-degree angles or if your book was made with acute fifteen-degree angles.

You'd sprain your back and your eyeballs and probably get a paper cut.

Or consider complementary colors—color pairs that, when mixed in the right proportion, create black or white. Amazing isn't it? The other thing we do with complementary colors, based on their place upon the color spectrum, is to determine which shades have the strongest contrast when placed next to each other. Wow, I am glad I know that—how about you?

Not sure?

Well it's helpful to know that a bright blue tie will "pop" with a black suit, or that black words will vanish when printed on black paper, or that purple highlights won't make a bit of difference with your naturally purple hair. As to why you were born with purple hair, I am afraid I have nothing to say except that the money spent on purple highlights should be spent on a complementary color—such as green. Lovely.

When it comes to human relationships—different people come together, hopefully, to enhance each other's unique qualities for the better. Thankfully, despite seasons of trial in their marriage, James and Ellen functioned as a dynamic team for Jesus in the church—and in their home.

The Whites' routine[1]

James and Ellen ran a tight ship—beginning with a 6:00 A.M. wakeup call. Brutal.

What's even more brutal is that, by that time, Ellen had already been writing for two or three hours. Seriously? By that time I am waking up to a puddle of drool on my pillow—or maybe, best-case scenario, I have managed to open one eye and stumble into the shower. And, for you worn-out moms reading this, here's another detail to upset you: Ellen and/or her cook had breakfast on the table by 6:30 . . . A.M.

Around the table, Ellen told her family something about what she had been writing. James would share with the kids what his work plans were for the day—and give reports about how the message was spreading across the nation. By 7:00 A.M. the family assembled for worship.

James read a scripture from the Bible, offered a few thoughts on what he felt it meant, and then led out in singing. Everyone joined in, with the favorite hymn being "Lord, in the Morning." The singing wasn't tepid, either. Willie recounted that the song "was sung with hearty vigor" (most singing in family worship sort of reflects "wimpy lazy"). Then came the Whites' prayer time.

James "prayed with earnestness and with solemn reverence." Dad prayed for blessings on the family and the "cause of God." Willie remembered that his parents' passion in song and in prayer would deeply impress people not used to it. When James had to leave on business, Ellen led out in family worship.

"The worship hour," said Willie, "was as regularly observed as the hours for breakfast and dinner."

After James left for work, Ellen spent a half hour in her garden—encouraging her kids to work with her. Then, heading indoors, she put in another three or four hours writing. Afternoons found Ellen chilling with sewing, maybe a little more tending to the flowers, shopping trips, and occasional visits to the sick.

If there wasn't a church meeting, the whole family would reconvene around 7:30 P.M. for evening worship. If everyone finished their work early enough, Ellen would read to the children from "religious papers or books." James, again, read from the Bible and prayed, "thanking God for the blessings of the day, and committing the family to God's care for the night."

Whatever arguments James and Ellen may have had between each other—they managed their family well. It's a testament to their commitment to each other and to their kids that they maintained such a solid schedule as well as they did—despite the fact (as we have already seen) that their boys occasionally acted up, travel schedules interrupted their routine, and a host of traveling "brethren" placed hospitality demands on them.

The Bible contains two letters from Paul to a young pastor named Timothy. One line, in the first letter, reads: "For if someone does not know how to manage his own household, how will he care for God's church?" (1 Timothy 3:5).

The White family held together when many others became a train wreck.

Train wreck

OK, I admit the transition from family routine to literal train wreck is a little strained—though metaphorically, if you have small children, especially more than one of them, "train wreck" resonates awesomely well. In any case, during the 1850s James and Ellen nearly died in a train wreck—and in the process we get a cool picture of the two of them defying death together.

The Whites were scheduled to leave for Wisconsin on the 8:00 P.M. train, but earlier that day James had some reservations *about* the trip—not *for* the trip. He said, "I feel strangely in regard to starting on this trip; but Ellen, we have an appointment out, and we *must* go." And "With my feelings, if I had not an appointment, I should not go tonight." Not a great premonition to have right before a big trip. The Whites and their friends united in prayer about it.

In spite of his concerns, James felt confident God would watch over them, so they left with their good friend, John Loughborough, for the train station. Matter of fact, it is Loughborough who recounted what happened next:

"At eight o'clock I went aboard the train with them [James and Ellen], to assist in getting . . . their parcels [on the train]. We went into one car with high back seats, called in those days a 'sleeping car.' Sister White said, 'James, I can't stay in this car; I must get out of here.' "

That's mildly unnerving when your prophet wife, who knows you've been feeling weird about the trip, suddenly doesn't feel safe to stay in a certain car. "That's not cool, Ellen. Don't be messing with me like that!" But she wasn't fooling around.

Loughborough helped the couple find a seat in the middle of the next car. He remembered that "Sister White sat down with her parcel in her lap, but said, 'I don't feel at home on this train.' The bell then rang, and I bade them 'goodbye.' "

At this point I would have followed Loughborough off the train. If the prophet doesn't like the train—I don't either. I'll walk to Wisconsin—no problem. Loughborough went to "Brother Smith's" house to get a little shut-eye—only to be awakened by a knock on the door at 10:00 P.M.

It was James.

"The train ran off the track three miles west of town," he said breathlessly. "Most of the train, with the engine, is a total wreck . . . a number have died."

The chilling tale was remembered by Ellen many years later:

The train had run about three miles from Jackson when its motion became very violent, jerking backward and forward, and finally stopping. I opened the window and saw one car raised nearly upon one end. I heard most agonizing groans. There was great confusion. The engine had been thrown from the track. But the car we were in was on the track, and was separated about one hundred feet from those before it. The baggage car was not much injured, and our large trunk of books was safe. The second-class car was crushed, and the pieces, with the passengers, were thrown on both sides of the track. The car in which we tried to get a seat was much broken, and one end was raised upon the heap of ruins.

The coupling did not break, but the car we were in was unfastened from the one before it, as if an angel had separated them. We hastily left the car; and my husband took me in his arms, and, wading in the water, carried me across a swampy piece of land to the main road. Four were killed or mortally wounded. . . . Many were much injured. We walked one-half mile to a dwelling, where I remained while my husband rode to Jackson with a messenger sent for physicians.[2]

Being married to Ellen guaranteed the occasional adventure with angelic intervention. The cause of the train wreck had been a bumbling ox having a nappy-poo on the tracks. The collision threw two second-class passenger cars off the tracks, and the "forward end of one of the first-class cars" was bent up pretty good.

A post-wreck inspection done by Loughborough revealed that the car the Whites rode in stood completely unharmed about two hundred feet away from the crash site—an answer to prayer, especially when it came to light that the Whites' car was uncoupled from the rest of the train. Yet, no one working on the train could explain how that could have happened—especially since no link, bolt, or chain had been broken; instead, the linkage lay "quietly on the platform of the unwrecked car."

"I have been shown," wrote Ellen some time later, "that an angel was sent to preserve us." That's an amazing image, and I am grateful they were supernaturally spared. But, for me, I like the picture of James carrying his wife across the swamp to safety best of all.

Colorado vacations

Every family needs vacations. Camp meetings were a popular destination for the early Advent people, but they did occasionally opt for something more traditional. The Whites frequently took the train to the Rockies for a little R and R. One such trip, in the summer of 1873, found the Whites in the mountains accompanied by their son Willie and Ellen's friend Lucinda. It gives us a glimpse into a very normal family at play.

They spent the first few days in Denver with extended family, the Wallings, before going into the mountains. Two "hair mattresses" (as in stuffed with horse hair . . . not even Walmart carries those) as well as pillows (not sure if they were "hair pillows") afforded a comfortable place to sleep. The Whites stayed there through the Sabbath, and after Sabbath came to a close, they made their way to Golden City (not stuffed with gold) in the mountains.

On July 3, Willie wrote to his brother, Edson, about all the fun they were having:

> We are here at Walling's old mill, two miles from where he is now operating. It is a good house which he lets us have the use of. There are a parlor, dining room, kitchen, two bedrooms, and a sort of underground room, which serves as buttery and cellar below, and two bedrooms above.
>
> We are nearly settled. Walling lends us nearly all the furniture we need. Day before yesterday we awoke in the morning to find an inch of snow on the ground and the thermometer two degrees above freezing. How is that for the first of July? . . .
>
> Father is quite well and cheerful. He is tinkering up shelves, bedsteads, et cetera, and keeps busy most all the time.

Sounds like the fam was having a great time frittering their time away, puttering and tinkering around. Even James was having a brief moment of relaxation. Willie went on to talk about mending the fence and planting a garden.

Diaries from the family also tell us that they prayed together atop mountains and along trails. Sometimes they wandered into the wilderness to just have quiet moments with their thoughts. They picked wild strawberries and raspberries—products that fetched high prices in the local general store.

All things considered, it sounds a lot like my family vacations to our cabin in the Smoky Mountains. The White family ate, puttered around the woods, tinkered with various projects around the house, and had devotions together. They knew how to do more than work and found pockets of time to just enjoy the world around them—even though it was a struggle for James.

Good advice for those of us stressed out with school, work, and book deadlines.

Of course, just like in normal families, vacations for the Whites didn't always go according to plan. Just as we struggle with missing the ferry and getting stuck on an island (happened to me twice), running out of gas, and ungrateful children who throw temper tantrums at Disney World, James and Ellen sometimes had to deal with unforeseen problems as well—even when they were trying to relax and get away from it all.

Travel failure

In spring of 1879, some poor Adventists needed a lift from northern Texas to Colorado to resettle. James got excited about helping them. It would be an adventure, he decided and dragged his dear family along. Their caravan included eight wagons, the

Whites' two-seater spring wagon, thirty-one people—and a very stormy night.

Ellen recalled that three days into their epic journey they camped in the open prairie. Shortly before they could set up camp, a storm erupted. "In ten minutes there were several inches of water in the tent,"[3] wrote Ellen.

I've been on camping trips like that . . . they're awful.

According to the prophet, everyone woke up "sick with colds and bowel complaints."

I have also been on camping trips like that . . . they're worse than awful.

Ellen managed to write her son Willie and express her displeasure: "I had rather attend twenty camp meetings with all their wear, knowing I was doing good to souls, than to be here traveling through the country. The scenery is beautiful, the changes and variety enjoyable; but I have so many fears that I am not in the line of my duty."[4]

Turns out, James's trip was a failure on multiple levels—including the fact that they found themselves camping out in Indian Territory. This was back in the old "cowboys and Indians" days—the historical period when arrows and bullets tore through people's heads and chests. Ellen wrote, "We have to be very well armed in passing through Indian Territory. We have our wagons brought up in a circle, then our horses are placed within the circle. We have two men to watch. They are relieved every two hours. They carry guns on their shoulders. We have less fears from Indians than from white men who employ the Indians to make a stampede among the horses and mules and ponies."[5]

Despite the dangers, several Indians joined their camp to hear Ellen preach . . . which was another point of angst for the weary woman.

Ellen had to speak to the camp every Sabbath, because "no one else seemed to feel the burden." Ellen complained that she had "not had time to keep a diary or write a letter. Unpack, and pack, hurry, cook, set table, has been the order of the day." Even more aggravating was the fact that James was clearly having a great time.

"Father [James] rides horseback a considerable part of the time," Ellen wrote. "He is enjoying the journey much."[6] A stark contrast from Ellen's experience.

"I have been sick the entire journey. . . . Lost twelve pounds. . . . We have worked like slaves," she griped in her letter to her son. "I went to Texas against my will."[7] James had promised her the chance of a lifetime, but the trip nearly killed her sense of adventure. Thankfully, James felt impressed to go to a camp meeting in Kansas—cutting the trip short.

It's amazing that Ellen ever traveled with him after that.

Team ministry

"At the present time I am destitute of means, and am some in debt," wrote a broke James in an issue of *Present Truth*. As you may recall, James had trouble launching a magazine early in his ministry. To make matters worse, their friend Joseph Bates had successfully published six pamphlets and had told James that pamphlets—not magazines, were the way to go.

Writing to his friends, the Hastings, James lamented, "As for the poor little paper, it has so little sympathy, and (I fear) so few prayers that I think it will die. I am in deep trial. . . . I want to work for God, but to publish is an uphill work unless there are many prayers ascending, and an interest to sustain a paper."[8]

Further letters had James using the metaphor of a "hot furnace" to describe his desire to publish a periodical. He couldn't let go of the idea, but he also lacked any hope to hang on to.

Like trying to find some college loans to keep you in class or enough change in the couch cushions to put gas in your car to pick up your date—James was scrambling to find any kind of support so that his dream could become reality. Thankfully, God, through Ellen, gave him what he needed.

A vision came to Ellen in which she saw "that it [the periodical] was needed." The vision was so intense that she told James that if his paper died, so would souls. Her words to him were, "*Write, write, write, write*, and speed the message and let it go." The vision filled James with spiritual adrenaline.

Fired up by his wife's vision and encouraging words, James wrote, "My way now seems to be made plain, and I hope all my brethren will do their duty, and no more, nor less." Throughout James's career, Ellen constantly encouraged and nudged him to fulfill his calling, and in turn, James helped his wife process what God revealed to her in vision.

"While my husband lived," penned Ellen, "he acted as a helper and counselor in the sending out of the messages that were given to me." As is often the case with inspiration, she received visions at all hours—late at night or even in the middle of preaching at church. She did her best to write them down when she had time. Then, she and her husband "examined the matter together." James corrected "grammatical errors" and eliminated "needless repetition." Kinda destroys the idea that Ellen's writings were all dictated verbatim from the mouth of divine beings, doesn't it?

Ellen recorded what she was shown in vision as best she could. Remember, God works with us; He doesn't hijack our minds and make our hands write. Once the editing was complete, they sent the written counsel to the person who needed the vision—or to the printer for mass distribution in some cases. Publishing took teamwork, and so did public speaking.

When Ellen first started speaking in front of the faithful, she "moved out timidly." If she had any confidence to speak of, "it was given to me by the Holy Spirit." Next time you have to give a presentation in front of class or read something in church, and you feel the strong urge to vomit—remember that prophets have stage fright too, and that the same Spirit who helped Ellen will help you.

"Our meetings were usually conducted," reflected Mrs. White, "in such a manner that both of us took part." She let James lead off with a "doctrinal discourse"— something about the Sabbath or Jesus' second coming—and then Ellen stepped up with "an exhortation of considerable length." She was long-winded but never boring. Also, know that back in her day local churches did not hear regular sermons—there were no settled pastors over churches. So people were willing to sit and listen.

James and Ellen were itinerant—meaning they traveled to a new church every week. That's why so many people loved for them to come to a camp meeting back then—because, for many, it was the only time they could hear any good preaching. The rest of the year, things functioned like a small-group Bible study. To have a live preacher preaching actual sermons was like opening night of a summer blockbuster.

And the Whites always brought a double feature.

For years, people found themselves challenged, blessed, exhorted, and encouraged by the dynamic duo—this unstoppable pair who continued to serve God despite tragedy, poverty, disability, and hostility. Yet, for all the incredible strength the Whites possessed they were still human . . . and humans don't live forever.

ENDNOTES

1. Source for this section is William C. White, "Sketches and Memories of James and Ellen G. White: XXX. Early Memories of Our First Home," *Review and Herald,* February 13, 1936.
2. James and Ellen White, *Life Sketches* (1880), 308.
3. E. G. White, letter to W. C. and Mary White, May 3, 1879; letter 20a, 1879.
4. Ibid.
5. Ibid.
6. E. G. White, letter to "Children," May 4, 1879; letter 36, 1879.
7. E. G. White, letter to Mary White, May 20, 1879; letter 20, 1879.
8. James White, letter to Leonard and Elvira Hastings, January 3, 1850.

Chapter 35

Death of James

Years ago I answered a phone call from my head elder informing me, "Ken has had a heart attack and passed away."

What? Ken? Ken is a husband and a father—barely fifty years old, if that . . .

"Are you serious?" I heard myself ask into the receiver. What kind of question is that? Like my sweet head elder is gonna prank call his pastor with stories of members suffering fatal heart attacks? No one jokes about that; why would I ask it?

"Yes, I'm serious," came the reply. "We're at the hospital."

"I'll be right there."

That moment of disbelief, when confronted with death, continues to haunt my mind. As common as death is, it always arrives as a surprise—even when someone has been hovering near dying for months. Which brings up another weird question we ask when we hear someone has died: "Was it expected?" Like the idea of someone passing away is the most foreign concept to ever be voiced on planet Earth—this world where everything from grass to grandpas dies.

All over the world.

All the time.

And yet we never seem to expect it.

Even in those rare moments when we do—when someone has been terminally ill for a long time—the moment of death still slips in so silently, so stealthily, as it steals our loved one's final breath away, that we still weep and grieve as though we never thought it would happen. In the Bible, death is considered an "enemy" (1 Corinthians 15:26), because God never intended for humans to die. So it always hurts when it happens—even to prophets.

On a warm day early in August 1881, James lay in Battle Creek Sanitarium in Michigan—he was dying. Friends, family, and fellow believers paced the grounds and the lobby, holding a vigil for the powerful spiritual leader. They knew death stalked close by—rumors suggested James was already unconscious. Tears, whispers repeating

Scripture, and hugs did their best to bring comfort to the grieving—shocked at how quickly James's health had failed.

Just a week earlier, James had preached by his wife's side at church. No one had any idea that the great pioneer of their faith would fall so ill so fast. The announcement came at 5:15 P.M.—James was dead, on the Sabbath, the day designed for human rest that James had spent his life promoting.

People reeled at the reality that he was gone.

Only a few days before he died, James wrote a piece for the *Review and Herald*, entitled "Words of Comfort"—speaking about the hope that Christians have beyond the grave, when they have lived a life trusting in the Lord. "The hope of the gospel," penned James, "dispels the gloom that enshrouds the grave."[1] The timing was eerily appropriate.

Ellen, now a widow, wrote about the last week of her husband's life—starting with Sabbath, July 30. She wrote that they took their usual prayer walk in the grove on Sabbath, and he helped her open the church service with singing and prayer. On Sunday, James felt God would give him strength to attend the "Eastern camp meetings." Pretty normal weekend so far . . . and then Monday happened.

"He had a severe chill," remembered Ellen. "Tuesday he did not rally as expected, but we thought the disease an attack of fever and ague [malaria], and supposed that it would soon yield to treatment." Making matters worse, Ellen, herself, succumbed to chills on Tuesday night.

Dr. John Kellogg—brother of the guy whose company makes Fruit Loops and Frosted Flakes—happened to be a buddy of the Whites and suggested they go to Battle Creek Sanitarium. A mattress was found for them, and, according to Ellen, "my husband and myself were laid side by side, for the last time, and thus taken to the Sanitarium." By Friday, Ellen had improved—but James struggled to wake up.

Immediately, Ellen was whisked away to her husband's room, but as soon as she saw him, she "knew that he was dying." She did her best to wake him, and he seemed to understand everything she said—responding well to "yes or no" questions, but not to much else. Their conversation must have gone something like this.

"James . . . you're dying," she said softly. He didn't seem to be taken off guard by the news. Looking at the love of her life fading away, she asked him, "Is Jesus precious to you?"

"Yes, oh, yes," he replied.

"Have you no desire to live?" she continued, feeling the time vanish.

"No," he said softly.

Ellen knelt by his bedside, with Edson, and prayed for her husband "in that solemn hour." She saw a peaceful expression come over him. "Jesus loves you," she told him. "The everlasting arms are beneath you."

"Yes, yes," he murmured.

Wanting to be certain he knew what was going on, Ellen asked him if he recognized who was around him. "You are Ellen," he said looking at the loving faces gazing on him. "You are Edson . . . I know you all." Others joined in the prayer around James's bed and resolved to pray through much of the night.

Mercifully, James felt no pain. The prayers of loved ones sustained him, and even revived him for a short spell, but he remained extremely weak. The following morning he ate some breakfast and, briefly, seemed to recover. However, around noon a chill shuddered through him, rendering him unconscious.

"He quietly breathed his life away," wrote Ellen, "without a struggle or a groan. . . . The scene was as pleasant as it was possible for a deathbed to be." Losing your partner of thirty-five years would devastate most people. Ellen seems a bit too calm here. She also goes on to say some things that appear a bit callous. Continuing to reflect on the loss of her beloved, she said,

> At times I felt that I could not have my husband die. But these words seemed to be impressed on my mind: "Be still, and know that I am God." I keenly feel my loss, but I dare not give myself up to useless grief. This would not bring back my husband. And I am not so selfish as to wish, if I could, to bring him from his peaceful slumber to engage again in the battles of life. Like a tired warrior, he has lain down to sleep. I will look with pleasure upon his resting place. The best way in which I and my children can honor the memory of him who has fallen, is to take the work where he left it, and in the strength of Jesus carry it forward to completion.

See what I mean? Her attitude is very admirable, but it seems a bit emotionally detached. She sounds more like a person losing a business partner—not a life partner.

Of course, as with many people who experience loss, the weight of what has happened often strikes much later. Later that afternoon, loss struck Ellen hard:

> The shock of my husband's death—so sudden, so unexpected—fell upon me with crushing weight. In my feeble condition I had summoned strength to remain at his bedside to the last; but when I saw his eyes closed in death, exhausted nature gave way, and I was completely prostrated. For some time I seemed balancing between life and death. The vital flame burned so low that a breath might extinguish it. At night my pulse would grow feeble, and my breathing fainter and fainter till it seemed about to cease.

Now that sounds more like it. Ellen was a strong woman, making her seem unfeeling to some people, but she was also vulnerable to all the same hurts we are—and she was brave enough to write about it.

ENDNOTE

1. James White, "Words of Comfort," *Review and Herald,* July 26, 1881.

Chapter 36

The Funeral

The funeral took place a week after James's death—and Ellen herself didn't look so good while she waited for friends and family to arrive. John White, James's brother, who had arrived the Friday before, remarked, "Ellen, I am deeply sorry to see you so feeble. A trying ordeal is before you in the funeral services of the morrow. God help you, my dear sister, God help you on this occasion."

Ellen dismissed his concern, saying that she would be able to hold it together and that God isn't glorified by abandoning oneself to grief—Jesus would sustain her.

On August 13, Sabbath afternoon, twenty-five hundred people showed up for James's funeral in the Battle Creek Tabernacle. Despite feeling ill, Ellen attended, though she had to be carried in a chair. She was laid on a "sofa prepared with pillows" while being watched by a doctor.

I never knew people could attend funerals on sofas until I read this.

One of the church's foremost theologians, Uriah Smith, gave the eulogy (a short talk praising the life of the dead), highlighting six major traits that James demonstrated: he was cool in times of confusion, he was never prone to "fanaticism," he made great decisions, he never collapsed under discouragement, he planned for the future work of the church, and finally, he knew how to make strong friendships and be generous with people.

Strengthened by these words, Ellen surprised everyone by taking the pulpit to speak for ten minutes. In a clear voice, she spoke about her Savior's ability to hold her up during intense grief—just as He had done when she experienced the loss of two of her children. Speaking to the thousands of sad souls in the sanctuary, Ellen said,

I thank my Saviour I have two sons He has given me to stand by my side. Henceforth the mother must lean upon the children; for the strong, brave, noble-hearted husband is at rest. The turmoil with him is over. . . . And now he upon whose large affections I have leaned, with whom I have labored—and we have been united in labor for thirty-six years—is taken away; but I can lay my hands upon his eyes and say, I commit my treasure to Thee until the morning of the resurrection.

Beautiful, affectionate words spoken from the lips of a grieving prophet.

Ninety-five carriages formed the funeral procession to Oak Hill Cemetery—almost one hundred people followed on foot to the family plot where James's two boys and parents rest until the resurrection. I have been there; it is a beautiful place with trees and small green hills.

After James was buried, Ellen returned to the sanitarium for the evening. The next morning she was taken back to her house—still resting on her bed—where family waited for her. I have often been told that the hardest part about experiencing a deep loss in the family is the return home—after all the arrangements, memorials, potlucks, and visits from sympathetic friends have ended.

There, as you lay in your bed in silence, you feel the emptiness of your house and the full weight of your sad thoughts, with nothing to direct you from them. Ellen felt the darkness around her. She said, "The light of my home had gone." However, she would do her best to carry on—as she moved into what her grandson would later call "the lonely years."

We will look briefly at that time toward the end of this book, but for now, watching Ellen leave behind her role as wife, we can stand back and look at a marriage that lasted well over thirty years despite circumstances that would have crushed most relationships.

Even though they had challenges, losses, disagreements, separations, and arguments over visions, James considered Ellen to be his "crown of rejoicing," and Ellen, writing years later, reflected on how she missed the "strong manly arm" she used to lean on—and that James was "the best man that ever trod shoe leather."

A marriage like this deserves our respect. We should all pray for the strength to love as dedicatedly and as deeply as they did.

Section IV: The Misery of Healing—Turning the Health Message Into a Mess

Chapter 37

Are You Gonna Eat That?

The world is full of gross.

Even in the area of culinary arts, we have managed to nasty-up mealtime around the world, with delicacies that make your stomach feel like crawling out through your own throat and running away from the dinner table. Allow me to elaborate.

In Japan and Korea, you may find yourself dining on *odori don*—live squid and/or octopus writhing in a bowl of sauce.

Not a fan? Well head on over to Canada and order yourself a "sourtoe" cocktail. This special drink has a severed human toe—drained of bodily fluid and pickled— swimming in the bottom of the glass. Apparently, in 1973, a man named Captain Dick Stevenson found a man's frostbitten toe floating in a jar of moonshine left over from an expedition in the 1920s. While you and I may have chosen the natural response of vomiting in the snow, the good captain saw potential.

He even created a little rule, "You can drink it fast, you can drink it slow, but the lips have got to touch the toe." I'm not sure which is worse—the alcohol or the dismembered phalange. Just to be safe, I'd avoid both at all costs—along with Guam's fruit bat soup.

You heard me—soup with a whole, boiled fruit bat bathing in the broth. Head, eyes, teeth, wings, and fur all intact and soaking among the vegetables and coconut milk. Please, please, I beg of you, don't Google that.

The world has countless atrocities like these, ranging from devouring live baby snakes as though they were green spaghetti, deep-fried tarantula fritters, and Greenland's technically edible pile of decomposed meat slurry—made by stuffing dead birds into a seal carcass and letting them ferment for three to eighteen months.

Gross.

And you Googled fruit bat soup, didn't you?

Unhealthy foods

It's easy to turn up our noses at some of these dishes, but every culture, and every person, has unhealthy dietary habits. I love McDonald's french fries—even though when left out to decompose . . . well, they never do. I tell my wife that's because the oil they are deep-fried in serves to lock in the nutrients. She doesn't believe me, and neither do nutritionists and filmmakers who continue to point out the dangers of fast food in films such as *Super Size Me.*

I am also a huge fan of soda—particularly root beer. Not far from where I live there exists a magical business known as The Root Beer Store. I love that place. They have over a hundred kinds of root beer. My favorite brand contains forty-six grams of pure cane sugar—per bottle.

Meaning they should probably rename it The Diabetes Store.

Beyond fried foods and sugary soda, we have a host of processed (premade in a factory) foods. Instead of the good old days when you went out and picked vegetables, slaughtered the best-looking bovine, and churned your own butter, we now buy everything in a box with contents waiting to be "zapped" in the microwave.

The result of this kind of diet is evident—an ever increasing number of people suffering from heart disease, diabetes, obesity, cancer, and general grossness. And our solutions to these problems are limitless.

Video exercise programs such as P90x, P90x2, P90x3 Insanity, Tae Bo, Tae Bo II . . . (yeah, you get the idea; we have a lot of them) are designed to punish your body's lack of muscle and stamina. Then there are multitudes of generic videos featuring yoga, Pilates, aerobics, and calisthenics.

Augmenting our videos are diets that offer freedom from any number of ailments. If you only eat meat, or bread, or raw veggies, or drink liquids by the light of the moon standing on one foot, you will never be sick again. It's exhausting keeping up with all the health trends—particularly when at least half of them seem a little cray-cray.

Ellen knew what it was like to live in an unhealthy culture that found itself constantly bewildered about how to keep people in decent shape. We have already seen how, in the nineteenth century, people were suspicious of fruits and veggies—going so far as to think they were unfit for children. They tended to gorge themselves on meals saturated with sweets and highly spiced foods, topping it all off with a stiff drink or a puff of pipe tobacco.

With life expectancy peaking in the forties during the 1800s, somebody needed to do something. Health reform—essentially societies of concerned people telling folks to eat their vegetables—emerged during this time, seeking to clean up the dirty health habits people had embraced. The idea was to improve and prolong life—and thereby increase the chances of you having great-grandparents.

On June 6, 1863, a vision revealed the role Ellen and the Adventist people were to have in this health movement—and it was huge.

Chapter 38

Health Visions

"I saw," wrote Ellen, "that now we should take special care of the health God has given us, for our work was not yet done." The vision directly linked health with the ability to serve God. Moreover, Adventists "should encourage a cheerful, hopeful, peaceful frame of mind, for our health depends upon our doing this." So, no "madventists" or "sadventists" allowed.

Continuing with her recollection of the vision she had seen, she wrote,

> I saw that it was duty for everyone to have a care for his health, but especially should we turn our attention to our health, and take time to devote to our health, that we may in a degree recover from the effects of overdoing and overtaxing the mind. The work God requires of us will not shut us away from caring for our health. . . .
>
> . . . It is not safe nor pleasing to God to violate the laws of health and then ask Him to take care of our health and keep us from disease when we are living directly contrary to our prayers.[1]

God did not call people to be workaholics, and He would not bless those who mistreated their bodies and then asked Him to bless them with healing.

Other major points from the vision included a refusal to remain silent on the issue of health. Adventists needed to encourage others to stop being unbalanced in the areas of "working, in eating, in drinking, and in drugging" and then "point them to God's great medicine, water, pure soft water, for diseases, for health, for cleanliness, and for a luxury."

Ellen's vision gave solutions, not just criticisms.

On Christmas Day 1865, she received a sequel health vision with implications for outreach. She wrote:

I saw that the health reform was a great enterprise, closely connected with the present truth, and that Seventh-day Adventists should have a home for the sick, where they could be treated for their diseases and also learn how to take care of themselves so as to prevent sickness. . . .

. . . Our people should furnish means to meet the wants of a growing Health Institute among us. . . .

God would have a health institution established which will in its influence be closely connected with the closing work for mortals fitting for immortality.

Ellen didn't call out people's bad habits just to make them mad—the health message was to be a way to bring healing to people and then point them to Jesus. If Adventists could be a people known for healing, it would create interest in their faith.

Ellen's vision also called for a "health institute." And just a year later, in 1866, the Western Health Reform Institute, located in Battle Creek, Michigan, opened. The swiftness of its construction testified to how powerfully Ellen's influence had grown since her first vision in 1844. Not too long after the health institute opened, Dr. John H. Kellogg took over and changed the name to the Battle Creek Sanitarium, which by 1900 had an international reputation for quality health care.

Since that time, Ellen's visions have sparked a health movement that now stands at 175 hospitals/sanitariums, 134 nursing home/retirement centers, 269 clinics/dispensaries, and 36 orphanages. Boom! That's a lot of medicine. Not only that, but studies consistently show Adventists to be some of the longest lived and most contented people on the planet—having one of the highest percentages of centenarians (people living to be at least one hundred years old).

While it's true that Ellen did not start the health reform movement—and that some of the health principles she came up with weren't original to her—she did enhance the movement by providing a unique perspective that linked physical health with spiritual health. This is sometimes called a holistic approach.

In other words, it is hard to maintain a strong connection with God and a commitment to serving others, when you're hunched over the toilet bowl revisiting your lunch, felling entire forests to provide enough Kleenex to damn up the rivers flowing out of your nose, or just generally feeling like a steaming pile of garbage while you await sweet death to come and rescue you from whatever ailment you have that might have been prevented had you not eaten deep-fried Twinkies for breakfast—every day of your life.

It is noteworthy to mention that recent studies comparing Ellen to her contemporaries who were writing and promoting health reform reveal that only a third of her writings regarding what people should do to be healthy could possibly have been borrowed from others. This means that two-thirds of her health principles appear to have come directly from the visions God gave her. Even though some of her reasons as to "why" the principles work tended to reflect the current scientific thinking of her day, her material is almost frighteningly impressive for a nineteenth-century woman with a third-grade education.[2]

Basics

Ellen had other visions, and testimonies, related to health—coupled with studies from biblical books such as Leviticus. Her health message can be summed up in eight principles: "pure air, sunlight, [moderation], rest, exercise, proper diet, the use of water, trust in divine power."[3]

Seems legit to me. Pretty normal sounding, right? While it may be hard to balance all of these things at the same time, no one can argue that these principles are legalistic or unrealistic. I mean, seriously, water? Sleep? Sunshine, for crying out loud! Who in their right mind suggests that things such as these are bad for you?

So how do people get so crazy with Ellen White's writings on health? Of all the things Ellen writes about, why do people get so defensive and argumentative about the subject that is supposed to help them live healthier lives?

ENDNOTES

1. E. G. White, *Selected Messages,* 3:280.
2. Don S. McMahon, *Acquired or Inspired?* (Victoria, Australia: Signs Publishing Company, 2005), 77.
3. Ellen G. White, *The Ministry of Healing* (Mountain View, CA: Pacific Press® Publishing Association, 1905), 127.

Chapter 39

Righteousness by Fork

When I was in seminary, a book on health, written by two supermodels, became tremendously popular among the students. What made it so strange was that the two authors used language that bordered on the abusive. While the health principles in the book mirrored much of what Ellen taught, the two lovey ladies called their readers names, and mocked their weight, energy levels, and even the smell of their breath.

People loved it.

Why? Why did that book become so popular, while Ellen White—whose writings often said exactly the same things (in strong, but never abusive, language)—remained unread or viewed as judgmental? I think part of the answer as to why people misuse Ellen's writings on health has to do with the very thing that makes them special—their spiritual connection, their holistic approach.

Some people misunderstand the link between the body and the spirit, particularly when it comes to food. They make judgment calls about the state of people's salvation based on what they put in their mouth. If they see someone eat too much meat, or bring a cheese dish to an all-vegan potluck, or order a salted caramel mocha—they immediately downgrade that person's walk with Jesus.

"Good" Adventists don't drink coffee or caffeinated sodas, eat steak, gain weight, order cheese on their pizza, or enjoy such "worldly" entertainments as roller coasters, movies, or board games. We take these externals and elevate them to a moral status—a litmus test to determine whether someone belongs to Jesus.

It's not a new problem; Jesus Himself ran into it. The religious leaders in His day, the Pharisees, were very concerned about holiness. How you handled your food was as important to them as what kind of food you ate. During one of their epic interactions, Jesus broke down their weak definition of holiness by saying, "There is nothing outside a person that by going into him can defile him, but the things that come out of a person are what defile him" (Mark 7:15). Jesus isn't suggesting that we can eat whatever we want without consequences, but He is making an important contrast.

What criteria characterize a follower of Jesus? Instead of cheese, maybe we should be looking at such things as love, mercy, forgiveness, sacrificial service, and faith. Jesus said that people would know His followers by how they loved other people (John 13:35). Compounding the issue of judging the state of people's souls based on their diet and how often they exercise is Jesus' pesky order not to judge those things at all (check out John 7:24).

Ellen had some words for people who elevated the health message to the same level as the gospel or the good news that Jesus is coming soon: "Health reform is closely connected with the work of the third [angel's] message, yet it is not the message. Our preachers should teach . . . health reform, yet they should not make this the leading theme in the place of the message."

Ellen knew how to keep her theological priorities straight. As vital as the health message is—it isn't *the* message. It is an amazing tool to help us, but it can't save us.

Now, before lovers of health think I am somehow minimizing its importance, let me reassure you. Although I cannot judge the state of someone's eternal destiny based on what he or she does—I *can* point out natural consequences (assuming the person knows me, loves me, and knows I love them) and challenge them to make positive changes.

In other words, I don't know if you are going to hell, but I can tell you that if you keep doing crystal meth, you will end up in the hospital . . . or the cemetery. See what I mean? And while, in one sense, the health message is about (surprise) health, it can also become a moral issue if you willingly/knowingly do things that destroy the gift of life you have been given. Doing so denies the special value that God places on each of our lives.

For example, if I know my cholesterol is 300, and if my doctor says that eating another triple cheeseburger will cause me to suffer a massive heart attack—leaving my wife and three kids destitute—then, yes, absolutely, the way I eat becomes a life-or-death issue that affects others. Or, if my daily addiction to Starbucks costs me a hundred bucks a month—leaving no room in my budget for church, charity, or even a couple bucks for the homeless guy outside my favorite coffee shop—then yeah, there's a problem.

In all these cases—and an infinite number of others you can imagine in your free time—my health choices have the potential to affect my ability to be loving and just. And those are big things that Jesus and His followers should care about. The other contributing factor to people making the health message a mess has to do with our old friend: context.

Chapter 40

Extremists

One of the most famous—or infamous, depending on who's quoting at you—Ellen White compilations (collections of her writings, organized by topic and crammed into one book) is *Counsels on Diet and Foods*. This nifty volume came into being in 1926 (eleven years after Ellen died) to be used as a textbook for students studying diet at the Adventist Church's medical school in Loma Linda, California. Back then, it was known as *Testimony Studies on Diet and Foods*. A second edition, bearing the current name, hit the market in 1938.

So, to answer the "who" question (as in, Who was the book meant for?), we see that this compilation was planned to fit squarely within a college classroom of medical students, under the direction of medical professors. This meant that if someone read a snippet of Ellen's work and had questions, they could find the context of the initial quotation in question, or they could draw on their medical knowledge to balance what they read, or the professor could call them out if they had a wild idea.

However, just handing the book to people who don't understand how context works is like researching your illness in a medical dictionary or WebMD. Got a sniffle? A quick flip or word search through the medicinal databases will convince you that you have a cold . . . or pneumonia . . . or maybe thyroid failure.

By perusing the pages of medical textbooks/resources without a clue how to use them properly, people make themselves nuts, hunting down all the potential symptoms, diseases, and treatments to cure whatever life-threatening thing they think they have. The same thing can happen with Ellen White's works—particularly ones such as *Counsels on Diet and Foods*.

A classic example of this is the case of M. L. Andreasen, a prominent Adventist theologian in the 1930s and 1940s. Early in his career, Andreasen canvassed (sold Christian books door-to-door) and embraced health reform to the extreme.

"I lived practically on granola and water only," he remembered. "I used neither milk, butter, nor eggs [for a period of years]. My older daughter was ten years old when she first tasted butter. We used no meat, of course, nor milk, butter, or eggs, and almost no salt and sugar. We did not have much left but granola. I canvassed on granola."

So much for variety being the spice of life . . . or the spice of anything, for that matter. Canvassing is very physical work—walking miles and miles at a time. While granola is hearty, and I use it myself on backpacking trips, to make it the sole source of nutrition isn't healthful.

The story gets better.

"I ate my granola," wrote Andreasen, "and drank water three times a day. Then my attention was called to the fact that two times were better and so I ate granola twice a day."

OK, so you're on foot for miles at a time as part of your job, and all you have are two bags of granola—and this isn't trail mix, the stuff that has coconut flakes and M&Ms in it. This is just oats.

The story gets better.

"But I got tired of granola alone after a while," complained Andreasen. "I wondered if it would be all right to eat raisins with it; and so I bought some raisins with a little trepidation and anxiety."

Anxiety over raisins? I might understand if you were approaching a cookie and were afraid of being duped with raisins when you expected chocolate chips—but this guy was afraid he was committing some grievous sin by adding raisins to his oats!

"Now it was granola and raisins," Andreasen continued, "but my conscience smote me, so I gave up the raisins."

Wow.

The story gets better.

Upon repenting of his raisins, Andreasen writes, "Then I bought a pineapple and ate all of it, with the result that my mouth became sore. I took that to be punishment for eating pineapples. So I went back to granola again."

Ha ha ha ha ha ha ha! . . . I'm sorry. What I meant to say is, how awful! This poor guy was doing his best to serve the Lord, and he actually thought God would begrudge him a pineapple.

You guessed it, the story gets better.

Having abandoned the iniquity of eating pineapples, Andreasen discovered more "truth": "Then I read somewhere in Sister White's writings that people eat altogether too much. I applied that to my two meals of granola a day. That statement in itself is true, but not under those conditions. I cut down on my granola and henceforth lived mostly on granola and a few simple vegetables and peanuts, not for a day or a month or a year, but for ten years."[1]

Thankfully, for Andreasen, he eventually grew to understand Ellen's writings better and backed off his extreme diet. He went on to warn people against applying her writings to "conditions other than those under which they were given." Good call.

Ellen repeatedly dealt with extremes like this. In her book *The Ministry of Healing*, she wrote,

> Another class, in their desire to set a right example, go to the opposite extreme. . . .
>
> . . . Some restrict themselves to a very meager diet, not having sufficient variety to supply the needs of the system, and they suffer in consequence.
>
> Those who have but a partial understanding of the principles of reform are often the most rigid, not only in carrying out their views themselves, but in urging them on their families and their neighbors. The effect of their mistaken reforms, as seen in their own ill-health, and their efforts to force their views upon others, give many a false idea of dietetic reform, and lead them to reject it altogether. . . .
>
> There is real common sense in dietetic reform. The subject should be studied broadly and deeply, and no one should criticize others because their practice is not, in all things, in harmony with his own. It is impossible to make an unvarying rule to regulate everyone's habits.[2]

Notice how the extremists operate? They adopt "meager" diets (a.k.a., "everything is bad for you") and then try to coerce and force others to follow their ideas of how to live a healthful life. Ellen does her best to appeal to common sense in the whole thing.

Tragically, as has been said by someone cleverer than I, "Common sense is a flower that doesn't grow in everyone's garden."

ENDNOTES

1. M. L. Andreasen, unpublished manuscript, November 30, 1948.
2. E. G. White, *The Ministry of Healing*, 318, 319.

Chapter 41

Ellen's Eatings

A lot of people are curious about what Ellen ate—no doubt some of them hoping for a grocery list to emulate on their next outing to the local grocer. Talking to some people, you'd think Ellen survived on nothing more than holiness and air. Haters also have an interest in Ellen's eatings—attempting to point out inconsistencies in her life that might nullify her message.

One favorite accusation among the haters is that she ate meat—which, in the grand scheme of things, is not much of a criticism, but they turn it into a charge of hypocrisy, not practicing what she so adamantly preached to others. Ellen officially swore off meat at a camp meeting in Australia in 1894, but did she mess up?

Part of the problem is that her critics can be as rigid as her supporters.

We know that Ellen wasn't perfect and that she messed up from time to time like the Bible prophets. So even if she did partake of some "flesh meat" now and then, that shouldn't be a surprise. But often there is a specific context to the times when she and her husband ate meat. For example, according to her son Willie:

> There were about 35 of us going from Battle Creek to Oakland in 1884 in two skeleton sleeping cars. . . .
>
> As we approached to the border line between Nevada and California, it was found that our provisions were running low. Some of us were able to make good meals out of the dried things that were left in our lunch boxes, but Sister White's appetite failed.
>
> We were in a country where fresh fruit was very expensive and so one morning at a station where our train had stopped for half an hour, I went out and purchased two or three pounds of beefsteak and this was cooked by Sister McEnterfer on an alcohol stove, and most of the members that composed Sister White's party partook of it.[1]

Uh-oh, beefsteak? Well, there you have it. Nearly twenty years after Ellen's first vision, her own son dooms the entire family. Except all that was available otherwise were some crusty, dried-out goods and exorbitantly priced fruit—not a lot of options. Willie continued to share his thoughts on the matter:

> When I bought the beefsteak, I reasoned that freshly killed ox from this cattle country, would probably be a healthy animal and that the risk of acquiring disease would be very small. . . .
>
> You will find in Sister White's writings several instances where she says flesh meats do not appear on our table, and this was true. During a number of years when on rare occasions a little meat was used, [it] was considered to be an emergency.[2]

Remember that line Ellen had about using common sense? Sometimes we find ourselves in less than ideal circumstances, and we have to make do with what we can. Not to mention that common sense should keep us from debating things such as whether or not she ate beefsteak.

Beyond emergencies, Ellen freely admits struggling with giving up meat. In 1870, she wrote about her experience: "I suffered keen hunger, I was a great meat eater. But when faint, I placed my arms across my stomach, and said: 'I will not taste a morsel. I will eat simple food, or I will not eat at all.' . . . When I made these changes I had a special battle to fight."[3]

The fight required a great effort, but she won. The year after her initial health vision she claimed she had "left off the use of meat." Five years later, she wrote to Edson, telling him, "We have in diet been strict to follow the light the Lord has given us. . . . We have advised you not to eat butter or meat. We have not had it on our [own] table."[4]

Good work, Ellen! And she continued the good work up to 1870, when she continued to write about success in removing certain deliciously detrimental items from the table.

Yet despite the strong language, she still ate meat . . . and admitted it. In 1890, Ellen wrote, "When I could not obtain the food I needed, I have sometimes eaten a little meat; but I am becoming more and more afraid of it."[5] Again, the context has everything to do with common sense—Jesus isn't glorified when people starve themselves to death. Even as late as 1901, Ellen flatly said, "I was at times . . . compelled to eat a little meat."[6]

Was she a hypocrite? What about all that talk about meat never being served on her table? Well, it wasn't—it was on other people's tables. Ellen did her best to hold to her vegetarian diet, yet sometimes in her travels, meat was all that was available.

About one incident, Ellen wrote, "Brother Glover left the camp today to go for supplies. We are getting short of provisions. . . . A young man from Nova Scotia had come in from hunting. He had a quarter of deer. He had traveled twenty miles with this deer upon his back. . . . He gave us a small piece of the meat, which we made into broth. Willie shot a duck which came in a time of need, for our supplies were rapidly diminishing."[7]

A few days later, Ellen and crew were eating meat again: "The sun shines so pleasantly, but no relief comes to us. Our provisions have been very low for some days. Many of our supplies have gone—no butter, no sauce of any kind, no corn meal, or graham flour. We have a little fine flour and that is all. We expected supplies three days ago certainly, but none has come. Willie went to the lake for water. We heard his gun and found he had shot two ducks. This is really a blessing, for we need something to live upon."[8]

When provisions run low, you do what you need to survive. This was a woman, living in the pioneer days of the United States; practicality was everything.

"How dare you, and your family, Ellen, try to survive on anything but faith! And imagine Ellen's son owning a firearm in nineteenth-century America!" Seriously people, grow up.

Walmart, the Internet, and Amazon.com had the nerve to wait until after Ellen passed away to offer anything you could ever want at the touch of a button. Companies such as Worthington Foods (with the brand MorningStar Farms)—offering ready-made vegetarian proteins—also chose to wait until Walmart, the Internet, and Amazon.com released their best products.

Despite caricatures (those goofball portraits artists draw at fairs), Ellen didn't go to extremes. In 1894, she wrote a piece for *The Youth's Instructor* in which she said, "A meat diet is not the most wholesome of diets, and yet I would not take the position that meat should be discarded by every one. Those who have feeble digestive organs can often use meat, when they cannot eat vegetables, fruit, or porridge."[9]

Personally, I remember being in Newfoundland in the early 2000s and not being able to find even a package of veggie hot dogs for less than eight bucks. It seemed a better idea to just eat some fresh fish and grab a few more veggies rather than pay for premium tofu. I think Ellen would be OK with that.

My stepbrother, serving as a student missionary in the Marshall Islands, was forced to eat fish raw. He is a staunch vegetarian, but when the locals caught a flopping fish, chopped it up, and handed my bro an icy flesh cube laced with saltwater, he had no choice. To refuse would have been considered the epitome of rudeness, and he would have lost his influence as a teacher.

Fish flesh brings up another interesting point. For many people, including Ellen for a time, seafood fits squarely within a vegetarian diet. Ellen liked oysters a lot, but as she studied and grew in her knowledge of health, she eventually stopped eating them. It might be a good idea to give each other a little more grace when it comes to diet.

Obviously, Ellen brooked no compromise with such things as tobacco and alcohol. You may be tempted to argue moderation—that although a steady diet of cupcakes isn't healthful, a cupcake once in a while is OK. Therefore, moderation should apply to tobacco and alcohol as well. A little tobacco or alcohol from time to time should be OK. But even secular society recognizes a qualitative difference between certain things —you don't get carded for buying cupcakes or ordering a pumpkin spice latte. Use your brain.

As for substances such as the caffeine in your latte (thankfully, Ellen makes no mention of chocolate), a few taps on the ol' computer keyboard reveal scores of scholarly articles about how people abuse caffeine. Of course, other studies show caffeine to aid in reducing headaches (ibuprofen, for example), or keeping someone awake who finds themselves driving at 3:00 A.M.

Again, the idea is to use common sense, avoid extremes, and stop judging someone's walk with God—including Ellen's—by what they put in their mouth.

ENDNOTES

1. W. C. White, letter to G. B. Starr, August 24, 1933, in *The Fannie Bolton Story: A Collection of Source Documents* (Washington, DC: Ellen G. White Estate, 1982), 119.

2. Ibid., 119, 120.

3. E. G. White, *Testimonies for the Church,* 2:371, 371.

4. E. G. White, letter to J. E. White, May 25, 1869; letter 5, 1869, in *Manuscript Releases,* 14:312.

5. Ellen G. White, *Christian Temperance and Bible Hygiene* (Battle Creek, MI: Good Health Publishing Company, 1890), 118.

6. E. G. White, letter to "Brethren and Sisters," July 15, 1901; letter 83, 1901.

7. E. G. White, diary entry, September 28, 1873; manuscript 11, 1873, in *Manuscript Releases* 20:211, 212.

8. E. G. White, diary entry, October 5, 1873; manuscript 12, 1873.

9. E. G. White, *The Youth's Instructor,* May 31, 1894; quoted in *Counsels on Diet and Foods,* 394, 395.

Chapter 42

Grandma's Kitchen

Grandmas' kitchens are phenomenal places to experience what I call "food comas." Food comas occur when you have filled yourself absolutely full of good food until all you can do is stare at the wall—or nap contentedly. Grandmothers don't have to put up with you 24/7, so they feel no hesitation in loading you up with cookies, pies, casseroles, and whatever else you want—things that your parents put strict regulations on at home.

When she was alive, my grandma gave me all the sugary cereals banned from my house . . . the ones that turn the milk an unnatural shade of purple (#fruitypebblesforever).

But how was Grandma Ellen at cookery? It seems that she indulged in tasties only in emergencies. It's easy to picture energetic grandbabies sitting up to a cold wooden table and served gruel by Granny White. Thankfully for the grandkids, Ellen knew better than that.

Grace, one of Ellen's grandkids, described Mrs. White's meals as "a happy time," and "a big occasion of the day," with delicious homemade bread and muffinlike creations called "gems." Grace wrote, "We put up strawberry jam and blackberry jam and loganberry jam, but we ate it sparingly, I would say. Grandmother was not one to say, 'No, you can't have any of this.' But, 'Eat it moderately.' You know, don't eat too much, but enjoy a nice slice of bread and cream and strawberry jam. It's delicious."[1]

Again, Ellen seems frustratingly balanced. She didn't forbid sweets, but she also didn't tell her grandkids to put a five-inch-thick blanket of berries on their toast, either.

Another of Ellen's grandkids, Arthur, noted that "beverages were often on the table, but used in modest amounts—tomato juice, grape and other fruit juices, carrot juice, milk, and buttermilk. Besides the cows on the farm, there were chickens fenced in under the apple trees. These supplied the family with eggs that were used in cooking and occasionally served soft-boiled on the table. For desserts, fruit was often used, and occasionally a little pumpkin or lemon pie, tapioca pudding, or bread pudding."[2]

It would seem that every grandma has a pie and pudding in their repertoire. During her ministry, Ellen went so far as to tell one of the Adventist health institutions that "lemon pie should not be forbidden."[3]

ENDNOTES

1. "Dinner at Elmshaven: An Interview With Mrs. Grace Jacques, Granddaughter of Ellen G. White" (Ellen G. White Estate, 1978); document file, 129e.

2. Arthur White, *Ellen G. White,* 6:395, 396.

3. E. G. White, letter to Brother and Sister [G. A.] Irwin, April 11, 1904; letter 127, 1904, in *Counsels on Diet and Foods,* 288.

Chapter 43

More Than Food

We could continue with many more examples of the gastrointestinal variety—but we would fall into the same trap so many have. The health message is so much more than food. Food is critical, and with so many types of food illnesses (bulimia, anorexia, etc.), addictive additives placed in our processed foods, and the junk they inject into even our fruit and veggies, we need to be mindful of how we approach our diet.

However, if we focus only on food, the heath message becomes a mess that makes us miserable. Just think about the lack of writing and preaching on sleep? How often do we check up on each other to make sure we are resting enough? What about sunshine and living an active life? Generally speaking, we can all do better taking good care of ourselves.

In her writings, Ellen linked diet with developing undesirable passions. Part of that reflected the thinking in her day, but it can't be denied that what we eat affects us deeply. Yet I have known people who never ate meat, drank only water, and abstained from all things cheese related—but who were passionate in their mistreatment of people.

Their perfect diets did nothing for their personalities.

We are more important than how much work we can put out or how healthfully we can eat. We need time to breathe, to sit among friends, to laugh, to reflect, to learn, and to grow. When we neglect the entire health message to focus only on diet, we exchange a ministry of healing for a misery of healing—irritating people by calling them to deal with the same things we have just happened to have mastered. Our own life becomes the standard by which we measure others—instead of Jesus, who, by the way, is the only one allowed to judge how close someone is mirroring His character.

Eternal life isn't gained by exercise, eating salad, or taking naps. We don't eat our way into, or out of, heaven. Salvation comes only through trust in Jesus and His love for you. Staying healthy is an important tool, only because it keeps our minds clear so we can discern His will for our lives and our bodies fit for serving Him by sharing His love with others.

Only to the extent that our health habits hurt our ability to respond to God's love and share it with others does it cross into the arena of evil. Hell has the potential to be full of mean-spirited vegans as well as drunk drivers . . . they might even be the same people. I have always been told that there is no such thing as a consistent legalist. We love to showcase our achievements in one area of life—while completely ignoring the rest of our mess.

Embrace and practice the health message—but don't make it a mess by confusing it with the gospel of Christ. Our life is a spectacular gift that demands care, but life also requires the freedom to enjoy itself with friends, laughter, reflection, learning, and growth. Take care of yourself; give yourself grace—and treat others with the same care.

If the health message is making you unhappy—you're probably doing it wrong.

"Let us be careful," wrote Ellen, "not to graft into health reform one false shoot according to our own peculiar overstrained ideas and weave into it our own strong traits of character, making these as the voice of God, and passing judgment on all who do not see as we do."[1]

ENDNOTE

---

1. E. G. White, *Manuscript Releases*, 2:104.

Section V: Sex in the Nineteenth Century

Chapter 44

The "S" Word

Sex.

The word makes people excited, uncomfortable, and awkward. Sex sells, enslaves, inspires, pleasures, pains, drives, scares, delights, confuses, and offends people. Say the word a little too loud in a conversation, and instantly everyone in the room looks at you with a raised eyebrow or a smile, hoping to be invited into the conversation.

Some people won't buy this book because the subject of sex is included—and some of you bought it solely to read this chapter—you probably skipped right to it, didn't you?

Sex plays a role in everyone's life. Without it, you wouldn't be here to read this book, and I would never have existed to write about it. People—more specifically, your parents—had sex, and that's how you got here.

How could my parents do that to me? Wasn't there some other way? Where's the stork when you need him!

It's too awful to think about, and yet we do think about it. A lot. We learn about sex by accident, by textbook, from that one weird friend we all have who seems obsessed with it, or because our bodies suddenly start feeling things that draw us to that annoying person, or, well, that person who used to be annoying but who we now think is kinda cute.

Or our parents, the ones responsible for all this, give us "the talk."

You know "the talk."

When I turned twelve, my dad took me on a walk in the woods by our house to give me "the talk." The talk about "birds and bees" and the "facts of life." It is this terrifying rite of passage that finally reveals the location where babies come from, what happens when "a man and a woman love each other—very much," and a host of other phrases we use so we don't have to say *that* word.

Sex.

Even in Ellen's day they used other words so they didn't have to say *that* word.

Some of my favorites from the 1800s are "basket-making," "amorous congress," "face-making," "blow the grounsils," "convivial society," "lobster kettle," "stitch," and "tiff."

"Come with me, son, I need to tell you about basket-making."

"Should I bring some weaving materials, Dad?"

"No, son."

Whether we are comfortable or uncomfortable talking about it, sex is biblical. That should be sufficient reason to explore the subject, but the harsh reality is that our contemporary culture is saturated with sexual imagery. The message embedded in much of our media is that sex is the greatest thing you can ever hope to experience—and as you transition from teen to adult, your body certainly feels that way. So it's important to know what to do with these feelings and how to interpret the messages we are bombarded with every day.

Modern tech lets us stayed connected with our media at all times—it's almost like an addiction; we can't unplug. The advent of Internet has also made accessible every conceivable sexual act in living—and moving—color.

When I was little, doing my own research on the subject before the dreaded "talk," the only sources available were the dictionary, the encyclopedia, and a few choice passages from Leviticus and Song of Solomon. Now we go to Google if we want to see something—and what we can see far surpasses basic medical diagrams or a few poetic lines about a woman's breasts.

Some estimate that the average age at which a child is exposed to pornography is eight or nine. Some of you reading this are among that average. And this pornography isn't some lame dirty magazine from years ago; this is visceral, audible, visible stuff that sears itself into your memory banks and changes the way you think and view other people.

Everyone seems to talk about sex, so the question isn't *if* we should talk about it, but *how* should we talk about it.

Victorian voices

In Ellen's day, lots of people had sex (as in any era), but fewer were willing to talk about it—and those who did, frequently didn't know what they were talking about.

John H. Kellogg. "Sexual life begins with puberty," wrote Doctor Kellogg, a fellow Adventist, in 1882, "and in the female ends at about the age of forty-five years, the period known as the *menopause* or *turn of life*. At this period, according to the plainest indications of nature, all functional [sexual] activity should cease." Hear that, ladies? When you turn forty-five, you had better cool it in the bedroom.

He had a lot more to say on the subject in his groundbreaking, and heartbreaking, work *Plain Facts* (free copies on Google!). This book influenced sexual thought throughout the latter nineteenth and early twentieth centuries. Kellogg warned women that past the age of forty-five, if they continued to have sex, "disease, premature decay [and] possibly local degenerations will be sure to result."

Bummer.

As for men, well, we are blessed—according to Kellogg—since the "generative power of the male is retained somewhat longer than that of the female, and by stimulation may be indulged at quite an advanced age." Amen. Of course Kellogg adds, "but only at the expense of shortening life and running the risk of sudden death."[1] Sudden death? That's a mood killer.

Regarding the long-awaited wedding night, Doc Kellogg quoted in his book a few words for newlyweds from nineteenth-century sexual expert William Acton: "As soon as they are wedded, intercourse is indulged in night after night; neither party having any idea that these repeated sexual acts are excesses which the system of neither can bear, and which to the man, at least, are absolute ruin. The practice is continued till health is impaired, sometimes permanently."[2]

You have been warned.

Kellogg, an Adventist at the time, was not the only influential voice speaking to things sexual—his buddy Sylvester Graham (of cracker fame) also had some things to share.

Sylvester Graham. Mr. Graham, in his *A Lecture to Young Men on Chastity,* published in 1837, gave this counsel, "When the dietetic and other habits are such as they should be, this intercourse is very seldom." In other words, if you are eating right, you won't be wanting to have sex very often. Which brings us to the subject of the "graham cracker." I'm about to change them forever for you.

Graham believed that bland foods would prevent people from having unnecessary "urges." He also believed that the practice of "self-abuse" (a nineteenth-century term for masturbation) was due to children eating crackers.[3] You see where this is going, don't you?

Enter the graham cracker—invented by and named for Mr. Graham—a gentle food designed to downshift your sex drive. Yes, within that box of airy wafers lies your victory over sexual temptation.

Graham also had some definite opinions about what young couples should practice in the bedroom. "Beyond all question, an immeasurable amount of evil results to the human family from sexual excess within the precincts of wedlock." What kind of evils? I am so glad you asked.

According to cracker man, too much sex leads to the following:

- muscular relaxation (that's a bad thing?)
- depression
- indigestion

- sinking at the pit of the stomach
- chilliness
- melancholy
- hypochondria
- impaired vision/loss of sight
- nervous cough
- loss of memory
- epilepsy
- insanity

All of these, he wrote, "are among the too common evils which are caused by sexual excesses between husband and wife."[4] Wow.

Other Victorian voices

The Victorian era, spanning 1837 to 1901, and named after Queen Victoria in England, was loaded with a wide variety of opinions on the subject of sex. Without any Internet, or sex-ed classes, most people's first encounters with reproduction happened on granddad's farm. Even back then, people knew the barnyard was not the best choice from which to draw wedding night inspiration.

So they wrote some things to help people . . . and what they wrote was amazing.

Back in 1883, a Methodist minister named George W. Hudson penned *The Marriage Guide for Young Men: A Manual of Courtship and Marriage.* One selection says that "besides being the universal aggressor, he [man] is obliged, in nine hundred and ninety-nine cases in every thousand, to break her [the wife] into the harness of passion, by dint of both stratagem and perseverance. True, when thus broken in, she often pays him in his own coin."[5]

Thanks, George—nice to be known as the "universal aggressor" who should "break in" my wife. Someone should put those sentiments on a Hallmark card . . . and then be served a restraining order for achieving maximum creepiness.

Karl Heinzen, in *The Rights of Women and Their Sexual Relations,* manages to insult both men and women simultaneously:

> There is, indeed, another kind of shame. It is that delicate shyness which the virgin feels when she is to step beyond the boundary of virginity, as well as that feminine reserve which strives to hide or to guard her charms. This "shame" is . . . a natural consequence of an emotional affection upon entering a new life. . . .
>
> *This "shame,"* which has nothing to do with the consciousness or the fear of seeing something improper disclosed, is an ornament to every woman, and

its absence is a proof of dullness and coarseness.[6]

Nothing turns a man on more than a woman feeling ashamed of her body? Really?

In *What a Young Wife Ought to Know,* author Emma Frances Angell Drake wrote, "From the wedding day, the young matron should shape her life to the probable and desired contingency of conception and maternity. Otherwise she has no right or title to wifehood."[7] Hear that ladies? Your sole purpose as a wife is baby-making, oops, I mean "basket-making."

Surely we have something better to say than this.

ENDNOTES

1. John Harvey Kellogg, *Plain Facts for Old and Young* (Burlington, IA: Segner & Condit, 1881), 123.

2. Ibid., 226.

3. K. W. Tompkins, "Sylvester Graham's Imperial Dietetics," *Gastronomica* 9, no. 1 (Winter 2009): 50–60.

4. Sylvester Graham, *A Lecture to Young Men on Chastity* (Boston: Light & Stearns, Crocker & Brewster, 1837), 68, 69.

5. George W. Hudson, *The Marriage Guide for Young Men: A Manual of Courtship and Marriage* (Ellsworth, ME: self-published, 1883), 34.

6. Karl Heinzen, *The Rights of Women and the Sexual Relations* (Boston: Benjamin R. Tucker, 1891), 80.

7. Emma Frances Angell Drake, *What a Young Wife Ought to Know* (Philadelphia: Vir Publishing, 1901), 100, 101.

Chapter 45

In the Beginning . . . People Had Sex

Making the arena of sexual health even more difficult back then were certain taboos (forbidden things) that prevented people from having a healthy sexual experience. For example, in the Victorian era, "it was considered noble for women to suffer from gynecological disorders rather than seek treatment."[1]

Also, with such scary warnings from "health experts" about too much sex, people often found unhealthy ways to release sexual tension—often via prostitution, which was rampant. This created a culture in which it was believed that too much sex in marriage was bad, so people acted out in unhealthy ways—which made them sick with STDs, but also caused them to avoid treatment, because it wasn't considered refined to do so.

What a disaster.

How did this happen? How did people become so confused about something so common to life on planet Earth? For that matter, why is there still so much confusion about sex today?

In the beginning . . .

The first command God ever gave to human beings was to have sex (see Genesis 1:22). Sex was designed for one male and one female in a committed, monogamous relationship we call marriage. In his exhaustive treatment of the subject, Richard Davidson points out that Adam and Eve weren't just "created" but, according to the original language Genesis was written in (Hebrew), "aesthetically designed." They were beautiful . . . attractive . . . even sexy.

Not in the cheap way modern marketers define sexy on bikini-clad billboards, but in the way a man and a woman can be deeply, perfectly, beautiful by complementing one another. The Hebrew language in Genesis carries the idea of sexual delight between the first two humans. Sex is a tremendous gift, not only for procreation, but also for pleasure and developing intimacy.

Sex. Is. Good.

Deal with it.

"The man and his wife were both naked and were not ashamed" (Genesis 2:25) goes beyond physical nudity—it is talking about complete, utter transparency. Adam and Eve had no secrets; they reveled in each other's love during the all-too-brief time they lived in paradise. It is only in Genesis 3, with the entrance of sin, that they become ashamed of their nakedness—and a whole, sad history unfurls—with sex being degraded and used in ways that don't foster intimacy but often drive a wedge between people.

You can read about it in Richard Davidson's *Flame of Yahweh*—more than eight hundred pages of everything you could ever want to know about how the Bible views sex.[2]

It's also important to note that Genesis 2:7 states that man was made a "living creature" or a "living soul" (KJV). The Hebrew word *nephesh* is used interchangeably to mean "breath" and "spirit." It is the "life force" (for lack of a better term) with which God animates (makes alive) humanity. When we die, the *nephesh* goes back to God, and the individual's personality/existence is in God's memory banks, so to speak, until the resurrection, when he or she is raised to meet Jesus at the Second Coming.

Scripture says Jesus is the "only Sovereign, the King of kings and Lord of lords, who alone has immortality, who dwells in unapproachable light, whom no one has ever seen or can see. To him be honor and eternal dominion. Amen" (1 Timothy 6:15, 16).

This isn't to say humans won't experience eternity, but we understand that our immortality is not "inherent" but rather "given" to us by Jesus when He comes again. Our immortality is "conditional" on our acceptance and dependence on Him.

This means that body and spirit are linked as a whole; we are holistic beings, and we are sexual beings. Body and spirit are interwoven by the Master. We can't exist without the body or the "breath" of life. This becomes important in our quest to see how even Christians have distorted the beautiful gift of sex.

ENDNOTES
_____

1. Reay Tannahill, *Sex in History* (New York: Stein & Day, 1980).
2. Richard M. Davidson, *Flame of Yahweh: Sexuality in the Old Testament* (Peabody, MA: Hendrickson Publishers, 2007).

Chapter 46

Dividing Body and Spirit

As time went on, both Jewish and Christian communities embraced a few ideas that the ancient Hebrews wouldn't have recognized. One of those ideas—dualism—sought to separate the body from what the Greeks called the "immortal soul."

Jewish scholar Martin Goodman says, "In the Hebrew Bible man was conceived as an animated body rather than an incarnated soul. . . . Most of the authors of the biblical books seem to have envisaged the *nefesh* as the vital principle which gives life to the body without imagining it as something which could survive separation from the flesh. For most biblical writers, an individual did not *have* a body. He or she *was* a body, animated by the life principle."[1]

Gradually, Christians began to believe that the "soul" was a separate entity from the body—and that everything related to the body was bad—including sex.

Strange, considering the sexual imagery in the Bible book Song of Solomon. Shouldn't that "song" be enough to convince Christians that sex is good? A quick survey of how people have interpreted this brazenly romantic book will show just how far away from the truth they have gone.

ENDNOTE

---

1. Martin Goodman, *Rome and Jerusalem: Clash of the Ancient Civilizations* (New York: Vintage Books, 2008), 242.

Chapter 47

The Wrong Song[1]

In A.D. 90 Rabbi Akiba declared, "He who trills his voice in the chanting of the Song of Songs . . . and treats it as a secular love song has no share in the world to come." He also said no one under the age of thirty should be allowed to read it. So what do we do with this book then?

Christian allegorists had some ideas. An allegory is a story, poem, or picture thought to have hidden meanings. So the allegorists were those who thought that the plain text of Scripture really pointed to "hidden meanings" instead of what it obviously talked about. These interpreters had swallowed the pagan, Greek idea of dualism—the idea that everything to do with the body is bad and everything to do with the spirit (which is immortal and separate from the body) is fabulous. Or, to put it simply, everything that feels good is bad, and everything that denies good feelings is great. The idea was to free the spirit by killing the body. Naturally, this puts sex in the unspiritual category. Sex is bad for the soul, they said. So what exactly did they do with Solomon's love song?

They decided that all the erotic imagery had to do with the yearning of the soul for union with God, or that it was an expression of God's love for His church. For the Jews, the book was talking about God's presence with His people throughout history and looking forward to the Messiah. Ever heard someone talk about how Song of Solomon is about Christ and the church?

In the third century A.D., a man named Origen gifted the church with a more sophisticated allegorical method of interpreting the Bible. In his Bible commentary, he wrote, "I advise and counsel everyone who is not yet rid of the vexations of flesh and blood [sexual urges] and has not ceased to feel the passion of his bodily nature to refrain completely from reading this little book [Song of Solomon]. . . . They must not take anything of what has been said with reference to bodily functions."

Vexation of the flesh? We need to bring that phrase back. It should also be noted that Origen not only clouded the plain meaning of the Bible, but in terms of sexual advice he is probably disqualified based on the fact that he castrated himself.

To make Song of Solomon allegorical results in some very strange stuff. Case in point: the interpretation suggesting that the breasts of the Shulamite woman (Song of Solomon 7:3, 7, 8; 8:1, 8, 10) represent Moses and Aaron. Pretty sure they wouldn't appreciate the comparison.

According to Adventist scholar Richard Davidson, "For fifteen centuries the allegorical method held sway in the Christian church, and the Song of Songs became 'the favorite book of the ascetics and monastics who found in it, and in expansive commentaries on it, the means to rise above earthly and fleshly desire to the pure platonic love of the virgin soul for God.' "[2]

Weird. That such a beautiful book—full of romantic poems between a husband and wife—should be deemed unfit for spiritual consumption.

A bishop of early Christianity named Theodore of Mopsuestia came up with the "radical" idea to interpret Song of Solomon literally. His views were condemned more than one hundred years after his death, at the Second Council of Constantinople (epic name for a conference) in A.D. 533. Even his own student Bishop Theodoret declared that his teacher's literal approach to the Bible was "not even fitting in the mouth of a crazy woman." I think I'd fail that student.

In the seventeenth century, the Westminster Assembly cursed Presbyterians who "received it [Song of Solomon] as a hot carnal pamphlet from some loose Apollo or Cupid." Apollo was the Greek god of poetry with a vigorous love life (would you expect anything less from the god of poetry?), and Cupid, you'll remember, is that fat, rosy cherub that shows up on Valentine's Day cards with the heart-shaped arrow heads.

Solomon's song was still "wrong" by the time that John Wesley, founder of Methodism—the church to which Ellen's family belonged—came on the scene in the eighteenth century. Wesley says of Song of Solomon that "the description . . . could not with decency be used or meant concerning Solomon and Pharaoh's daughter . . . if applied to them, [it] would be absurd and monstrous. . . . It therefore follows that this book is to be understood allegorically."

Monstrous? Absurd? Remember, this is sex within the context of a husband and wife. With a history such as this, no wonder the church has had such a hard time talking about sex.

So how did Ellen view sex? With all the bad information running around her world, and fifteen hundred years of, if I may borrow the words, "monstrous" and "absurd" handling of the Bible on the matter—what on earth could she say that wouldn't just contribute to the problem?

Quite a lot, actually.

ENDNOTES

1. The information in this chapter is a *highly* condensed version of how Song of Solomon has been interpreted—as given in Richard Davidson's *Flame of Yahweh: Sexuality in the Old Testament*.

2. Davidson, *Flame of Yahweh*, 548.

Chapter 48

The "Marriage Privilege"

Every era has its "code words" for sex; some of them aren't crude, but quite lovely. In Ellen's writings about sex she uses the terms "marriage relation," "privacy and privileges of the family relation," and "marriage privilege." Some might think this is just Victorian "prudery" (being easily shocked by anything sexual) avoiding the word *sex*. In one sense, perhaps it is; she wouldn't have gotten very far as a messenger of the Lord using terms that offended and shocked people in the culture she was ministering in. But the terms also give us insight into her philosophy of sex.

A "privilege" is a good thing. It isn't a right to be demanded and forced; it is a blessing to be enjoyed and handled with care. Privileges are amazing advantages that should never be used to take advantage of someone else. Ellen's word choice reveals that she thought sex was a good thing, in the context of marriage, and that it was not something to be taken for granted, or forced on someone—no "breaking in" your wife, in other words.

She writes, "Very few feel it to be a religious duty to govern their passions. They have united themselves in marriage to the object of their choice, and therefore reason that marriage sanctifies the indulgence of the baser passions. Even men and women professing godliness give loose rein to their lustful passions, and have no thought that God holds them accountable for the expenditure of vital energy, which weakens their hold on life and enervates the entire system."[1]

Because our culture is saturated with sex, our first reaction to words like these tends to be negative. But if you carefully extract the principle, she is basically saying that you can't base a marriage just on sex.

If you have ever watched *Pride and Prejudice* (the BBC version is the best), you have gotten a glimpse into the silliness with which some people approached lifelong commitments in those days. Marriages then (and today, as well) were often about status or simply letting your passions run wild because of a very restrictive culture. Anyone with two brain cells to rub together knows that you can't create a happy marriage just because someone looks good and you are "in the mood."

Ellen continued this line of thought when she wrote, "It is not pure love which actuates a man to make his wife an instrument to minister to his lust. It is the animal passions which clamor for indulgence. How few men show their love in the manner specified by the apostle: 'Even as Christ also loved the church, and gave Himself for it; that He might [not pollute it but] sanctify and cleanse it; . . . that it should be holy and without blemish' [Ephesians 5:25–27, KJV]. This is the quality of love in the marriage relation which God recognizes as holy."[2]

Notice her careful juxtaposition (placing alongside) of the text talking about sacrificial love with husbands who make their wives into a sex tool. The words "animal passions" aren't condemning our sex drives—they are condemning sex drives that are beyond control and that are used to control other people. That's wrong in any era.

We see it today in such horrible practices as human trafficking, rape, and prostitution, which strip people of the image of God and turn them into a "thing" for pleasure.

"Love is a pure and holy principle," wrote Ellen, "but lustful passion will not admit of restraint."[3] Again, this is less about sex itself and more about being controlled by sex. She says lust is "blind to consequences; it will not reason from cause to effect."[4] One of the increasingly common examples of this is online porn addiction.

Scores of books, articles, and studies—Christian and secular—have been released warning against the potentially compulsive behavior that accompanies viewing online porn. While space prohibits a long discussion about it here, some of the findings suggest it results in a loss of intimacy with one's spouse, damages the self-esteem of your spouse, sets up unrealistic sexual expectations, contributes to an industry that reduces people to play things and that has a reputation for being steeped in drug abuse, and leads to a compulsive need to view the material that can't be controlled.

Now, back to Ellen's views on sex. Speaking of the marriage purpose, she wrote, "God never designed that marriage should cover the multitude of sins that are practiced. Sensuality and base practices in a marriage relation are educating the mind and moral taste for demoralizing practices outside the marriage relation."[5]

Again, this isn't simple sex bashing; it's criticism of sex that is fueled by a certain spirit. Biblically speaking, sex is designed to create not only pleasure but intimacy with one's spouse. Ellen seems to indicate that there are people with some weird sexual ideas who think that, just because they have a marriage license, they can practice whatever they want sexually.

The author of Hebrews, speaking of loving like Jesus loves, tells us to be hospitable to strangers, visit those who are in prison, not value money more than people, and be content with what we have been given. In the middle of this list, the author says, "Let marriage be held in honor among all, and let the marriage bed be undefiled, for God will judge the sexually immoral and adulterous" (Hebrews 13:4). Ellen's counsel seems to be in line with this—that sex in marriage is sacred and that nothing should be introduced that would "defile" that sacred relationship.

Sex requires respecting the other person's boundaries and well-being. In writing to women in a culture that did not give them as strong a status as men, Ellen stated, "It may be necessary to humbly and affectionately urge, even at the risk of his [the husband's] displeasure, that she [the wife] cannot debase her body by yielding to sexual excess. She should, in a tender, kind manner, remind him that God has the first and highest claim upon her entire being, and that she cannot disregard this claim, for she will be held accountable in the great day of God."[6]

It doesn't matter if she is his wife; the husband cannot demand her body whenever he feels like it. She has every right to, with a kind spirit, put *reasonable* boundaries in place on her body, and the husband should respect that. I emphasize the word *reasonable* because Ellen, by using the softer phrase "may be," is not advocating sexless marriages.

Wives and husbands should never refuse sex in order to punish each other or because they feel that it is something dirty and wrong. While sex is not the sole purpose for marriage, it is a great gift that bonds two people—a gift that, as far as physically possible, both husband and wife should enjoy as much as they can.

Ellen has many other things to add on this subject—including warning young women about how to conduct themselves in public in terms of being flirtatious and how a lack of sexual control in marriage may affect the kids. The most influential people in our lives are the parents or guardians who raise us; we take our relationship cues from them. Ellen's challenge to husbands and wives is to be loving, generous people—not controlling and abusive. We are to model a selfless, affectionate love for our kids to copy.

ENDNOTES

1. E. G. White, *Testimonies for the Church,* 2:472.
2. Ibid., 473.
3. E. G. White, "Give Unto the Lord the Glory Due His Name," *Review and Herald,* September 19, 1899.
4. E. G. White, *The Adventist Home,* 124.
5. E. G. White, "The Sin of Licentiousness," *Review and Herald,* May 24, 1887.
6. E. G. White, *Testimonies for the Church,* 2:475.

Chapter 49

Sexual Stupidity

The church owes many of its youth an apology for the lack of good information about sex. One of the dumbest things the church has done, while advocating the biblical idea of sex only within marriage, is to indirectly make sex seem like the most important accomplishment of one's life.

Well-meaning adults have given the impression that, simply by waiting until you are married to have sex, your sex life will be this window-rattling, earth-shaking, pleasure explosion that will finally make you a man/woman and complete your life. That is a steaming pile of stupid.

Truth is, with few exceptions, sex life within marriage often starts off rather awkwardly—it can even be painful. And when your wedding night doesn't match all the euphoric descriptions of earnest youth pastors and protective parents—you feel cheated, disillusioned, and you may even be upset with your freshly minted marriage partner.

The way some adults have communicated ideas about sex to young people has also led them to think that sex is all there is to being married—otherwise, why not just be friends? This is the kind of thing Ellen fought against. She tried to let people know that sex is great, but it isn't all there is, and you need to be smart about the person you choose to marry.

Sex. Is. Good. But sex is not god.

One of the best examples of Ellen practicing what she preached occurred when she helped a terrified new couple navigate their wedding night.

Seriously, it's a real story.

Chapter 50

Ellen Helps a Honeymoon

Daniel T. Bourdeau married Marion Saxby in Bakersfield, Vermont, in 1861. Dan had been wife hunting for three years when he finally found his twenty-three-year-old beauty. James White officiated at the ceremony in a private home, with his bride, Ellen, looking on. The ceremony finished late in the day, and so their host invited them to spend the night in his home.

You'd think Dan, at twenty-five years old, would be more than ready to participate in a little "basket-making." However, Danny boy had a nervous personality, and instead of going into the wedding suite, he paced the hallway up and down. My guess is that if you are a fourteen-year-old boy reading this, that fact alone makes you question this story's authenticity.

I assure you, it happened.

Where would this man find the courage to enjoy his wedding night? Surprisingly, Ellen White came to his rescue. She and James had also been invited to stay in one of the many rooms in the house, and she was not a little surprised to see the groom ruminating outside a closed bedroom door.

Gently, she approached Dan, and told him, "Daniel, inside that room there is a frightened young woman in bed totally petrified with fear. Now you go in to her right now, and you love her, and you comfort her. And, Daniel, you treat her gently, and you treat her tenderly, and you treat her lovingly. It will do her good." She paused, and then added, "Daniel, it will do you good, too!"[1]

The couple was grateful. How do we know? We have this story only because Dan chose to share it with others.

ENDNOTE

1. Maguerite Bourdeau Gilbert Fields, interview, 1982; quoted in Roger W. Coon, "Counsel to a Nervous Bridegroom," *Adventist Heritage* 13, no. 2 (Summer 1990): 16–23

Chapter 51

"Be a Man"

Of course, Ellen not only helped sexually nervous newlyweds; she also confronted sexual crazies who thought sex was unspiritual—even in marriage. The following story is ranked among my personal list of Ellen's All-Time Greatest Prophetic Hits.

J. N. Loughborough had been good friends with the Whites since 1852. He had worked with them diligently in the ministry and contributed significantly to helping the health message along. In 1907, J. N. received a letter from a recently married young man. He had embraced the Adventist faith and wanted to know what role sex should play in his home—asking several point-blank questions of the aging Adventist pioneer.

Here is a sample portion of Loughborough's reply. I think you will find it amusing. I've highlighted certain portions.

Mountain View, California, April 21, 1907

DEAR BROTHER:

. . . These quotations will show you that your idea expressed in your letter to me of "a moderate indulgence" and exercising judgment as to the number of children in the family is sanctioned. **I never saw anything in any testimony that sexual indulgence should only be for the raising of children.** And I know Sr. White has given no sanction to those who have advocated that position.

One man here in California had written a tract to that effect and wanted to get her sanction to his printing it. He went down to see her, **but she said she could not see him but sent word to him that "he had better let that matter alone."**

He pressed the matter and wanted to see her and finally she consented to see him. When he had finished what he had to say to her she asked him if he

194

was through. He replied that he was and she said: **"Go home, and be a man."**
He took the hint and the tract was never printed.

The above testimonies you and your wife can read for yourselves and draw your own conclusions in harmony therewith, **instead of being condemned by some radical teaching that in some cases has divided families.**
Yours for right and temperance in all things,
J. N. LOUGHBOROUGH[1]

"Be a man." I love that line!

Ellen did not think highly of reducing the role of sex in marriage—or in printing anything that would tend to reduce its role. J. N. also includes a warning to the young husband that the "radical" view that sex is only for making kids destroys families. Ellen was cool with sex, as long as it wasn't controlling and the context was right.

ENDNOTE

1. Quoted in Arthur White, "Ellen G. White and Marriage Relations (Concluded)," *Ministry*, April 1969.

Chapter 52

Self-Abuse

Masturbation is a more uncomfortable word than *sex*.

Yet if statistics are true, it is something most people will experience as they grow and discover how their bodies work. Biblically speaking, the Bible doesn't say anything about masturbation (save a vague possibility in Song of Solomon)—although, in the past, some people have made valiant attempts to show that it does.

The classic example, and one that is seldom cited anymore, is found in Genesis 38:8–10: "Then Judah said to Onan, 'Go in to your brother's wife and perform the duty of a brother-in-law to her, and raise up offspring for your brother.' But Onan knew that the offspring would not be his. So whenever he went in to his brother's wife he would waste the semen on the ground, so as not to give offspring to his brother. And what he did was wicked in the sight of the LORD, and he put him to death also."

People suggest that because Onan wasted his semen, not impregnating his sister-in-law, that masturbation is evil because it wastes semen. The term *onanism* has become a replacement word for *masturbation*.

And, as you can plainly see from the text, God will kill you for it.

Not!

Besides terrifying children everywhere with divine retribution and making people feel shame for discovering how their body works, this interpretation takes the passage grossly out of context.

First off, in that culture Onan had a responsibly to take his deceased brother's wife, marry her, and give her offspring. This would make sure his sister-in-law was provided for. Instead of "being a man" and performing his responsibility, Onan bailed—leaving his sister-in-law without a child and without a husband, simply because he didn't want any more kids. Lame. The sin of Onan was failing to be responsible and take care of his family . . . not masturbation—if, indeed, that is even what the text is saying Onan did.

Most Christian books on sexuality approach masturbation with a bit of indifference. With no clear command in Scripture regarding masturbation, how can it be a sin? The danger, as people point out, is that masturbation is accompanied by lust, and lust *is* something Jesus soundly condemns (Matthew 5:27, 28). Some go so far as to say that when Jesus links the "eye" and the "hand" in sin (verses 29, 30) He has masturbation in mind.

Now, don't get confused—lust is not the same thing as finding somebody attractive. You will always find people attractive—even after you are married. *Gasp.* We are wired to appreciate beauty; that's a good, natural thing to do. But we are forbidden to abuse beautiful things for selfish desires.

For example, Horace, a ninth-grader at Imaginary High School, sees Beatrice sitting in the lunchroom wearing a new blue cashmere sweater that fits her very well. Horace walks over to Beatrice and says, "I just wanted to tell you that your new sweater is very pretty and really brings out the color of your eyes." Nice, normal appreciation of beauty. Beatrice thanks him for the compliment, and they continue on with high school life—probably sometime in the 1930s based on their names.

Now, same situation, only this time Horace tries a different approach.

"Hey Beatrice, I want you to know I fantasize about what's underneath your sweater every night before I go to bed." *Well, that got awkward in a hurry.*

Beatrice shoots him a horrified look, picks up her food tray, and tries to find school security, who in turn finds Horace a good counselor to help him eliminate the creepy factor in his life.

In both imaginary, but real, examples, being attractive, or being attracted, isn't the problem—it's how we process it. Beatrice's value was suddenly reduced to what was underneath her sweater—instead of how her choice in clothing accented her natural beauty as a whole. Not to mention, she felt violated by having someone use her body as a private fantasy.

It's a lack of respect. And the same warning goes for girls—though they usually aren't as visual as guys. Bottom line, sex is a sacred gift for marriage that creates *both* pleasure and intimacy. It isn't a way to control someone else out of selfish desire. This strikes at the heart of masturbation, because masturbation is a sexual experience rooted in self.

Ellen used the term *self-abuse* when dealing with the sensitive subject for her Victorian readers. She gave this warning regarding one individual:

> He had practiced self-abuse until he was a mere wreck of humanity. This vice was shown me as an abomination in the sight of God. . . .
> . . . The results of self-abuse in them [those who practice masturbation] is seen in various diseases, such as catarrh, dropsy, headache, loss of memory and sight, great weakness in the back and loins, affections of the spine, the head often decays inwardly. Cancerous humor, which would lay dormant in the system their life-time, is inflamed, and commences its eating, destructive work. The mind is often utterly ruined, and insanity takes place.[1]

Well, based on this, masturbation seems to be more dangerous than skydiving without a parachute. Remember, though, some of the reasons behind Ellen's words reflected current medical thinking in her day—which she often worked to change—as she communicated to the people of her time. However, that last line about the mind is interesting.

We have already noted that masturbation, especially when combined with pornography, can become a compulsive behavior—meaning that it's difficult to stop even when you want to. I remember chatting with a counselor who told me that some of his clients had a sexual addiction that they fed seven or eight times a day. They wanted to stop, but they couldn't. They had become so attached to the images, coupled with the sexual rush they felt when masturbating, that their brain functioned similarly to those withdrawing from drugs. In a sense, it made them crazy. They had a behavior that wasn't consistent with their values, but the drive to continue doing it overpowered their will to stop. That's a scary place to be.

"They do not realize," wrote Ellen, "the exceeding sinfulness of this degrading sin, which is enervating the system and destroying their brain nerve power."[2] It makes the most sense, when reading her on this delicate issue, to understand her as pointing out that masturbation as a mode of sexual expression has a negative effect on the mind, which can lead to acting out in other sexually self-centered ways.

Ellen's point seems to be that repeated "self-abuse" not only creates an unhealthy attachment to the practice; it leads, unintentionally, to the idea that sexual relationships should be all about "me," not something shared with another person. If our goal, as followers of Jesus, is to be selfless in our love, a fixation with "self-abuse" seems out of harmony with that goal.

ENDNOTES

---

1. Ellen G. White, *An Appeal to Mothers* (Battle Creek, MI: Seventh-day Adventist Publishing Association, 1864), 25, 27.
2. E. G. White, *Testimonies for the Church,* 2:347.

Chapter 53

Summarizing Sex

Sex is good. But sex is not god.

Adventists believe we are created holistically, a blend of body and spirit. This makes sex part of who we are, not something to be ashamed of. Sex is an amazing gift designed to bring us pleasure and deep connection—as long as it's in the right context. God never intended sex to create a fragmented, self-centered experience, and He weeps when it is used in a way to control and hurt people.

God is also good and gracious to give us forgiveness when we mess up, think wrong thoughts, become a little too enamored with our own sexuality, or even have sex out of the right context. The Bible makes it clear that Jesus gives us fresh starts (1 John 1:9), and stories such as that of David and Bathsheba teach us that although poor choices have consequences, we can still work through them and be a person "after his [God's] own heart" (1 Samuel 13:14; see 2 Samuel 11, 12; Acts 13:22).

God's grace is sufficient for you.

In closing, I think Ellen's best summary on sex, especially for young people, is when she says, "The young affections should be restrained until the period arrives when sufficient age and experience will make it honorable, and safe to unfetter them."[1]

Affections are great; they are good. But they shouldn't be treated carelessly out of the right context. And when the right context comes along—they should be set free to be enjoyed.

Thanks, Ellen.

ENDNOTE

1. E. G. White, *An Appeal to Mothers*, 8.

Section VI: Ellen's Oddities

Chapter 54

Oddities

A couple of years ago, while cable surfing at a hotel, I found a show called *Oddities* on the Science Channel. Even though it was late and I had to work the following morning, the bizarre show hooked me, and I settled in for a ten-episode marathon—this is also why I can't have things such as cable in my house.

The show revolves around a unique antique store called Obscura Antiques and Oddities—located in the East Village in Manhattan, New York. The viewer spends thirty-minute episodes looking at all the weird stuff owners Mike Zohn and Evan Michelson purchase—and all the weird stuff they sell to their weird customers.

A few of the bizarre products available in the store include mummified cats, old bottles of embalming fluid, giant centipedes soaking in formaldehyde, a purse made out of a giant frog's body, and a monkey head in a jar. So odd. And then there are the people who come to do business there.

Some of the characters that wander into Mike and Evan's shop are a man who wants to rent a straightjacket for a play he is writing (really creepy), a puppeteer in search of a prosthetic limb (uh, what kind of puppet is this?), someone trying to sell an ancient book he believes to be bound in human skin, a performer who buys a throwing knife used by Harry Houdini, and a man who paints with his own blood (seriously, and what's even crazier is that his paintings are quite good).

The fun part of the show is to see whether the "oddities" are authentic or fabrications—and to watch Mike and Evan go on trips on behalf of clients in order to hunt down strange and rare items that match the personalities and tastes of their unusual shoppers. Next time I am in New York, I plan on visiting; hopefully, I won't blend in.

Ellen's oddities

Ellen wrote a lot. I mean *a lot*. Thousands upon thousands upon thousands of pages. Most of what she says makes a lot of sense as long as you are reading it in its context. However, we do find a few obscure oddities on the shelves of her massive corpus. Some of these items have shipwrecked people's faith in her and led others to make fun of her—or condemn her to Hades.

When we discover oddities in anyone's writings, it's sometimes helpful to take a step back and realize, first and foremost, that they are *oddities*. They aren't the norm. When 90 percent of what someone writes makes perfect sense, but 10 percent seems a bit off, we should give the writer the benefit of the doubt—maybe it's our issue, not hers.

In C. S. Lewis's classic work *The Lion, the Witch, and the Wardrobe,* the littlest sister, Lucy, discovers a magic portal to another world. Her mean older brother, Edmund, also stumbles upon it, but when they both come back, Edmund tells their other two siblings that Lucy is lying. Edmund is kind of a jerk for most of the book. Lucy bursts into tears, leaving the older two siblings, Peter and Susan, confused. Eventually they take their concern to the old professor whose house they are living in. He is frustrated by Peter and Susan's lack of "logic" (which he grumbles is because logic isn't taught in school anymore) and asks them which of the two—Edmund or Lucy—is the most truthful.

Without hesitation, they answer that Lucy is far more honest than Edmund.

"So," the professor continues, "either your sister has gone mad or she is telling the truth. And you can plainly see she isn't mad." The siblings reconsider. Maybe Lucy is right. A number of astonishing events happen at this point, and they all wind up in the magical land of Narnia, and—well, you should probably just read the book.

It's easy to dismiss Ellen as nuts when we encounter a strange phrase or idea. But when we examine her life, she doesn't seem to be prone to madness. Maybe a closer look at some of these oddities will help us see that, although she was imperfect and sometimes influenced by the current thinking of her times, she is still worth listening to.

Chapter 55

Revolutionary War II?

The fight for the United States' independence concluded in 1783—long before Ellen arrived on the prophetic scene. But in her writings she seems to declare that the end of independence might be at hand. Check it out:

This nation will yet be humbled into the dust. England is studying whether it is best to take advantage of the present weak condition of our nation, and venture to make war upon her. She is weighing the matter, and trying to sound other nations. She fears, if she should commence war abroad, that she would be weak at home, and that other nations would take advantage of her weakness. Other nations are making quiet yet active preparations for war, and are hoping that England will make war with our nation, for then they would improve the opportunity to be revenged on her for the advantage she has taken of them in the past, and the injustice done them. A portion of the Queen's subjects are waiting a favorable opportunity to break their yoke; but if England thinks it will pay, she will not hesitate a moment to improve her opportunities to exercise her power, and humble our nation. When England does declare war, all nations will have an interest of their own to serve, and there will be general war, general confusion.[1]

That last sentence is what usually trips people up. It seems as though she is making a prediction that Britain will declare war on its former colony. But, as we all know, that never happened. So what gives?

In the English language—in all languages, for that matter—there are "conditional" statements. They go like this:

"If you punch me in the face, I will kick you in the head."

Have I kicked you in the head? No? That's because you haven't punched me in the face. Following so far? Let's continue . . .

"When I kick you in the head, I will pull a muscle that will require physical therapy."

Do I need therapy? (I mean, *physical* therapy.) No? That's because you haven't punched me in the face, and I haven't kicked you in the head, and therefore I haven't pulled any muscles.

Now, take a closer look at what Ellen says in that statement about fightin' it up with Britain for the second time. I count at least two "ifs" and one "hoping" before Ellen says "when." I guess Britain decided it wasn't worth it. No harm done, to Ellen or the United States.

ENDNOTE

1. E. G. White, *Testimonies for the Church,* 2:259.

Chapter 56

Amalgamation

Science fiction fans drool over the idea that man and animal could share DNA, creating powerful combinations resulting in the likes of Spider Man, Hawkgirl, and any number of permutations resulting in the ability to fly, jump, run, and see in ways that only comic books can imagine.

In 1864 (and republished in 1870), Ellen crafted a few statements that have fueled wild speculation because she seems to suggest that, back in Noah's day, man and beast combined to make abominable creations:

> But if there was one sin above another which called for the destruction of the [human] race by the flood, it was the base crime of amalgamation of man and beast which defaced the image of God, and caused confusion everywhere. God purposed to destroy by a flood that powerful, long-lived race that had corrupted their ways before him.

> Every species of animal which God had created were preserved in the ark. The confused species which God did not create, which were the result of amalgamation, were destroyed by the flood. Since the flood there has been amalgamation of man and beast, as may be seen in the almost endless varieties of species of animals, and in certain races of men.[1]

There you have it. Ellen clearly states that humans and animals formed hybrids. (Can you imagine the epic felts we could create to teach kids about the Flood?) People have gone so far as to suggest that Ellen believed some of the differences in human races we see today are a direct result of these dark pre-Flood experiments.

Truth?

Well, here's the deal. The whole theory revolves around that crazy word *amalgamation*. Scholars point out that no dictionary has ever defined it as "a combination of man and beast." The main use of the word has to do with fusing metals, or elements, together to make different substances. It is true, however, that nineteenth-century usage of the word did include using it to mean the mixing of various races.

The problem is that Ellen's statement can be understood in a couple of ways. Is she saying that man and animals were "amalgamating" with each other? Or does she mean that men and animals were amalgamating separately—with their own kind? We have endless varieties within species today—from spiders that dance to human beings who carry genetic material that predisposes their children to certain illnesses.

The other difficulty is that Ellen doesn't use the word *amalgamation* very often. The only other times she uses it are references to Christians and nonbelievers getting their values mixed up or to poisonous biological life resulting from sin (which is why parents freak out when you eat unidentified berries and mushrooms on camping trips). When compared with her other writings on the Flood (see *Patriarchs and Prophets,* for example), her purpose in using the word seems to be to create a distinction between good and evil—what is holy and what is corrupt.

The big picture she paints of life before the Flood is of Satan actively corrupting human and plant life since Adam and Eve first ate the forbidden fruit. Amalgamation could be a general expression for the results of sin and the awful things we do that "deface the image of God" in our lives. One thing for certain, Ellen never hinted at, or elaborated on, alien, subhuman, superhuman, or hybrid species—no matter how weird your sister is.

ENDNOTE

1. Ellen G. White, *Spiritual Gifts* (Battle Creek, MI: Seventh-day Adventist Publishing Association, 1864), 3:64, 75.

Chapter 57

"I'm Saved!" Or Not

There are certain words good Christians shouldn't say. Which is why I can't give you any examples. But you know them. I discovered one on my eighth birthday. You can imagine my parents' delight, as pastors, when upon its discovery I ran around the house yelling it at the top of my lungs in front of church members and their children.

I'm sure you have your own bad-words memory that made things awkward for all involved. Ellen warns us about not saying bad things, and one of the baddest things she warns us not to say is:

"I'm saved."

Well . . . that's unexpected.

However you might protest, Ellen is certain that your certainty of salvation is sinful. Here's what she wrote: "Those who accept the Saviour, however sincere their conversion, should never be taught to say or to feel that they are saved."[1]

Don't you feel better knowing that you can't feel that you're saved? I know I don't—and many others don't either. This quotation has been so misused and has hurt countless Christians in their walk with Jesus.

Maybe it's time to take Ellen in context. Here is the pesky quote set in its proper framework:

> Peter's fall was not instantaneous, but gradual. Self-confidence led him to the belief that he was saved, and step after step was taken in the downward path, until he could deny his Master. Never can we safely put confidence in self or feel, this side of heaven, that we are secure against temptation. Those who accept the Saviour, however sincere their conversion, should never be taught to say or to feel that they are saved. This is misleading. Every one should be taught to cherish hope and faith; but even when we give ourselves to Christ and know that He accepts us, we are not beyond the reach of temptation.[2]

So it's not a sin to feel you are saved, but it isn't safe to think that you are beyond temptation—just because you have made a commitment to Jesus. The problem is presumption.

I can work hard for six months and lose a bunch of weight—and that's amazing. But if I then declare that "I'm in shape" and begin thinking I can stop working out and eat whatever I want, I'm going start breaking the scales again. Or if I get my PhD—declare myself an expert—and then stop reading books and studying, I will lose all my credibility in a few years. Make sense?

So if we say, "I'm saved," thinking we can't sin, fall to temptation, or do anything wrong, we may find ourselves an enemy of Jesus instead of His friend. Not that Jesus stops loving us, but we might stop loving Him. As for feeling assured of Jesus love, Ellen has a lot to say on that.

Check out a couple of examples:

> Each one of you may know for yourself that you have a living Saviour, that he is your helper and your God. You need not stand where you say, "I do not know whether I am saved." Do you believe in Christ as your personal Saviour? If you do, then rejoice.[3]

> The message from God to me for you is "Him that cometh unto me, I will in no wise cast out" (John 6:37). If you have nothing else to plead before God but this one promise from your Lord and Saviour, you have the assurance that you will never, never be turned away. . . . Cling to that promise and you are safe. "Him that cometh unto me I will in no wise cast out." Present this assurance to Jesus, and you are as safe as though inside the city of God.[4]

Thanks for clarifying, Ellen. Now, let's make sure we do the same whenever we see someone struggling with believing whether or not they have salvation.

ENDNOTES

1. Ellen G. White, *Christ's Object Lessons* (Battle Creek, MI: Review and Herald® Publishing Association, 1900), 155.
2. Ibid.
3. Ellen G. White, "The Need of Missionary Effort," *General Conference Bulletin,* Extra no. 7, April 10, 1901.
4. E. G. White, *Manuscript Releases,* 10:175.

Chapter 58

Shut That Door!

Ever seen those doors that have a sign reading, "Please Keep This Door Closed"? Why even have a door there? If you never intend to open it, then it might as well be a wall. Of course, imagination can run wild at the thought, *What are they hiding behind that door?*

I had a door like that in my high school.

I speculated that the "administration" was performing secret experiments on students in a diabolical underground lab. Or maybe they raised funds for the school district by allowing the CIA to train their ninja operatives in a hidden base—behind the door. They may have also put gold, weapons, spaceships, straightjackets, and bottles of "anorthex" in there.

It could also have been a closet.

Whatever lay behind that door, it was fun to wonder about it. Every closed door keeps things out and keeps things in. Sometimes it's stuff that doesn't matter, like clothes we don't wear anymore, outdated cleaning products, and random stuff we have crammed in there because company came over and we don't want to look like slobs.

But sometimes it does matter—like when we close doors to keep people out.

The Millerites believed Jesus would return in 1844. One of the Bible passages they drew inspiration from is in Matthew 25—the story of the ten virgins. Basically, five of the girls weren't ready when the groom came to the wedding, and they got locked out of the festivities. The Millerites interpreted this to represent the "closing of probation"—that point in history when people have made their final choice for or against Jesus.

After 1844, many Millerites believed that even though Jesus didn't come as expected, salvation was no longer available for anyone—like when your favorite show gets canceled, or they run out of your favorite soda at the store, except in this case it was much, much, much more serious.

Seventeen-year-old Ellen was among those who believed salvation had sold out.

To believe otherwise, she and those who were like-minded felt, would be rejecting the prophecies in Daniel 8 and the spiritual experience that had accompanied the events in 1844. This belief, that salvation was no longer available, received the name "the Shut Door theory," because Matthew 25 says that when the wedding began the door was shut—leaving the unwise virgins outside and unable to enter. The phrase "shut door" occurs in Ellen's writings, and this has led many to believe that she, in her prophetic office, promoted this erroneous theory.

Before we look at what she said, it's critical to note that the Millerites' ideas about the shut door shifted—by necessity. As they studied their Bibles and shared the truths they found with others, some of these "others" believed and accepted the Saviour. People who hadn't been involved in the Millerite movement at all. Did the "shut door" mean there was no salvation for them? After a while, the "shut door" took on new meaning for the Millerites; they saw that it referred to Jesus closing one phase of His work in heaven and replacing it with another.

You can read all about that in my book *What We Believe for Teens* (#shamelesspromotion).

What this means for our Ellen studies is that when she used the phrase "shut door," she wasn't referring to the old theory (that there was no more salvation for anyone after October 22, 1844) but the new idea (that Jesus had begun something new in heaven). It's also important note that, while Ellen initially held to the old theory, she never had a vision telling her that theory was correct.

Ellen put it this way:

> For a time after the disappointment in 1844, I did hold, in common with the advent body, that the door of mercy was then forever closed to the world. This position was taken before my first vision was given me. It was the light given me of God that corrected our error, and enabled us to see the true position.
>
> I am still a believer in the shut-door theory, but not in the sense in which we at first employed the term or in which it is employed by my opponents.[1]

She went on to point out that a "shut door" existed in Noah's day (Genesis 6:3), in Abraham's day (Genesis 19:4–14), and in Jesus' day (Matthew 23:38). The idea that there comes a time when the opportunity for redemption ends permeates Scripture.

Ellen expounded further on her concept of the shut door when she wrote,

> I was shown in vision, and I still believe, that there was a shut door in 1844. All who saw the light of the first and second angels' messages and rejected that light, were left in darkness. . . .
>
> Those who did not see the light, had not the guilt of its rejection. It was only the class who had despised the light from heaven that the Spirit of God could not reach.[2]

In other words, people who rejected the experience and the truths that emerged out of the 1844 experience, when they knew them to be true, had the door closed on them.

That sounds harsh, but it makes sense. We are challenged to follow God and live out what we know to be true. When we knowingly live lies, we are really closing the door of God's light and love on ourselves.

ENDNOTES

1. E. G. White, *Selected Messages,* 1:63.
2. Ibid., 63, 64.

Chapter 59

Apocrypha

Everyone loves a good secret.

We want to know what our crush whispered to their friend at the party, what people really say about us when we aren't in the room, how much money our parents actually have when they tell us they are broke, and what happens behind "shut doors."

A group of writings called the "Apocrypha" appears in Catholic Bibles. The word *apocryphal* means "secret" or "obscure"—they are oddities, in other words. The authors of these books, which include such amazing names as Bel and the Dragon, Maccabees, Susanna, and Wisdom of Solomon, remain mysterious and highly suspect. Like if I handed you a letter, scrawled in crayon, and told you George Washington wrote it . . . you'd probably have a few questions.

While these apocryphal books offer some interesting insights into history, they are not considered part of the inspired biblical canon. Which is why it's weird that Ellen referred to them as something the "wise" should understand in the last days.

Ellen White had a vision in New York. It is described in a document dated January 28, 1850:

> I [Ellen] then saw the Word of God, pure and unadulterated, and that we must answer for the way we received the truth proclaimed from that Word. I saw that it had been a hammer to break the flinty heart in pieces, and a fire to consume the dross and tin, that the heart might be pure and holy. I saw that the Apocrypha was the hidden book, and that the wise of these last days should understand it. I saw that the Bible was the standard Book, that will judge us at the last day. I saw that heaven would be cheap enough, and that nothing was too dear to sacrifice for Jesus, and that we must give all to enter the kingdom.[1]

Yes . . . we can finally have Scripture readings from Bel and the Dragon! Right? The trouble with this particular oddity is twofold. One, the document is a report of a vision Ellen had; it wasn't written by Ellen herself. In a highly charged moment of spiritual excitement, we can sometimes hear and see things that might not quite capture everything correctly. After all, the words *apocrypha* and *apocalypse* are similar, and another name for the book of Revelation is the Apocalypse. *Apocalypse* simply means "to reveal" or "a revelation," whereas *apocrypha* means "hidden" or "secret." Maybe Ellen's vision referred to the Apocalypse—the book of Revelation—and not the Apocrypha. Just a theory, but on to the next problem with Ellen's seeming endorsement of these odd books.

She never mentions "apocrypha" at any other time—ever. She doesn't refer to it; she doesn't encourage people to study it; she doesn't even make fun of it. Nada, zilch, nothing. If the Apocrypha was critical to our understanding, you'd think she would have spent more time talking about it.

Or maybe the vision's reference to "understanding" the Apocrypha simply meant we should understand that it is not the "standard" book that the Bible is—which is the ultimate standard of judgment, according to Ellen.

I guess I can't preach my Susanna sermon.

ENDNOTE

---

1. E. G. White, *Manuscript Releases,* 16:34.

Chapter 60

The 1843 Chart and God's "Mistake"

Is God the author of mistakes? Does God cause people to mess up? Most of us would quickly shout an emphatic NO! But then how do we explain why God allowed William Miller to mess up the interpretation of prophecy so badly in 1844? Better yet, why did God show Ellen, in vision mind you, that God had led William in the creation of his error-laden 1843 prophecy chart?

Oh snap.

In 1850, Ellen penned that she saw "that the 1843 [prophetic] chart was directed by the hand of the Lord, and that it should not be altered; that the figures were as He wanted them; that His hand was over and hid a mistake in some of the figures, so that none could see it, until His hand was removed."[1]

Well, isn't *that* problematic. Kinda messes with your theology, doesn't it? Does God author mistakes?

To begin solving this conundrum, we have to understand that God allows people to use their own language to describe circumstances, both good and bad, that are said to be caused by Him. The classic example is found in Exodus 10:1, which says that God hardened Pharaoh's heart. Wow, that's kind of a rude thing to do—considering it led to the death of all firstborn Egyptians. Yet when we flip back to Exodus 8:15, 32, and 9:34, the same author says that Pharaoh hardened his own heart. Maybe the big idea is that, regardless of Pharaoh's obnoxious decisions, God was still in control of His people's destiny.

We do have an example of God playing apocrypha with people. Following His crucifixion, Jesus hid His identity on the road to Emmaus, He watched while His grieving disciples tried to recover from their great disappointment because of the Crucifixion (Luke 24:16). Later on, after they had sorted out Scripture, Jesus appeared to them (verse 31) and relieved their pain. Something about that Emmaus experience was vital to their spiritual walk.

As for the 1844 situation, it is possible that the interest in prophecy would never have reached the intensity it needed to reach if people hadn't expected the end of the world. Had Miller simply expounded on the changing of Jesus' ministry in heaven (again, check my book, *What We Believe for Teens,* for more details), the interest may not have surged to the place that God could call a new religious movement into being.

The point is that God can still lead His people, even through mistakes, and bring them to a place of deep Bible study and revitalized spiritual health.

ENDNOTE

1. Ellen G. White, *Early Writings* (Washington, DC: Review and Herald® Publishing Association, 1945), 74.

Chapter 61

No Slaves Resurrected

Most of us have been taught (hopefully) of the atrocities suffered by slaves in the early days of the United States. Our country had a big fight over it called the Civil War; it was kind of a big deal. Books such as *12 Years a Slave* and *The Help* tell stories that help us understand the awfulness of racism and make us sensitive to the mistreatment of any human being.

Which is why it is so odd when Ellen had the audacity to suggest that slaves wouldn't be resurrected.

In the late 1850s, our friend Ellen composed a few lines that border on the incredibly insensitive: "The slave-master would have to answer for the soul of his slave whom he has kept in ignorance. . . . God cannot take the slave to heaven, who has been kept in ignorance and degradation, knowing nothing of God, or the Bible, fearing nothing but his master's lash, and not holding so elevated a position as his master's brute beasts. But he does the best thing for him that a compassionate God can do. He lets him be as though he had not been."[1]

If that kind of cruel statement doesn't make you an Ellen hater, I don't know what will . . . unless, of course, this isn't a cruel statement.

Remember what we said about the rules of context? We need to read *all* Ellen wrote about a certain topic. In this case, all potential haters have to do is turn a few pages further, where they will be greeted with Ellen seeing "the pious slave rise [in the resurrection] in triumph and victory."[2] So, not all slaves are doomed. I feel a little better.

It should also be noted that Ellen fought against slavery. She lamented that human beings were treated like beasts when "many of the slaves had noble minds."[3] Not all humanity will be saved, and Ellen carefully contrasts the "pious" with the "ignorant" slaves. What makes Ellen, and her family, less hate worthy is (as previously mentioned) her son Edson's effort to take the message of Jesus to the slaves in the South.

The Whites loved the blacks.

It may seem harsh that Ellen believed that some slaves, because of ignorance forced upon them by their masters, would not be resurrected—and that is understandable. In her mind, it was an act of mercy on God's part, not one of viciousness, that these slaves would not be resurrected only to be judged again.

Bottom line is that whether slave or free, master or servant, black or white, red or yellow, or whatever—not everyone makes a choice for Jesus based on the truth they know to be true. Jesus doesn't force anyone into heaven, but He makes the offer to everyone.

Additional oddities

These are just a sample of some of the strange statements you can find in Ellen's writings. There are more—and there are places to find good answers. No doubt, there will be times when you will have questions. We still have questions about certain Bible passages too—such as 1 Peter 3:17–20, where Jesus appears to preach to "spirits in prison" (meaning the grave). Wow, what did Peter say? How do we make sense of this strange verse?

Or what about the old question, based on Genesis 4:16, 17, about where Cain found his wife after being banished from his family's presence? We don't know everything, but we know a lot of things. In these odd moments, it's best to take a step back and look at the big picture instead of getting hung up on individual puzzle pieces that don't seem to fit. I am sure you have said and done of things that don't accurately portray the whole of your life, either.

Also, enjoy the oddities you find—they may very well lead you to some of the most fruitful and exciting studies of your life.

ENDNOTES

1. E. G. White, *Spiritual Gifts,* 1:193.
2. Ibid., 206.
3. E. G. White, "An Example in History," *Review and Herald,* December 17, 1895.

Section VII:
Wonder Woman—Miracles in Ellen's Ministry

Chapter 62

More Than a Good Trick

Not too long ago I witnessed a street magician pull off a trick that seemed nothing short of miraculous. I have wracked a few brain cells trying to figure out how he did it—with no luck. The magician's name is Stuart Edge, and this particular trick not only helps him amaze crowds and make money but also kiss cute girls.

What Stuart does is troll the sidewalks of college campuses looking for a willing female participant; yes, I know that sounds creepy, but stay with me. When he finds a young lady curious enough about the trick, he has her pick a card from a deck of playing cards and sign her name on it. Easy enough. Next, he has her fold the card in half, then in half again, and stick it in her mouth.

Yes, I know that's weird—just pay attention.

Then Stuart takes another card from the deck, signs his name on it, folds it the same way, and sticks it in his mouth. Then through gritted teeth, he tells the girl that they need to kiss, just a quick peck, nothing wild. Stuart tells her that the magic is in the kiss—which is a great line to use, but only if you are a professional magician. Otherwise, you will indeed look creepy and will probably receive a slap instead of a smooch.

After a moment's reluctance, the girl, the card with her signature still in her mouth, acquiesces to Stuart's request, and both magician and perfect stranger lean in for a kiss that lasts barely a second.

Now, here comes the miraculous part.

The girl opens her mouth, removes the card, unfolds it—and it isn't hers! Her eyes widen, and her mouth drops open, as she sees that she is holding the magician's card with his signature. Then to her amazement, Stuart extracts her signed card from his mouth! I have no idea how this works. Again, this is a quick, kosher, kiss—no "frenching." Yet, somehow, the cards switch; it's an incredible feat.

Think of how many kisses you could get with a stunt like that.

You can see it for yourself on YouTube at http://www.youtube.com/watch?v=Jo0gY4EjW2o.

Let me know if you figure out how it's done. Oh, and just to make it more complicated, he performs the same trick with couples kissing—meaning that he doesn't even have to do the kiss himself for it to work. I am completely at a loss to explain what he is doing.

One thing I do know, as miraculous as the trick appears, it *is* a trick. I have watched magicians explain their tricks and, sadly, the miracle immediately vanishes—and I always feel a little dumb for not figuring it out. Maybe you have had the same experience. Yet, I do believe that there are supernatural powers, good and evil, operating in the world.

The Bible is full of miracles, particularly ones that accompany the work of prophets. Scripture talks about prophetic people inviting fire to fall from out of the sky (1 Kings 18:36–38), paying taxes with coins found in the mouths of random fish (Matthew 17:27), dead children returning to life (1 Kings 17:17–24; Matthew 9:18–26), women turning into salt (Genesis 19:26), water turning to blood (Exodus 7:17–21) and wine (John 2:1–11), visions of the future (Daniel and Revelation), and calling bears to eat rude people (2 Kings 2:23, 24).

So, did Ellen have any miraculous things in her ministry?

Yes—and they were cooler than any card trick you can find online.

Chapter 63

Breathtaking Visions

When Ellen went into vision mode, a few things happened to her that amazed those around her. Ellen's husband, James, compared notes with others who had seen her in vision more than fifty times since 1852 and wrote down the miraculous things that people witnessed. While there were several wonders that happened to Mrs. White during her visions, the most dramatic involved supernatural strength, unblinking eyes, and, strangest of all, no breathing.

When a vision began, Ellen felt faint for a few moments and teetered a bit as though she would fall. But then a surge of strength rushed through her. Ellen walked around the room, making gestures with her hands, arms, and head. J. N. Loughborough described the movements as "free and graceful." We have already seen that, in 1845, she held up an eighteen-and-a-half-pound family Bible with her outstretched left hand for half an hour. I can't do that, and neither can Arnold Schwarzenegger. What's more, Loughborough says that when she was in vision her hands and arms could not be controlled or hindered by anybody in the room.

Yet she weighed only eighty pounds at the time she lifted the Bible—that's like a third-grader.

The next unnerving item in Ellen's vision experiences had to do with her unblinking eyes. She didn't blink in vision—and sometimes those visions lasted hours. I am sure you have, out of profound boredom, conducted staring contests with a sibling or a classmate. They usually don't last longer than a minute or two. Go ahead; try to keep your eyes open as long as you can. Seriously, try it.

Try it.

Don't be lame.

OK, my guess is either you couldn't keep them open longer than thirty seconds or you didn't even try, because you have a sour attitude and you know that Ellen has the world record for staring contests. When she did it, she also had a "pleasant expression, only differing from the normal in that she appears to be looking intently at some distant object." Which means she wasn't straining her eyeballs; she was transfixed on something only she could see.

Finally, and most impressively, she didn't breathe the entire time she was in vision. I have heard that Navy SEALS can hold their breath for two minutes—pretty impressive. Ellen once didn't breathe for three hours, and yet her pulse kept right on beating as it should, and she didn't turn red, purple, or blue. She maintained a pleasant look while she didn't breathe for three hours and managed to stay alive.

I can't do that—neither can Stuart Edge.

Chapter 64

The Hairnet

Willie White, one of Ellen's sons, tells an incredible story of a vision that helped catch a thief. When she was older, Ellen had several young people boarding at her house; some of them were helpers and others were students and teachers in the local school. One day, a "peculiar temptation" got the better of one of the teachers.

Mrs. White possessed a "nicely woven hair net"—and the teacher decided it would look better on her. She snatched it and slipped it into her trunk. A hairnet? Not exactly an item that you'd think would create a temptation. The only time we think of hairnets is when we are working fries at a fast-food restaurant—because who wants greasy human hair with their value meal?

It's a good reminder that Ellen didn't live in the present day. Back then hair nets were a lot more popular than they are today. Try to imagine someone taking your Gucci purse, your iPhone, or your favorite water bottle that cost you thirty bucks at REI. Maybe those things would make you desperate enough to try to pull a fast one on a prophet. Naturally, Ellen asked around the house for her hairnet, muttering, "It could not go away by itself." Sounds like something my mom used to say to me when I lost stuff.

Some time went by, and then one day, as Ellen walked through the teacher's room, she heard a voice say, "Lift the lid of the trunk." What would you have done? I'm not sure I would have lifted the lid. Running down the hall screaming might be the more natural response for me. But Ellen felt at peace with the voice—and the action, which normally would have been considered quite rude. Like selling off the secrets in your sister's diary; anyway, such an incredible story.

When the voice told Ellen a second time to check the trunk, she lifted the lid and saw her missing hairnet. The clever old lady left it there and decided to ask around again to give the little stinker a chance to confess. Instead, the educator with the fast hands snuck back to her trunk when Ellen wasn't looking and destroyed the hairnet.

Wow, teacher of the year, ladies and gentlemen.

A few days later, as Ellen sat by the fireplace, an image flashed before her. She saw a young woman burning the hairnet over a hot lamp. Now she knew this teacher had no intention of doing the right thing. Calling the thief to her, she shared what she had seen, and the young woman broke.

"I do not know why I took it," she said truthfully. "I do not know why I did not bring it back when you first spoke of it."

"YOU EVIL CHILD!" roared Ellen, leaping from her seat. Then, with supernatural strength and speed, she pushed the young girl into the mouth of the blazing fireplace.

Wait, no, nope—I think I got the end of "Hansel and Gretel" mixed up in there somewhere. Sorry.

What actually happened was beautiful and involved no writhing in flames of judgment. Ellen's confrontation helped reveal a serious character flaw in an otherwise lovely young lady. As the relationship between them deepened, it became clear that the young teacher had grown up spoiled and had been led to believe that she could just take whatever she wanted. Ellen's firm, but not mean, confrontation helped her change and probably saved her from far worse things later on.

Just because someone confronts our behavior doesn't mean they don't love us. It takes strength to confront and to be confronted, but God can work through those kinds of conflicts to make us more like Christ.[1]

ENDNOTE

1. W. C. White, "W. C. White Statements Regarding Mrs. White and Her Work," White Estate, http://www.whiteestate.org/issues/VisionsofEGW.html.

Chapter 65

Healings

All of us have sick stories.
The time you were so sick that

- you threw up thirty-eight times in fifteen minutes;
- you slept on the bathroom floor next to your new BFF—the toilet;
- an acre of forest fell to supply you with enough Kleenex;
- your family cooked breakfast on your feverish forehead to save money on gas and electricity;
- a small alien tried clawing its way out of your abdomen—or maybe it was gas;
- or you had to finish your sermon on Bible prophecy in time to make it home before you vomited on stage in front of two hundred people. #truestory

I am sure you have gorier details than I have listed here about "that time" you succumbed to intense illness. Even if it lasted only twenty-four hours, you probably prayed several times for the Lord to spare your life.

Most of our illnesses, as awful as they feel, don't compare with more serious diseases such as pneumonia, cancer, or Ebola. But in Ellen's day even the illnesses that seem common to us could easily turn lethal. Without proper medicine, a chest cold or common flu had the potential to pummel your insides to a bloody paste.

You're welcome for that image.

Miraculous healing lent power and credibility to Ellen's ministry. When doctors failed, the prayer of faith offered by the prophet and her friends often resulted in a cure. Numerous accounts exist from Ellen's decades of ministry, so we will peruse only a few—beginning with Sister F.

Sister F.

Early in Ellen's ministry, we read of Sister Frances Howland who became extremely sick with rheumatic fever (fever, swollen joints, involuntary jerking of the muscles, generally awful feelings). Her joints had become so swollen "we could not see the joints." The docs caring for her found themselves unable to do any more—and that's when Ellen asked Mr. Howland if he had faith that prayer might heal his daughter.

"I will believe," he replied.

"Do you believe?" came the question a second time.

"I do," he said with more confidence.

So they began to pray, claiming the promise, "Ask and ye shall receive." As Ellen told the story:

> Sister F. was in the chamber above. She had not stood on her feet for two weeks. The Spirit of the Lord indited [composed] prayer. We had the assurance of God's willingness to heal the afflicted one. Bro. D. cried out in the Spirit, and power of God, "Is there some sister here who has faith enough to go and take her by the hand, and bid her arise in the name of the Lord?" Sister C. was on her way as the words were spoken. She ascended the stairs with the Spirit of the Lord upon her, and took F. by the hand, saying, "Sister Frances, in the name of the Lord arise and be whole." Sister F. acted out her faith, rose from her bed and stood upon her feet, and walked the room praising the Lord that she was healed. She dressed and came down into the room where we were, her countenance lighted up with the blessing of God.[1]

While Ellen herself did not take Frances by the hand, she was nonetheless present for the prayer, and as her ministry grew so would the number of stories. Frances was checked out by the doc and given a clean bill of health. Shortly thereafter, she was baptized by James White.

Mr. Hyde

In the 1870s, Ellen recounted a story in *Spiritual Gifts* about a man named Hyde who received healing:

> At this time Bro. Wm. H. Hyde was very sick with the bloody dysentery. His symptoms were alarming. A physician said that unless he received help in a short time, his case was hopeless. There was much unbelief and darkness in the place where he was staying, and we wished to get him away where there was more faith. We prayed for him around the bedside, that the Lord would raise him up and give him strength to leave that place. He was blessed and strengthened, and rode four miles. After he arrived at Bro. P.'s he grew worse, and seemed to be sinking every hour. Some things had hindered faith in his

case. Faithful testimony was borne to him, and humble confessions were made on his part, where he had erred, and a few who had faith were permitted to enter his room. Our earnest, fervent prayers went up to God, that the progress of disease might be stayed, and then faith grasped still more, immediate restoration. God's children seemed to groan in spirit. Such a reaching out after God and bringing the promises near, I have seldom witnessed. The salvation of God was revealed. Power from on high rested upon our sick brother, and upon those in the room. He called for his clothes, arose and dressed himself, and walked out of the room, praising God, with the light of heaven shining in his countenance. A farmer's dinner was ready. Said Bro. H., "If I was well I should partake of this food, and I believe God has healed me, and shall act out my faith." He ate heartily, and it did not hurt him.[2]

Again, Ellen worked within the community of believers; she didn't often go off by herself and lead giant healing crusades. Ellen never tried to put the *I* in *team;* her gifts always uplifted the group, reminding us that following Jesus isn't just a personal thing—it's a community thing.

I am also struck by the audacity of the prayers these early believers prayed. They didn't waffle or waver with sentiments such as "if it's Your will"—they just believed. Not that we shouldn't care about God's will, but too often we use it as an escape clause in case we don't get the answer we want, and so we don't have to invest too much of ourselves in wrestling with God.

Father Andrews

In the 1850s, J. N. Andrews's father became quite ill with inflammatory rheumatism. Another group prayer was offered, only this time Ellen herself laid her hands on the man's head and boldly stated: "Father Andrews, the Lord Jesus maketh thee whole." Just freeze this moment for a second. What would you do if someone did that during one of your prayers?

Imagine having prayer for an elderly relative in the hospital, a sick friend recovering in his or her room at home, or even a homeless guy on the street corner who can't afford the medicine he needs. Imagine holding hands and circling around the sick person, with everyone saying the usual "if it's Your will" cliché when someone breaks the circle, slaps his hands on the head of the ailing person, and shouts, "JESUS CURES YOU!"

What?

Seriously, I'll bet that's how people would respond.

What?

How awkward would you feel? It's one thing to hope for the possibility of healing, but to hear someone *claim* it as a reality? That feels a little weird to some people but not as weird, or as thrilling, as if the healing actually took place.

Mr. Andrews "was healed instantly."

According to Ellen, "light seemed to shine all through the house."[3]

Kinda makes me want to infuse my prayers with more boldness. In Scripture, God never seems offended when we ask for what is truly in our hearts. Matter of fact, the only prayers God seems annoyed by are the ones we ask with a hypocritical spirit. Let's ask honestly and receive gratefully the miracles God wants to give us.

Getting off the couch

In the 1880s, Ellen attended a meeting in Healdsburg, California. She had to be carried in on a "sofa" because she was so sick. Attendees noted how weak she looked—and also "deathly" pale. From her position on the couch, Ellen noted that it seemed "as if nearly all of Healdsburg was present."[4] That's an awkward place to be; imagine being a major leader in a church and having to attend services sitting, maybe even lying, on a couch where everyone can see you.

Of course, depending on how boring the speakers are, a couch might be nice.

Thankfully, the meeting proved exciting as speakers like J. H. Waggoner talked about how the Adventist Church had grown over the years. When he finished, Ellen turned to her son and Mrs. Ings who were sitting by her on the sofa.

"Will you help me up," asked Ellen, "and assist me to stand on my feet while I say a few words?"

"Uh, is that such a good idea, Mom?" Willie might have asked. "You look like death, and I am pretty sure people wouldn't find it very encouraging if you passed out or collapsed on the platform. How about you take a nappy-poo, and I'll wake you when it's time to go?"

Had he said that to her, Willie might have been the only one to look like death. Seriously, who's gonna argue with a prophet who wants to preach? So they helped her to the pulpit. And, according to Ellen, "For five minutes I stood there, trying to speak, and thinking that it was the last speech I should ever make—my farewell message."

Thankfully, as Ellen gripped the pulpit, she "felt a power come upon me, like a shock of electricity." Cool. She went on to say, "It passed through my body and up to my head. The people said that they plainly saw the blood mounting to my lips, my ears, my cheeks, my forehead."[5] Color raced back into her face; her strength returned to her body; and her ability to get her preach on reached out and captured the attention of her audience.

"We are seeing a miracle performed before our eyes!" shouted a businessman named Mr. Montrose. "Mrs. White is healed!" Her voice continued to build in power, her words crisp and articulate, and when she called for people to commit their hearts to Jesus "a goodly number answered to the call."[6]

Fit stricken

In another early incident, sometime in the 1840s, Ellen was staying at a house when "a young sister" was stricken with "fits." Whether this was the result of anxiety, fear, panic, or seizures, the records don't say. However, while at the house, she had a "most distressing" attack that made others in the house send for the doctor, and others suggest putting on a tea kettle for hot water.

"I felt the spirit of prayer," remembered Ellen. The teen prophet later wrote, "We prayed to the Lord to deliver the afflicted. In the name and strength of Jesus, I put my arms around her, and lifted her up from the bed, rebuking the power of Satan, and bidding her, 'Go free.' She instantly recovered from the fit, and praised the Lord with us."[7]

You don't have to be old in order to have powerful answers to prayer. Pray for healing, my friends. Don't be afraid to tell Jesus where you hurt and trust Him to help you when you need it.

ENDNOTES

1. E. G. White, *Spiritual Gifts,* 2:43, 44.
2. Ibid., 45.
3. E. G. White, Manuscript 135, 1903, quoted in *Selected Messages,* 1:207.
4. E. G. White, Letter 82, 1906, quoted in Arthur White, *Ellen G. White,* 3:204.
5. Ibid.
6. Ibid.
7. E. G. White, *Life Sketches Manuscript,* 150.

Chapter 66

The Shady Lady

This is my favorite miracle story. This epic tale occurs in the early 1850s when Ellen was still a young prophet. It is a prime example of the miraculous power that held Ellen's ministry in place when confronted with diabolical people masquerading with facades of holiness, when inside (much like the Pharisees of Jesus' day) lurked nothing but death.

The story begins with Ellen having a vision concerning a woman who professed "great holiness" in front of the believers in Michigan. Ellen didn't recognize the woman in the vision—had never seen her before. The only details she knew came from the vision. Ellen learned that M. E. Cornell, a new believer in the Advent message, had met the woman a few days before the Whites had arrived in Michigan.

Cornell heard about Ellen's vision from J. N. Loughborough but told him that he wouldn't give him further details about the woman. Cornell wanted to test if the prophet's vision would play out. The only thing Cornell said to Ellen was, "If there is such a woman you will probably find her, as you have appointments where you will be apt to see most, if not all, of the Sabbathkeepers in the State." Already this is an awesome story—visions of people you haven't met and are expecting to meet them at an undisclosed location in the near future.

Someone should make this into a skit for church.

Loughborough wrote about the vision and gave the following additional insights:

> In [Sister] White's written description of the woman she not only told her mode of procedure, but that when she [Ellen] should reprove her [the woman], she would "put on a sanctimonious look, and say, 'God—knows—my—heart.' " She [Ellen] said this woman was traveling about the country with a young man, while her own husband, an older man, was at home working to support them in their course. [Sister] W. said the Lord had shown her that "with all this woman's pretensions to holiness, she was guilty of violating the seventh commandment."[1]

The Shady Lady

Oh snap! This shady lady acts spiritually snooty at the same time that she is having an illicit affair with a young man traveling with her in "ministry." Maybe this isn't a great skit for church, after all; but it's a great story for this book. Let's continue.

On June 11, 1853, Ellen and crew reached the home where they were to be hosted. Good buddy Loughborough picks up the story:

> As we alighted from the carriage, and were standing under a large apple tree in front of the house, [Sister] White said to her husband, "James, we have got to the church where that woman lives whom I saw in the Tyrone vision." "Why," said Bro[ther] White, "this is not the house where she lives, is it?" "No," said [Sister] White; "but I saw this man and woman in connection with the case. The woman in this house has no confidence in that woman, but the man here thinks she is all right."[2]

We are getting closer to a showcase showdown between Young Prophet and Shady Lady. The house where the Whites are supposed to stay is divided in its opinions: the wife thinks Shady Lady is bogus, but the husband seems cool with her. This is too good not to make into a skit!

> **Wife:** Methinks that lady be shady.
>
> **Husband:** How can you say that, dear wife, when she has professed such holiness?
>
> **Wife:** Her holiness is a farce, my husband. Why do you give her such credence?
>
> **Husband:** Would such a strapping young man accompany her if her testimony were not true?
>
> **Wife:** I fear you are a simpleton, my blockheaded beloved.

Maybe a Christian school would let you do the skit for chapel.

Loughborough related how, as various carriages passed by, while everyone reclined under a tree by the road, Ellen identified some passersby as being supportive of the shady lady, and others not. As one load of people in a carriage drove by, Ellen said, "None of that load have any confidence in that woman's pretensions." That's good news.

When a second carriage passed by, she commented, "That load is divided on the case. Those on the front seat have no confidence in the woman; those on the back seat think she is all right." That's OK news.

When the third load rolled by, Ellen said, "They are all under the woman's influence." That's bad news. Her insight into the various groups of people only firmed up

Ellen's conviction that the gathering where she and the lady were destined to meet "must be the church where that woman lives; for I have seen all these persons in connection with that affair."[3]

Ellen seems to be outnumbered here, only heightening the drama that occurred Sabbath morning when it all went down in a large barn three miles away from where Ellen was staying. Even the location is awesome. A theological fight in a barn—beautiful!

Loughborough recalled the Sabbath barn party:

While Bro[ther] White was preaching, an old man, a young man, and a woman came in. The two former sat down directly in front of Bro[ther] White, while the woman took a seat close to the barn door. After a brief discourse from Bro[ther] White, [Sister] White arose to speak. She introduced her remarks by speaking of the care ministers should have that they mar not the work committed to them. She said God could not call a woman to travel about the country with some other man than her husband.[4]

Uh-oh, here we go . . .

Narrowing her focus and steadying her gaze on the woman sitting next to the door, the young prophet drops an epic truth bomb:

"That woman who just sat down near the door claims that God has called her to preach. She is traveling with this young man who just sat down in front of the desk, while this old man, her husband,—God pity him!—is toiling at home to earn means which they are using to carry on their iniquity. She professes to be very holy—to be sanctified. With all her pretensions and talk about holiness, God has showed me that she and this young man have violated the seventh commandment."[5]

Booooooooooooooooooom! This is such a gorgeous moment. How would you feel as a member of the congregation? The service would be awkward, exciting, supernatural, confrontational, and unforgettable.

Everyone knew that Ellen doesn't know these people, so when she selected them out of a crowd (from those who did know them) she immediately established her credibility. As would be expected, according to Loughborough, all eyes turn to the shady lady—Mrs. Alcott. How on earth could she save face after such a prophetic smackdown?

She sat for "about one minute," "slowly arose to her feet," and (just like the vision said) "put on a sanctimonious look." If you are unfamiliar with sanctimonious looks, imagine someone turning his or her nose up in the air, while having just taken a bite out of a lemon, and looking at you with one suspicious eye. Yeah, not pretty. But what Mrs. Alcott said next is pretty awesome.

"God—knows—my—heart."

That's it.

She sat back down firmly convinced she had refuted Ellen but sadly unaware that her response fit the vision exactly. If I had been there, I would be tweeting that thing all over cyberspace: #bestchurchserviceever.

During the following weeks, people began losing faith in the woman and her young male "friend." He decided to leave for Canada, admitting to people that Ellen's vision "was too true." After that, Shady Lady Alcott also received some intense questioning as to the content of Ellen's vision. Her reply?

"I consider Sister White a good, devoted, Christian woman," she said. "While I may not regard her visions just as you do, I shall not say one word against her or her work."

My guess is she wasn't wearing her "sanctimonious" look when she spoke those words.

ENDNOTES

1. J. N. Loughborough, "Recollections of the Past—No. 6," *Review and Herald,* May 6, 1884, 11.
2. Ibid., 12.
3. Ibid.
4. Ibid.
5. Ibid.

Chapter 67

Perspective on Miracles

Miracles are awesome, no question. They are given to lend credibility to someone's ministry, but they shouldn't be the only thing we look for. Jesus is clear that only wicked people search after signs (Matthew 12:39). Signs and wonders aren't bad; they just can't be the only things our faith is based on.

They serve practical purposes for mission; they aren't for our personal entertainment like tricks from sleight-of-hand artists such as Stuart Edge.

While Ellen had incredible spiritual power throughout her ministry, she did suggest, at times, that miracles weren't helpful. Six years before she passed away she addressed the issue as to why people should put energy into creating health centers rather than simply praying for healing.

Here is what Ellen said regarding prayer for healing in this context:

> In letters received from our brethren, the questions are asked, "Why do we expend so much effort in establishing sanitariums? Why do we not pray for the healing of the sick, instead of having sanitariums?"
>
> There is more to these questions than is at first apparent. In the early history of our work, many were healed by prayer. And some, after they were healed, pursued the same course in the indulgence of appetite that they had followed in the past. They did not live and work in such a way as to avoid sickness. They did not show that they appreciated the Lord's goodness to them. Again and again they were brought to suffering through their own careless, thoughtless course of action. How could the Lord be glorified in bestowing on them the gift of health?[1]

Sadly, this experience mirrors what happened to Israel in the Hebrew Scriptures.

God did countless miracles among the Israelites; He even promised them that if they simply obeyed, they would be blessed—and that if they didn't, they would be cursed (see Deuteronomy 28). God took all the guesswork out of wondering what His will might be and even promised them huge blessings. A quick glance reveals a pillar of fire, miraculous food showing up, oil jars that never run dry, healings, resurrections, and more.

Yet even more frequent than God's miracles were His children's disobedience and preference for self-destructive behavior. The miracles never last because our human problem runs deeper than hunger, thirst, poverty, sickness, and even death. We need a heart change; we need our whole perspective, and how we relate to the world around us, altered.

Mercifully, that is just what God offers each of us when He says, through one of His miracle-working prophets, "I will give them one heart, and a new spirit I will put within them. I will remove the heart of stone from their flesh and give them a heart of flesh" (Ezekiel 11:19). Even during the seemingly miracle-filled days of the Old Testament, God's intent was clear—our hearts need to be healed more than our circumstances do.

Jesus offered the perspective of first seeking God's kingdom and His righteousness—His saving power and love—and then trusting that "all these things will be added to you" (Matthew 6:33). Our primary focus must be to know Jesus, and as we seek to know Him, He will tell us what we need to do, what we are supposed to do.

I will add, in closing, that Ellen does speak of a time when miracles would erupt within the church again, just before Jesus comes: "It is with an earnest longing that I look forward to the time when the events of the day of Pentecost shall be repeated with even greater power than on that occasion."[2]

I can't wait for that time, but in the meantime I will seek Jesus and trust Him to give me what I need to accomplish great things—which probably doesn't include learning that amazing kissing card trick.

ENDNOTES

1. E. G. White, "Why Conduct Sanitariums?" *Review and Herald,* December 16, 1909.
2. E. G. White, "Among the Churches of Switzerland," *Review and Herald,* July 20, 1886.

Section VIII: Her Writings and Losing Her Voice

Chapter 68

What White Wrote

This year Ellen White will release a daily devotional book—strange, since she has been dead since 1915. I wasn't aware she was still working on material. I'm rather inspired actually. I hope something as trivial as my own death won't prevent me from publishing more books long after I'm gone.

Of course, not everyone is happy with Ellen's posthumous literary output. As one of my former college professors says, "I prefer to read the books she wrote before she died." So how does this happen? How can Ellen continue to "write" books when she is clearly buried in Battle Creek, Michigan?

This illustrates one of the tricky elements in reading Ellen's writings: she didn't write all of them. Let me clarify. All of the books bearing her name contain her writings, but not in the way she originally organized them. We have a variety of books, made up of Ellen's writings and organized around various themes, prepared by people who love her and what she wrote.

We call these books *compilations.*

Some are carefully put together with a general audience in mind, while some, as we saw with *Counsels on Diet and Foods,* have a very specific audience in mind. Ellen wrote so much in her lifetime that, combined with all the compilations, it can be very confusing to know what to read, what you're reading when you have decided what to read, and when exactly Ellen wrote it and why.

Well, it's a good thing you found this chapter because I am going to walk you through the major works *she* wrote, when she wrote them, the purpose for writing them, and give you some suggestions of when to read them. Keep in mind that while you can read her books in chronological order, and that has certain merits, I am going to give you a thematic order—moving from the simple and fundamental to the complex.

Steps to Christ (1892)

Translated into more than 150 languages (83 more than the Harry Potter series), this book is, by far, Ellen's most famous and most read work. The title describes the goal perfectly—moving us closer to Jesus. In the book, Ellen talks about God's love for us, how Jesus saves us, and how we can know Him better.

Start here.

Not only does this book masterfully explain the basics of knowing Jesus, it's also super short—barely over a hundred pages. There is even a translation in modern English called *Steps to Jesus* to make it even easier to understand. Short of having someone read it to you, and I am sure someone would be willing to do that, I don't know how this could be any easier for you.

One of my favorite quotes from the book:

> He [Satan] pictured the Creator as a being who is watching with jealous eye to discern the errors and mistakes of men, that He may visit judgments upon them. It was to remove this dark shadow, by revealing to the world the infinite love of God, that Jesus came to live among men.[1]

This book paints a beautiful picture of the loving Savior Ellen worshiped. Don't miss it. If more people read this book first, and more often than the rest, we might not have so many people with such a negative view of Ellen.

The Desire of Ages (1898)

This book is much larger than *Steps to Christ*, and it was intended to be much larger than it is now, except that Ellen decided to break it into three books, with this one being the first. *The Desire of Ages* follows the life of Jesus—and it's awesome.

The title of the book is taken from a prophecy about Jesus found in Haggai 2:7, which says, "And I will shake all nations, and the desire [or treasure] of all nations shall come: and I will fill this house with glory, saith the LORD of hosts" (KJV). If the Bible considers Jesus to be the ultimate desire, then He should be ours, and any book about Him should be at the top of our reading list.

A great quote from this book, which I would recommend reading second, says, "In Christ is life, original, unborrowed, underived."[2] Although this book is longer than *Steps to Christ*, it is very readable. Jerry D. Thomas has produced an even easier-to-read version called *Messiah*.

So, what are the other two books connected to this one? I am so glad you asked.

Christ's Object Lessons (1900)

You like stories? You like Jesus? This entire book is about the stories told by Jesus.

I'll give you a moment to catch your breath. This work follows right after *The Desire of Ages* and comes third in the reading order I recommend to you. Ellen offers some cool insights into stories that we think we already know.

For example, there is a story in which Peter thinks he is being forgiving, and Jesus blows his mind—and the minds of anyone listening to Him. Check it out:

> The rabbis limited the exercise of forgiveness to three offenses. Peter, carrying out, as he supposed, the teaching of Christ, thought to extend it to seven, the number signifying perfection. But Christ taught that we are never to become weary of forgiving. Not "Until seven times," He said, "but, Until seventy times seven."[3]

Hear that? The church leaders said you have to forgive someone only three times and you were good; you could start holding a grudge after that. Jesus messes up that number by suggesting 490 times—a divine exaggeration, letting us know we are never to hold a grudge.

That's helpful to remember when we are really angry with someone or someone puts on a "sanctimonious look" and tries to judge us for a mistake. Ellen says other cool stuff in this book, but I know you'll read it for yourself.

Thoughts From the Mount of Blessing (1896)

The greatest sermon ever preached happened on the Mount of Olives. The sermon spans only a few chapters (Matthew 5–7) but embedded in those chapters are the most profound verses in all of Scripture. In that sermon Jesus paints a picture of His kingdom and how we can be a part of it—now, even while we wait for Him to return.

Ellen takes that sermon and offers some fresh ways to look at Jesus' words—in only 152 pages. Short and sweet, with helpful insights into things like the Lord's Prayer. Most of us know this prayer; it's probably crocheted on something in your grandma's house. We say it and think we know it, but then we read insights like this:

> When you pray, "Hallowed be Thy name," you ask that it may be hallowed in this world, hallowed in you. . . . God sends you into the world as His representative. In every act of life you are to make manifest the name of God.[4]

You make God's name holy. Wow, that's heavy. How you love people (including forgiving them more than three times—yes, even your little brother) reveals God's character to people.

Oh, and Jerry D. Thomas also has a paraphrase of this book called *Blessings*—pick it up.

So, once we complete Ellen's Jesus studies, where do we go from here? Honestly, if you stayed with just these books, you would have an incredible grasp of the heart of her theology and passion.

But there is more and, thankfully, these writings point to Jesus too.

Conflict of the Ages: *Patriarchs and Prophets* (1890)

Patriarchs and Prophets is the first book in the five-book Conflict of the Ages series—which, incidentally, includes *The Desire of Ages* as book 3. This series walks you through the Bible, and *Patriarchs and Prophets* starts right smack in the beginning when God started creating things. Actually, it goes further back than that—into heaven when Satan picked a fight with Jesus and was booted out of heaven, only to arrive on earth and mess up humanity.

Follow Adam and Eve in the Garden of Eden (their first home until they ate the wrong groceries) and follow the story until you come to King David (of giant-killing fame). Giving an overview of Genesis through 2 Samuel in this book, Ellen grapples with huge questions that everybody has asked.

As I write this chapter, the school attached to our church is reeling from a robbery that occurred in the wee hours while it was still dark. Thousands of dollars' worth of instruments have been taken, the local news station has showed up, and the story is all over the Internet. While looking through the various comments on Facebook regarding the situation, I came across one that agitated me.

Some girl wrote, "Where was God when the instruments were stolen?"

Obviously this female troll (She-troll? Trollette?) is trying to provoke some kind of retaliatory response, but this question has been fought over for centuries. Where is God when this kind of stuff happens to His people? Or, in another variation, Why does God let bad things happen to good people?

The very first chapter in *Patriarchs and Prophets* is titled "Why Was Sin Permitted?"

Ellen deals with difficult stuff right from the beginning, capturing the hearts of all those who have been hurt and can't explain why. Want to know the big background reason why God allowed cancer to take your loved one, why your new kitten was run over by a truck, or why Justin Bieber is somehow still allowed to make "music"?

You'll have to read . . .

Prophets and Kings (1917)

Now *waaaaaaiiit* just a minute! Ellen died in 1915, and this book was published in 1917. Did I lead you astray? Have I slipped you a compilation just as you were filling your Amazon.com cart with Ellen Gould goodies?

Gould? Who's Gould?

That's Ellen's middle name; it's an old way of saying "gold." That's right, Ellen had a little bling for her middle name, and I used it to make an alliteration—putting words together that start with the same sound. I think it was worth the effort. But seriously, what's up with these dates?

Well, there is always a time period between when an author writes a book and when the publisher releases it. I am writing this book in 2014, but people won't read it until 2015 and beyond. The publisher has to edit, select the right type font, create a cover design, and so on. That takes time. Ellen had nearly finished this book right before she passed away. Her literary assistants pulled together material from her writings to complete the book, and the publisher released it as fast as possible.

We all cool here? Great, now back to the contents of this book.

Prophets and Kings picks up where *Patriarchs and Prophets* leaves off—beginning with Solomon. You've heard of him, right? The wisest man who ever lived, who, ironically, also made some of the dumbest mistakes in human history—seven hundred wives? Not a great idea, but an interesting read. Not to mention the überprophets Elijah and Elisha and all their (literally) fiery escapades—serious, lots of real, literal, hot fire.

The book surveys the Old Testament up until the prophecies of Isaiah that point to Jesus, which is where we pick up *The Desire of Ages* (if we're reading in chronological order).

The Acts of the Apostles (1911)

Following *The Desire of Ages* in the Conflict of the Ages series comes *The Acts of the Apostles*. This book runs through the rest of the New Testament, filling in important details as it weaves a narrative of people like Paul, Peter, Barnabas, and John.

Follow Ellen as she summarizes Paul's quest to clean up church messes in places like Corinth:

> At the very beginning of his labors in this thoroughfare of travel, Paul saw on every hand serious obstacles to the progress of his work. The city was almost wholly given up to idolatry. Venus was the favorite goddess, and with the worship of Venus were connected many demoralizing rites and ceremonies. The Corinthians had become conspicuous, even among the heathen, for their gross immorality.[5]

How did Paul deal with Gross Church? And what difficulties did other churches get into?

Read *The Acts of the Apostles* and see. More importantly, this book contains a lot of information on the often misunderstood Holy Spirit, who gives amazing gifts, such as prophecy, to the church.

The Great Controversy (1858, 1884, 1888, 1911)

This is Ellen's definitive work.

The call to write this epic came to her in 1858 through a vision in Lovett's Grove, Ohio—and there are four editions of the book that people like to fight over.

The first edition, in 1858, was much shorter than the current version. It simply recounted what she had seen in the two-hour vision. It was initially published as volume 1 of *Spiritual Gifts: The Great Controversy Between Christ and His Angels, and Satan and His Angels*. It's written in the first person, with Ellen writing "I saw" 161 times.

The 1884 edition expanded on the first by covering the entirety of Christian history for a largely Adventist audience; whereas the first edition had an Adventist audience in mind and focused on the experience leading up to 1844. To give you an idea of how much bigger this second edition was, the *Spiritual Gifts* version has 48,800 words, whereas this one has 136,700.

That's a lot of words.

The 1888 edition has 237,400 words. Part of this increase came from "de-Adventizing" the language. That might sound scary to some people. All I mean is that the 1884 edition of the book still contained phrases that wouldn't make sense to non-Adventists. The next edition (1888) changed these. Ellen also worked on the expanded edition while she was in Europe—the land where people such as Martin Luther inspired the Protestant Reformation. So in the 1888 edition Ellen threw in a few extra chapters on Reformers such as Huss, Jerome of Prague, Zwingli (yes, that's a real name), and John Calvin.

The book sold in phenomenal numbers, and in 1911 the definitive edition came into being due to the printing plates for the 1888 edition being completely worn out. The 1911 version reflects the shifting attitude toward quoting sources (citations were added to many of the references); some references to time were changed, because of the years that had elapsed between 1888 and 1911; some of the wording shifted to be more exact; references were selected by availability (after all, what's the point of referencing something no one can find?); and finally, and most controversially, some of the more pointed truths about the Catholic Church were expressed more gently so not to put off readers.

Some people think the mission of the Adventist Church is to attack Catholics—but being an Adventist simply means looking for Jesus to return. Our mission is not to hate Catholics; it's to help people fall in love with Jesus. Too many pastors and evangelists forget that point and wind up talking more about the pope than about the Prince of peace.

Sorry, I'm ranting.

The final edition of *The Great Controversy* weighs in at 241,500 words discussing, in great detail, the history of the church from the days of the disciples to the glorious day when Jesus comes again. At more than six hundred pages, this book can be a beast to work through and, at times, a little scary when it's dealing with world events before the Second Coming.

I once made a girl cry by skipping right to the most intense parts of the book in order to show her where she was wrong; it wasn't my finest hour. This is a book that tells the sweeping story of the followers of Jesus, and it includes some of the uglier parts of human history—and human future—that might be a bit much if you don't have the assurance of God's love.

Ultimately that's what this book is concerned with—God's love. The final sentence of the book (spoiler alert) says, "From the minutest atom to the greatest world, all things, animate and inanimate, in their unshadowed beauty and perfect joy, declare that God is love."[6]

Keep that goal in mind when you decide to dive into this one.

Gospel Workers (1892, 1915)

The title of this book is self-explanatory. In it, Ellen gives counsel about how to share everything you have presumably read in the aforementioned books. After all, with such an amazing picture of God and the story He is directing in human history, why wouldn't we want to share it?

There are two editions of this book because Ellen later expanded the 1892 version with more counsel. Some of that counsel includes gems such as the following:

> In the work of soul-winning, great tact and wisdom are needed. The Saviour never suppressed the truth, but He uttered it always in love. In His . . . [conversation] with others, He exercised the greatest tact, and He was always kind and thoughtful. He was never rude, never needlessly spoke a severe word, never gave unnecessary pain to a sensitive soul.[7]

In other words, don't be rude and obnoxious when talking about Jesus. You ever heard of rude Christians? Yeah, me too. Ellen can't stand it.

> Many of our ministers have merely sermonized, presenting subjects in an argumentative way, and scarcely mentioning the saving power of the Redeemer.[8]

Boring sermons? Ellen can't stand them. She goes on to tell people to preach from the heart about Jesus. Don't use corny gimmicks, either; just be real.

Then there is this one:

> Christ's method alone will give true success in reaching the people. The

Saviour mingled with men as one who desired their good. He showed His sympathy for them, ministered to their needs, and won their confidence. Then He bade them, "Follow Me."[9]

This is one of the most famous "Ellenisms" ever uttered by the prophetess. Sometimes we put the message before a relationship with the people we are speaking to. Ellen points out that Jesus worked hard to build rapport with people before inviting them into a deeper understanding of the truth. Too often we skip to the "follow me" part and forget to mingle.

Start mingling.

Finally,

Many do not realize the necessity of adapting themselves to circumstances, and meeting the people where they are.[10]

Irrelevant presentations? Ellen (surprise!) can't stand them. We need to be flexible, understand the language people speak, the cultural realities they live in, and share with them in ways that make sense.

As Ellen says, "Christianity is intensely practical."[11]

P.S. Don't confuse this book with *Evangelism,* which is a compilation.

The Ministry of Healing (1905)

The Ministry of Healing is the answer to the health mess mentioned in a previous chapter. Based on Ellen's 1863 health vision, this book expounds her philosophy on how to take care of our bodies so we can serve Jesus better.

This book, although it sometimes relies on nineteenth-century reasons for why certain things happen, has a lot of good stuff for us to consider. If you read it, I recommend you read the chapter "Extremes in Diet" first.

Here Ellen tries to qualify her counsels by encouraging us not to be dumb in our application of health principles:

It is impossible to make an unvarying rule to regulate everyone's habits, and no one should think himself a criterion for all. Not all can eat the same things. Foods that are palatable and wholesome to one person may be distasteful, and even harmful, to another. Some cannot use milk, while others thrive on it. Some persons cannot digest peas and beans; others find them wholesome. For some the coarser grain preparations are good food, while others cannot use them.[12]

Even the gifted Mrs. White tells us that no hard and fast rules can automatically apply to everyone.

Just because you happen to love the fermented cabbage in kimchi does not mean your sister will. It doesn't matter that your mother is wild for brussels sprouts; many people (including yours truly) think them a diabolical agent of Satan. I have a friend who is allergic to onions, but I cherish them—particularly when they are fried with butter. What an amazing smell! Someone should make it into a candle or an air freshener.

Yet, regardless of allergies and taste preferences, the principle is there—we should find vegetables that work for us, unless they are brussels sprouts.

In this book, Ellen also chats about mental health, serving others, and studying about God. Good stuff. Add it to your reading list, but don't confuse it with *Counsels on Diet and Foods,* another compilation.

Education (1903)

I'll give you three guesses what this book is about.

One of Ellen's legacies is the award-winning Adventist education system. Within the pages of *Education* dwells Ellen's philosophy of how people should be taught. If you attend an Adventist school, it would be interesting to dig into this book and see what she has to say—especially because some people have stories that aren't so great about being in Adventist schools.

As a pastor I have heard, too many times, about people who had crabby teachers or were picked on by other kids and by the time they leave the Adventist school, they have lost their faith and harbor some pretty ugly feelings toward the school and the church. On a purely logical level, this is a little stupid.

I know I just offended someone with that word, but stay with me.

I have had bad service at Pizza Hut, but I still eat there sometimes. I have seen movies that I hated, but I have also seen good ones. I know some "true believers" strap bombs to themselves and run into public areas, blasting everybody to smithereens; but I also know others who are horrified by that behavior. Church members have hurt me many times (and I'm a pastor!), yet I remain and work in the congregation.

The point is that it is not fair to judge a *huge* group of people based on the sins of a few. You and I have had many moments in our lives that we would never want people to use in order to define us—why would we do that to others? Especially in light of Jesus' words to forgive at least 490 times.

Now, on an emotional level, I, as a pastor, feel terrible whenever I hear teachers, preachers, and "sanctimonious" Christians mistreating people. Beyond feeling terrible, I feel angry, and whenever I am close enough to the situation, I do not keep silent. If you have been hurt in school, I hope you won't give those hurting you the power to ruin your faith—they don't deserve that.

Also, know that even if you think otherwise, that kind of behavior has never been OK—not even with Ellen. In the very first chapter of *Education,* she defines the foundation of Christian education , writing: "Love, the basis of creation and of redemption, is the basis of true education."[13]

Well said, Ellen.

Spiritual Gifts, vol. 2 (1860)

Moving away from theology and practical instruction, this little number (seriously, the older editions of this book can fit in your pocket) covers Ellen's life through 1858. Some great stories here—many more details than I have given in this book. Visions, untimely deaths, family fights, travel, and strange characters await you.

> Presently an angel bid me rise, and the sight that met my eyes can hardly be described . . .[14]

Want to know what she saw? Then you know what to do.

Life Sketches of Ellen G. White (1915)

Continuing the autobiographical thread, *Life Sketches of Ellen G. White* takes us past 1858—all the way down to the death of James. Lots of cool stuff in here, like this:

> On one occasion, while Elder Stockman was preaching, Elder Brown, a Christian Baptist minister, whose name has been mentioned before in this narrative, was sitting in the desk listening to the sermon with intense interest. He became deeply moved, and suddenly his face grew pale as the dead, he reeled in his chair, and Elder Stockman caught him in his arms just as he was falling to the floor, and laid him on the sofa back of the desk, where he lay powerless until the discourse was finished.
>
> He then arose, his face still pale, but shining with light from the Sun of Righteousness, and gave a very impressive testimony. He seemed to receive holy unction from above. He was usually slow of speech, with an earnest manner, entirely free from excitement. On this occasion his solemn, measured words carried with them a new power.[15]

Passing out in church as if dead? That's worth a read.

Early Writings (1882)

While this work contains some autobiographical details, it's really a collection of Ellen's earliest writings—didn't see that coming, did you?

Ellen wrote down the contents of her first visions and words of encouragement to the recently disappointed believers. One selection from this book, titled "To the 'Little Flock' " says, "I saw that some of the people of God are stupid . . ."[16]

Yes, yes, I know I put in an ellipsis (three dots indicating there is more to this quote than has been given), but you will have to read it for yourself to see if what she said is as awesome as it appears.

Testimonies for the Church (a.k.a. Letters to Crazy People), vols. 1–9 (1855–1909)

Now, let me explain my alternate title before you demand a refund for this apparently disrespectful book. As you have seen, Ellen dealt with some pretty spectacular characters from the time she was a little girl right up until old age. From time to time, God impressed her to write what was called "straight testimony" to people on the edge of making their lives complete disasters.

Most of the writing in the *Testimonies* is the strongest statements given to deal with some of the most extreme of circumstances. To pick up the *Testimonies* and think that this is what Ellen sounded like at the general store, at church, or at the family dinner table is completely bogus. This is why it's good to start with her general works, followed by her biographical stuff, so you don't end up doing crazy things with the *Testimonies* and making everybody hate Ellen—and you, in the process.

As fiery as the prophet's pen could be, I have found these writings to be cathartic (healing) since I became a pastor. In any profession dealing with people, you are bound to run into some very sad, and very aggravating, situations. In those moments, it would be nice to just blast people with "straight testimony," but, at least for me, I don't usually have the authority to speak that way.

Ellen did, however.

In dazzling displays of pointed prophetic prose, Mrs. White grabbed the subject of her letter firmly by the person's delusion and roundhouse kicked it in the face—metaphorically speaking.

Just look at the following examples.

From the first volume of the *Testimonies,* we are told the story of two wannabe health nuts who wanted to give a "sanctimonious" look to others' shortcomings and who had also become incredibly cheap in sharing their resources. Ellen breaks down on them:

> You are noticing little things that you do not understand, that you have not the least to do with, and that in no way concern you. . . .
>
> Brother A, you are naturally close [not generous] and covetous. . . . I saw that you had wrong ideas. God requires economy of His people; but some

have stretched their economy into meanness. . . .

. . . Brother and Sister A may decide in this matter, and be all wrong. Your judgment is imperfect, and can be no evidence in this matter. . . .

Now God invites you to get right, to try your motives, and to press into harmony with His people.[17]

Take that Mr. and Mrs. A! Quit judging people and not being nice—and please be part of our community. Ellen never lays the smackdown intending to reject people. On the contrary, she wants them to be happy and healthy.

In the second volume of the *Testimonies,* we have several more treats to consider. We will begin with Sister G—a woman who was consumed with stuff, neglected her stepchildren, and caused fights wherever she went. Ellen wasted no time assessing her situation:

> Sister G, I have a message to you. You are far from the kingdom. You love this world, and this love has made you cold, selfish, exacting, and penurious. The great object of interest with you is the powerful, mighty dollar. . . . Self- ishness and self-love are exemplified in your life to a great degree. You have not overcome this unhappy defect in your character. If this is not remedied, you will lose heaven, and your happiness here will be greatly marred. . . . The dark cloud which has followed you, overshadowing your life, will grow larger and blacker until your whole sky is clouded. You may turn to the right, and there will be no light, and to the left, and you cannot discover a ray.
>
> You make trouble for yourself where there is no trouble, because you are not right. You are unconsecrated. Your complaining, penurious spirit makes you unhappy and displeases God. During your life you have been looking out for yourself, seeking to make yourself happy. It is poor work, unprofitable business. The more you invest here the heavier will be the loss. The less stock you take in this business of serving yourself the greater will be the saving on your part. You are a stranger to disinterested, unselfish love, and while you see no special sin in the absence of this precious trait you will not be diligent to cultivate it.
>
> You loved your husband and married him. You knew that when you mar- ried him you covenanted to become a mother to his children. But I saw a lack in you in this matter. You are sadly deficient. You do not love the children of your husband, and unless there is an entire change, a thorough reformation in you, and in your manner of government, these precious jewels are ruined.[18]

BAM! She also calls out Bro. G, for not stepping up and putting a stop to the abu- sive shenanigans.

Skipping ahead to the fifth volume of the *Testimonies,* we are greeted with an unnamed church (Ellen was merciful) full of crabs who nitpicked at each other and made life unpleasant. Ellen had the following words for this situation:

> There are some in the church in —— who will cause trouble, for their wills have never been brought into harmony with the will of Christ. Brother E will be a great hindrance to this church. When he can have the supremacy he is satisfied, but when he cannot stand first he is always upon the wrong side. He moves from impulse. He will not draw in even cords, but questions and takes opposite views, because it is his nature to be faultfinding and an accuser of his brethren. While he claims to be very zealous for the truth, he is drawing away from the body; he is not strong in moral power, rooted and grounded in the faith. The holy principles of truth are not made a part of his nature. He cannot be trusted; God is not pleased with him.[19]

Ellen mentions that it's in human nature to "run to extremes," and sadly this poor church was a living example. Maybe you've attended one like it; this story might make you feel better, knowing that Ellen is annoyed by this kind of stuff too.

There's also a story about church members raising money by making wine—seriously. Maybe just one more story from *Testimonies,* volume 5:

> I cannot see how, in the light of the law of God, Christians can conscientiously engage in the raising of hops or in the manufacture of wine or cider for the market. All these articles may be put to a good use and prove a blessing, or they may be put to a wrong use and prove a temptation and a curse. Cider and wine may be canned when fresh and kept sweet a long time, and if used in an unfermented state they will not dethrone reason. But those who manufacture apples into cider for the market are not careful as to the condition of the fruit used, and in many cases the juice of decayed apples is expressed. Those who would not think of using the poisonous rotten apples in any other way will drink the cider made from them and call it a luxury; but the microscope would reveal the fact that this pleasant beverage is often unfit for the human stomach, even when fresh from the press. If it is boiled, and care is taken to remove the impurities, it is less objectionable.[20]

Ellen is exasperated—as evidenced by her incredulous first sentence. You could paraphrase it as, "I can't even imagine what you are thinking . . ." It's not so much that the juice is bad, but that these people can't even make it correctly.

Making the matter even worse is the fact that this church, according to Ellen, participated in temperance societies—groups of people dedicated to removing alcohol from the community. So the same group of people preaching against liquor was also making its own moonshine.

"I saw that some of the people of God are stupid . . ."

Sorry, couldn't resist that one.

The last one I will show you (because this could go on for quite some time with nine volumes—each with hundreds of pages) provides a good example of some of the general counsel we find in the *Testimonies*. Ellen frequently comments on general trends within the church and weighs in on the issues in order to keep people from being, well, stupid.

In the seventh volume of the *Testimonies,* in a chapter called "Committee Meetings," Ellen shatters one of the most irritating, obnoxious, lame practices within nearly every church on planet Earth. Check this out:

> I have been instructed that committee meetings are not always pleasing to God. Some have come to these meetings with a cold, hard, critical, loveless spirit. Such may do great harm; for with them is the presence of the evil one, that keeps them on the wrong side. Not infrequently their unfeeling attitude toward measures under consideration brings in perplexity, delaying decisions that should be made. God's servants, in need of rest of mind, and sleep, have been greatly distressed and burdened over these matters. In the hope of reaching a decision, they continue their meetings far into the night. But life is too precious to be imperiled in this way. Let the Lord carry the burden. Wait for Him to adjust the difficulties. Give the weary brain a rest. Unreasonable hours are destructive to the physical, the mental, and the moral powers. If the brain were given proper periods of rest, the thoughts would be clear and sharp, and business would be expedited.[21]

STOP HAVING LONG MEETINGS. STOP IT! Ellen deals a deathblow to the idea that the longer a meeting goes, the more spiritual it must be. She also has a few things to say to those who show up to a meeting intent on making it lengthy with their bad attitudes.

You go, girl.

So much more . . .

We have covered Ellen's major works, but we haven't even scratched the surface of the hundreds of articles she wrote—you heard me, hundreds. As you learn the story of her life, it is fascinating to see what she wrote and when. The articles take on a whole new meaning when you know what she was dealing with and the background.

So where do you access all of these articles? And where do you access the money tree to pay for this massive stack of books?

Good news—they are all free.

Not only can you download the *free* EGW Writings app on your tablet or smartphone, but you can also go to the following Web sites to access all of what Mrs. White wrote:

http://www.ellenwhite.com
http://text.egwwritings.org

Enjoy!

Psst! Hey, right here; got a little trade secret for ya. If you ask any Adventist pastor for a hard copy of one of these books, he or she will probably give you one for free. #themoreyouknow

ENDNOTES

1. Ellen G. White, *Steps to Christ* (Mountain View, CA: Pacific Press® Publishing Association, 1921), 11.
2. Ellen G. White, *The Desire of Ages* (Mountain View, CA: Pacific Press® Publishing Association, 1940), 530.
3. E. G. White, *Christ's Object Lessons,* 243.
4. Ellen G. White, *Thoughts From the Mount of Blessing* (Mountain View, CA: Pacific Press® Publishing Association, 1956), 107.
5. Ellen G. White, *The Acts of the Apostles* (Mountain View, CA: Pacific Press® Publishing Association, 1911), 243, 244.
6. Ellen G. White, *The Great Controversy* (Mountain View, CA: Pacific Press® Publishing Association, 1950), 678.
7. Ellen G. White, *Gospel Workers* (Washington, DC: Review and Herald® Publishing Association, 1915), 117.
8. Ibid., 156.
9. Ibid., 363.
10. Ibid., 381.
11. E. G. White, *Manuscript Releases,* 19:92.
12. E. G. White, *The Ministry of Healing,* 319, 320.
13. Ellen G. White, *Education* (Mountain View, CA: Pacific Press® Publishing Association), 16.
14. E. G. White, *Spiritual Gifts,* 2:61.
15. Ellen G. White, *Life Sketches of Ellen G. White,* (Mountain View, CA: Pacific Press® Publishing Association, 1915), 55.
16. E. G. White, *Early Writings,* 48.
17. E. G. White, *Testimonies for the Church,* 1:204, 207–209.
18. E. G. White, *Testimonies for the Church,* 2:56.
19. E. G. White, *Testimonies for the Church,* 5:304, 305.
20. Ibid., 356.
21. E. G. White, *Testimonies for the Church,* 7:256.

Chapter 69

Losing the Voice

The world is full of ways to lose your voice. Though why you would want to is beyond me.

Maybe you have a solo in the school choir coming up, and you aren't ready. Or you suspect that someone will ask you something that you can't answer. Or your mom just found out that it was you who ate the cupcakes she baked for your brother's birthday party, and she wants an explanation.

First of all, why would you eat that many cupcakes? That's not only mean, it also isn't normal. Sure, two or three is fine, but *twelve*? What's the matter with you? Have you no sense of proportion?

Sorry, I'm starting to sound like your mother. Maybe I should just tell you how to make your voice vanish.

The first method involves yelling—not helpful when you need to lose your voice right before an interrogation. You might get into more trouble. Closely related to this method is singing off-key as loud as you can; the way some people do in church—into the microphone (shudder). A third thing you can do is to bite your tongue, but this helps only when you *want* to say something but need to refrain out of good manners.

Coughing will disrupt your vocal cords' ability to speak; of course, you may need to do this for a while, and it may draw more attention than you want. You may end up at the doctor's office, and that could be worse than answering uncomfortable questions. Cold foods and drinks can lead to voice loss, but in the moment of crisis you are unlikely to find a half gallon of ice cream lying nearby, which is a shame; the world would be a better place with gallons of ice cream nearby.

Canker sores won't mess up your vocal cords, but they will ignite your mouth with excruciating pain, making it impossible to talk. I get these from time to time and can highly recommend avoiding them at all costs. By the way, health tip: my dentist treats my canker sores with a laser. Pretty sweet, huh? Didn't know lasers took out canker sores as well as alien spaceships, did you? Use that information wisely.

The next method involves whispering. Prolonged whispering will strain your vocal cords. This is probably your best option in a classroom or home setting. However, the whispering will have to be rather vigorous if you plan to do away with your speaking ability in a short time.

The final method is the most dangerous because you may never get your voice back. To completely misplace your voice—including your thoughts and feelings—you need to depend on other people. These people need to be louder than you; they need to argue, scream, fight, and create distractions so that nobody can hear you, see you, or even remember that you were there in the first place.

By the late 1800s, this was the way people began to lose Ellen's voice.

1888–1893

During their first decades of existence, Adventists fought to distinguish themselves from the general Christian culture around them. They argued so much about things like prophecy, the Sabbath, and what happens after you die that they lost sight of Jesus. They argued until all they knew how to do was argue.

They became more concerned about being Adventists than about being Christians, which is not very Adventist, because all *Adventist* means is someone looking for Jesus to return.

Thankfully, around 1888, two strong preachers named Jones and Waggoner, with help from Ellen, helped to refocus the church though the 1888 General Conference (GC) Session (meetings where the world church gets together). This General Conference session in which these issues were fought out was one of the most brutal, mean-spirited events in Ellen's life. Like a spiritual MMA (mixed martial arts) match—with no gloves.

Messy.

Ellen praised Jones and Waggoner's message, known as "righteousness by faith." But the nasty attitude displayed by some of the church leaders (which was later referred to as "the spirit of Minneapolis" since the 1888 General Conference Session was held in that city), along with some weird theological ideas Jones and Waggoner picked up later and some personality issues, caused these two young preachers to leave the church some years later. They made some great contributions to the church, but they left a few thorns in its theological flesh as well.

A. T. Jones was a passionate man—a little too passionate. For all of his good qualities, his mood could go from hot to cold like a busted thermostat. His zeal would cause him to overstate things, and when corrected, his soul would then wallow in self-reproach. And who do you suppose was frequently the focus of Jones's mood swings?

Yep. Ellen.

In 1893, five years after the brutal Minneapolis meeting, Jones preached some interesting messages. Instead of the Bible, Jones based his sermons on some of Ellen's writings. He felt this was cool when preaching to Adventists. Ellen didn't attend these meetings, but a man named S. N. Haskell did. He commented that Jones used so many of Ellen's quotes "that they had heard more from her in her absence than if she had been there in person."[1]

That's a little weird—what happened to the Bible?

In an article published the next year, Jones said, "The right use of the *Testimonies,* therefore, is not to use them as they are in themselves, as though they were apart from the word of God in the Bible; but to study the Bible through them."[2]

So, just to be sure I'm following here, we are supposed to study the Bible THROUGH Ellen's writings? Something ain't right.

Ellen noticed it, too, and rebuked Jones for it. As time went on, A. T. Jones, his partner E. J. Waggoner, and even Dr. J. H. Kellogg found themselves in frequent battles with Ellen over her writings, church organization, and beliefs about God.

Making the issue of how to understand her writings even more complicated was the fact that church leaders had "exiled" Ellen to Australia between 1891 and 1900, so that while these confusing views were crashing around, any communication from her, trying to settle conflicts, would take weeks to arrive. No e-mail, remember, in the 1890s.

ENDNOTES

---

1. George R. Knight, *From 1888 to Apostasy* (Hagerstown, MD: Review and Herald® Publishing Association, 1987), 230.

2. A. T. Jones, *The Home Missionary Extra,* December 1894, 12, quoted in George R. Knight, *A. T. Jones: Point Man on Adventism's Charismatic Frontier* (Hagerstown, MD: Review and Herald® Publishing Association, 2011), 259.

Chapter 70

Australia

During the General Conference Session of 1891, Ellen received an "urgent" call to help the Adventist work in Australia. That sounds cool. Who wouldn't want to go live among the koala bears, kangaroos, wallabies, poisonous snakes, giant spiders, and killer sharks off the Great Barrier Reef?

Wow, that list started so positive and then took a rather drastic turn. In any case, most of us would be excited, however exotic the wildlife—or maybe because of the exotic wildlife—to travel to a faraway land and work there. As I'm writing this chapter, I am looking forward to traveling to South Africa next month to share Jesus with others.

However, a few circumstances surrounding Ellen's departure to Down Under help us to see that this trip was more politically motivated than spiritually. In an 1896 letter, written to the General Conference president, O. A. Olsen, Ellen let it be known: "I have not, I think, revealed the entire workings that led me here to Australia. Perhaps you may never fully understand the matter. The Lord was not in our leaving America. He did not reveal that it was his will that I should leave Battle Creek. The Lord did not plan this, but he let you all move after your own imaginings."[1]

Why would the church's leadership try to exile Ellen to Australia? Conflict had erupted due to the theological fights at the 1888 General Conference Session and Ellen's subsequent preaching tours with Jones and Waggoner in the hope of refocusing the church on Jesus.

Refocusing on Jesus, once you have taken your eyes off Him, can be painful—even for churches. Jesus said, "Do not think that I have come to bring peace to the earth. I have not come to bring peace, but a sword" (Matthew 10:34). Ellen's views didn't sit well with the leadership, so they created a call especially for her.

How thoughtful.

I guess sending someone out of the country is one way to silence that person. Luckily for the church leaders, social media didn't exist back then, or Ellen's voice could have gone viral with negative messages directed at the church leaders.

Ellen, her son W. C. White, and a few other helpers arrived in Australia in December 1891, and she was welcomed warmly. Quickly, Ellen became aware of the need for an Australian educational facility to teach youth in a Christian atmosphere so they might be of service around the world for the Savior.

A Bible school opened in Melbourne in 1892. Ellen felt impressed that it should be moved to the country, and eventually the school grew into Avondale College—still in operation today. The school was molded toward Ellen's developing philosophy of education.

You can go to school there if you want. The Web site is http://www.avondale.edu.au.

In 1900, Ellen announced that the time had arrived for her voice to return to the United States. As we have already seen, trouble was brewing in the church over the nature of her inspiration, and although many in Australia felt this was a terrible time for her to leave, hindsight shows that she left at just the right time.

It is interesting to note that, in spite of the shady leadership move ejecting her into the Outback, God still moved through her voice in a powerful way, and great things were accomplished. Ellen saw this and penned, "God sent me to Australia."[2] Sometimes we find ourselves in places we didn't intend to be, but God is everywhere, and He can transform any situation into something for His glory.

ENDNOTES

1. E. G. White, letter to O. A. Olsen, from "Sunnyside," Cooranbong, December 1, 1896, quoted in *The Ellen G. White 1888 Materials,* 4:1622.

2. Letter 175, 1899, quoted in Ellen G. White, *Manuscript Releases,* 12:85.

Chapter 71

Elmshaven

I'm going to freely confess to you that I love houses—big houses. I like observing the architecture, seeing how the layouts work and, most important, envisioning myself living in them. What would life be like with five hundred acres to wander around in? How much better could I live if I had a place with secret passages leading from my personal library to my personal pantry—well stocked, of course.

I also think it's cool when houses have names.

Mine currently doesn't; we just call it "Home," which in many ways is a great name since not all houses *are* homes. But maybe we should give it a proper name. No, not like "Murray," "Bill," or "Beatrice." Houses need distinguished names like all of the big ones in the nineteenth century seem to have had.

Names such as "Ravenhurst," "Biltmore," "Lockwood," "Butternut," and "Cupcake Hill"—I'd love to live at Cupcake Hill.

When Ellen returned from her Australian exile, she moved to "Elmshaven," a lovely place in Northern California. Robert Pratt built Elmshaven in 1885, naming it "Robert Pratt Place." Not as creative as Ellen, who christened it Elmshaven—after the elm trees in the front yard. Ellen lived at Elmshaven for fifteen years until she passed away in 1915. In 1993, it became a National Historic Landmark, and it's open to tours should you ever want to go.

My friend Olivia went this past summer and got kicked out—along with her grandparents. Want to hear that story? OK, here's what Olivia told me:

> While on a road trip to visit Pacific Union College with my grandparents, they thought it was necessary that we visit Ellen White's home. As we turned into the driveway/entrance there was a sign posted that read, *"Closed for maintenance and repairs."* I saw the sign and mentioned it to my grandparents, who hadn't seen it.
>
> They either didn't hear me or I was ignored.

We parked and got out of the car. Grandma said she felt we were on holy ground and that we should say a prayer. After the prayer, we headed up to the door. Grandpa tried the door and found it unlocked.

We went inside because, clearly, rules don't apply to Grandma Sharon and Grandpa Harley.

My grandma started spouting off what I'm sure was fascinating information about Ellen. After a few minutes, an employee emerged and asked us to "please leave the premises." He also pointed out that there was a sign posted saying the house was closed. My grandparents both claimed they saw no such sign.

We left.

The end.

Hilarious, isn't it? So, if you do decide to take a tour, please call ahead and pay attention to any "holy ground" that might have a Keep Off sign attached to it.

Not long after Ellen settled into her new house, her friends at the General Conference sent her a request to attend their meetings in Battle Creek, Michigan. At the meetings, strong personalities pummeled each other while vying for power over building projects and the use of certain job titles.

Chapter 72

FIGHT!

Dr. Kellogg wanted to create an opulent medical facility to replace the old one that had burned down earlier in the year. Ellen White and A. G. Daniells (the executive chair of the Adventist Church) disagreed. Daniells also clashed with Dr. Kellogg over how much to spend on a medical facility in Britain.

To get his way, Kellogg partnered with A. T. Jones in an attempt to oust Daniells from his position. Making matters worse was Kellogg's recent book *The Living Temple,* which argued that God is *in* all things—instead of being the Creator of all things. This belief is known as *pantheism,* and Ellen hated it. Jones loved it.

Kellogg and Jones also took issue with the fact that Daniells had begun to sign his papers with the title "president," instead of "chairman." Ellen had previously expressed concern in her writings over the title "president," but Daniells pointed out that, for legal reasons, the title needed to be used. He said that "the meaning of the expression in the Testimony was not that the General Conference should have no president, but that the president of the General Conference should not be the one person to whom the details in the various parts of the field should be referred."[1]

In other words, "president" was a practical title, not one that meant that he had absolute authority over the whole church. W. C. White agreed. Jones did not.

Remember, Jones had a rigid view of Ellen's writings, holding that every little word was dictated to her by God. So things like this blew his mind and made him upset. As the fights grew more intense, questions revolving around Ellen's writings permeated everything—and inevitably led to Jones and Kellogg leaving the church by 1907.

By 1906, fights over her writings exploded to the point that Ellen sent out a request (like a mass e-mail) via church leaders encouraging people to ask her questions directly instead of speculating among themselves.

One man, Dr. David Paulson, wrote Ellen on April 19, 1906. He held a view of her writings that a lot of people still hold more than a hundred years later. He wrote to her: "I was led to conclude and most firmly believe that every word that you ever spoke in public or private, that every letter you wrote under any and all circumstances, was as inspired as the ten commandments. I held that view with absolute tenacity against innumerable objections raised to it by many who were occupying prominent positions in the cause."[2]

Should he continue to hold that position? How would you answer someone, today, who told you they believed this way?

Thankfully, we have Ellen's reply:

> My brother, you have studied my writings diligently and you have never found that I have made any such claims, neither will you find that the pioneers in our cause have made such claims.
>
> . . . "[Inspiration] is conveyed through the imperfect expression of human language."[3]

That kind of balanced position really poked holes in Jones's rigid view of her inspiration.

After all, Jones was so extreme that he suggested, in a letter to Ellen in 1909, that if her writings were really of God, "they need no explanation."[4] In other words, context didn't matter; God had dictated every word, and those words were as good as the Bible.

Ironically, Ellen was losing her voice due to people who thought they were preserving it.

ENDNOTES

1. A. G. Daniells, quoted in George R. Knight, *From 1888 to Apostasy*, 190.

2. David Paulson, letter to Ellen G. White, April 19, 1906, quoted in "Some Principles for Correctly Interpreting the Writings of Ellen G. White," White Estate, http://www.whiteestate .org/issues/herm-pri.html.

3. E. G. White, *Selected Messages*, 1:24, 26.

4. A. T. Jones, letter to Ellen G. White, April 26, 1909, quoted in Knight, *A. T. Jones*, 263.

Chapter 73

Final GC Session—1909

The last General Conference session that Ellen attended took place in 1909 on the campus of Washington Foreign Mission Seminary (now Washington Adventist University)—in a tent. The first meeting began at 10:45 A.M. on Thursday, May 13, with Ellen finally taking the platform on Sabbath, May 15, at 11:00 A.M.

Over a thousand people gathered to hear what the aging prophet had to say. Once a shy teenage girl too terrified to testify in her parents' living room, Ellen faced off against a world church that God had called into existence and which had not wrestled with itself sufficiently, trying to figure out how to organize and move forward.

Ellen was the last speaker of the meetings. "With trembling lips and a voice touched with deep emotion," wrote one attendee, "she assured the ministers and other workers that God loves them, and Jesus delights to make intercession in their behalf."[1] Ellen knew how important encouragement was to people, and many took comfort in her words.

Toward the end of her sermon she gave an indication that she knew her voice was vanishing. She said,

> Brethren, we shall separate for a little while, but let us not forget what we have heard at this meeting. Let us go forward in the strength of the Mighty One, considering the joy that is set before us of seeing His face in the kingdom of God and of going out no more forever.[2]

Ellen knew her time on earth was dwindling. When she ended her message, she made her way back to her seat—but then turned and came back to the podium.

With almost eerie premonition, she held up the Bible she had just preached from. So many times she had held up the Bible in vision—immovable and strong. Now, her old hands trembled under the weight, but her voice remained firm. "Brethren and Sisters," she said, "I commend unto you this Book."[3]

Ellen knew her church would struggle with the issue of her writings and their relationship to the Bible after she was gone.

ENDNOTES

1. Arthur White, *Ellen G. White,* 6:197.
2. Ibid.
3. Ibid.

Chapter 74

The Accident

Usually when someone falls down it's funny—and it ends up on the Internet.

We might object to people laughing at us when we step on a Lego, fall down (or up, if you are really coordinated) stairs, or trip over our own feet ("I meant to do that"); but we smirk whenever we see a supermodel slip on the runway (so much for nine-inch heels), a distracted shopper fall into a mall fountain (stop texting while walking), or a skateboarder miscalculate the icy railing he is now straddling (you kinda asked for it).

The possibilities are endless and have made YouTube what it is today.

Of course, most of us are sensitive enough to recognize when a fall isn't just a fall but a genuine injury. A person doing something dumb and reaping the consequences (as long as he or she walks away reasonably unhurt and a little smarter) is different than watching a person get hurt in a genuine accident.

There is a fine line between funny and a compound fracture.

On February 13, 1915, Ellen fell.

Not the funny kind of fall that everyone seems to have footage of on their smartphones to share with everyone on planet Earth, but the kind of fall that fractures bones and sentences you to bed rest.

Willie reported on the incident in the *Review and Herald:*

> Sabbath morning, mother appeared to be as well as usual. About noon as she was entering her study from the hallway, she tripped and fell. Her nurse, May Walling, who was in the hall about twenty feet away, hastened to her assistance, and endeavored to help her onto her feet. When mother cried out with pain, May lifted her into a rocking chair, pulled the chair through the hall to mother's bedroom and got her to bed. Then May telephoned to Dr. Klingerman at the sanitarium, and at once applied fomentations to the hip, where the pain seemed to be the greatest.
>
> When the doctor came, he said that it was either a bad sprain or a fracture,

and advised an X-ray examination at the sanitarium. This examination showed an "intracapsular fracture of the left femur at the junction of the head and the neck." Mother bore very patiently all the painful experiences of being carried from her room to the sanitarium and back again.[1]

Ouch, no good. Even though Ellen was a trooper throughout the experience, the injury slowed her down considerably.

She still managed to pray with clarity of mind, but she confided to her son that she felt that her work was coming to an end. She said that she was "willing to lie down and sleep till the resurrection morning, unless there is yet some special work the Lord has for her to do."[2] Reflections, reading, and prayer characterized the next five months until the middle of July.

Some days were good, and others not so good.

On March 3, around 10:00 A.M., Ellen White summoned Mrs. Hungerford (that would be a cool house name; I live at "Hungerford") in order to tell her about a vision she had had late the night before. Willie, her son, also arrived on the scene and wrote down his mother's words:

> There are books that are of vital importance that are not looked at by our young people. They are neglected because they are not so interesting to them as some lighter reading. . . .
>
> I do not expect to live long. My work is nearly done. Tell our young people that I want my words to encourage them in that manner of life that will be most attractive to the heavenly intelligences, and that their influence upon others may be most ennobling.
>
> In the night season I was selecting and laying aside books that are of no advantage to the young. We should select for them books that will encourage them to sincerity of life, and lead them to the opening of the Word.[3]

Her last vision was about the youth—not the Catholic Church, rock music, the Illuminati, meat eating, or anything else—except the youth and her desire for them to read the Bible.

That's heavy. Ellen's final "testimony" wanted you to read books that ultimately lead you to read Scripture.

"I do not think I shall have more Testimonies for our people," she continued. "Our men of solid minds know what is good for the uplifting and upbuilding of the work."[4]

Wow, I hope this book would make her happy, and I hope it inspires you to dig deeper.

As Ellen drifted closer to death, her mind felt pain at the mounting world tensions that would lead to World War I. "Are our people affected by the war?" asked Ellen one day while talking to her son.

"Yes," answered Willie gently, "hundreds have been pressed into the Army."

Making matters worse were those Adventists who judged their brothers and sisters who were forced into very difficult situations by the government's drafting of soldiers. Ellen didn't say much, but she did seem to indicate that people should be led by conscience in the difficult spots of life—and not do things simply because a government forces them or their fellow Christians judge them.[5]

As the summer of 1915 rolled around, Ellen's strength deteriorated.

Willie remembered that on bad days she wasn't even aware of people in the room. What a strange contrast for a woman who, for decades, seemed to be aware of nearly everything. She stopped eating, save for an occasional egg white in water—which she ate only sometimes.

Can't blame her there; that sounds worse than cherry cough syrup.

On Thursday, July 8, Ellen said, "I do not suffer much, thank the Lord. . . . It will not be long now."[6] The next day, surrounded by the prayers of loved ones, she said, "I know in whom I have believed." Those are the last words she spoke.

Ellen lingered for several more days, silently "breathing her life away."

On July 16, the frail little girl with such a mighty voice slipped into a slumber that can be awakened only by the voice of the Savior in whom she believed. When Jesus comes again, His voice will be so loud that graves will erupt with life—and Ellen will find her voice once again. And those who have heard Ellen's voice only through her writings, or through the well-meaning "buzzards" who misquote her, will hear her sing perfect loving praises to Jesus.

But on July 16, 1915, as her family watched her die, "It was like the burning out of a candle, so quiet."[7]

ENDNOTES

1. Willie C. White, *Review and Herald,* March 11, 1915, 17.
2. Ibid.
3. E. G. White, *Review and Herald,* April 15, 1915, 3.
4. Ibid.
5. Arthur White, *Ellen G. White,* 6:427.
6. Willie White, letter to "Friend," July 14, 1915, quoted in ibid., 430.
7. Arthur White, *Ellen G. White,* 6:431.

Chapter 75

Saying Goodbye . . . Three Times

Ellen had three funerals.

I know what you are thinking—and no, she didn't come back and then die two more times.

Late on Friday afternoon, July 16, 1915, telegrams and telephone calls rocketed across the country informing the world that Ellen was dead. The funeral arrangements for three services were crafted at Elmshaven by friends and family. The first service would happen on the lawn at Ellen's house, the second at a camp meeting not too far from Elmshaven, and the third, and final, service would be held in Battle Creek, Michigan where she would be buried alongside her husband and two sons.

In addition to the three services, Ellen "would lie in state" at Elmshaven on Sabbath and Sunday, July 17 and 18, meaning people could visit and see her—uh, well, as she was. Visitors arrived and were escorted up to her writing room. Ellen lay in a "simple cloth-covered black coffin bearing a modest silver plate with the engraved words 'At rest.' "[1] Most visitors came Sunday afternoon and were content to just hang out in the living room or on the lawn for the funeral service.

Funerals

Attendees at the first funeral noted how simple and informal it was. At the end, Willie commented how, even after the service ended, people lingered around, displaying no rush to leave. Some said they wanted the funeral to go on longer because the words shared by church leaders were so moving, and because it was hard to say goodbye to someone they loved and respected.[2]

The second funeral took place in Richmond, California, where the California Adventists were holding their annual camp meeting. Several of those conducting the camp meeting were old work buddies of Ellen during her "propheting" days when she first moved back to America from Down Under. Upon hearing of Ellen's death, they sent a request to Elmshaven.

" 'If Sister White were alive and well, she would be right here at this meeting, telling us how to live the Christian life. Why not let her be brought here and someone tell us how she lived it?' "[3]

Well, that's . . . different. Can you imagine attending camp meeting with (and I say this with all due respect) the dead body of a prominent leader used as an object lesson for a sermon?

To be fair, while the wording of the request seems strange, what they were really asking for is a funeral service and the chance to say goodbye to a woman that meant so much to them. A thousand people attended the service. By three o'clock, Ellen was aboard a train headed for Battle Creek for her final resting place.

On Sabbath, July 24, instead of Sabbath School, the congregation in Battle Creek could view Ellen in her coffin from 8:00 A.M. until 10:00 A.M., with the funeral taking place during the regular church time at 11:00 A.M. Churches around the area canceled their own services for a chance to say goodbye to God's messenger. Lines formed outside the church doors before they opened—just like people waiting outside an Apple Store for a new iPhone.

The *Battle Creek Enquirer* was on the scene and reported:

> During the two hours between eight and ten, there was a steady stream of humanity viewing the body. Men with gray heads and stooped shoulders, many who knew Mrs. White during the early days of the Advent movement, were at the Tabernacle to pay their last respects. They stood before the casket and tears flowed down their cheeks, as they thought of her wonderful work for the denomination.[4]

Even for people who have the hope of the resurrection when Jesus returns, goodbyes are still painful. And when they come in this life, it's important to take time to grieve.

The *Battle Creek Moon Journal* (don't even ask; I've no idea why they named it that) wrote that about two thousand people passed by Ellen's open casket in front of the podium. "An honor guard of six ministers alternated in pairs every twenty minutes and stood, one at the head of the casket and one at the foot."[5] Other news sources reported on the beautiful arrangements of carnations and, interestingly enough, forget-me-nots.

Also placed on the black coffin was an arrangement of flowers, pink-and-white carnations, in the shape of an open Bible, given by the publisher of this book—Pacific Press. In purple flowers, within the floral Bible, was written, "Behold, I come quickly; and my reward is with me."[6] Other funeral décor included a cross of white roses that hung from the pulpit with a ribbon attached, containing Ellen's last words: "I know in whom I have believed."[7]

Making the occasion even grander were thirty-five hundred mourners that the Tabernacle could barely contain. That little child, once devastated by injury, plagued by poor health, crushed so many times by people's harsh words, rejection, and her own lack of self-worth, had grown into a woman whose words brought the love of Jesus to countless numbers who now showered her with loving words of their own.

She lived a life worthy of her final rest in Jesus.

Thank you, Ellen, for staying faithful through darkness and death. May your life give us the courage to do the same and may Jesus help us when we forget who you really were and what you really said. You deserve better than what we have done to you.

ENDNOTES

1. Arthur White, *Ellen G. White,* 6:433.
2. Willie White, letter to David Lacey, July 20, 1915, quoted in ibid., 434.
3. Ibid.
4. Arthur White, *Ellen G. White,* 6:435, 436.
5. Ibid., 436.
6. Ibid., 436, 437.
7. Ibid., 437.

Chapter 76

The 1919 Bible Conference

Despite the forget-me-nots on her casket, we began losing Ellen's voice in earnest by 1919. After she passed away, and as time went on, fewer and fewer people who had actually known her and worked alongside her were able to defend a balanced approach to her writings—a shame since the Christian church as a whole got into a huge fight in the early twentieth century.

The fight began with what is called *liberalism*. This way of thinking popped up in major Protestant churches and in university settings and involved some of the following ideas:

- Humans are essentially good, and the idea of sin is essentially bad.
- Sin is just ignorance, and it can be educated out of people.
- Evolution is awesome.
- The kingdom of God will arrive via evolution—Christianity being the most "evolved" religion.
- The Bible is more human than divine.
- Miracles don't happen.
- Science and faith can't be BFFs anymore.

Guess how the conservative churches felt about these ideas? You got it. And they retaliated with some studies of their own that resulted in an idea called *fundamentalism*.

Fundamentalism reacted to the liberalism found in educational institutions by affirming the traditional accounts of Jesus' life; the reality of miracles; and the literal, visible second coming of Jesus. That's all well and good, but then, in their freaked-out state of mind, the conservatives slipped in a couple dumb ideas, such as the following:

- All colleges and universities are suspicious places that make you lose faith—a concept called *anti-intellectualism*.

- Every word in the Bible was dictated directly by God—an idea that became known as *biblical inerrancy.*

Although Adventists didn't agree with liberalism, they didn't quite fit in with fundamentalism, either. But as often happens in fights, sometimes you feel like you need to take sides.

Guess which side Adventists took?

Yep, they decided to have some FUNdamentalism—and view anything that disagreed with the truth they already had, especially if it came from a college or university, as "new theology." I used to think that was a compliment.

"Oh, I see you have the new theology."

It sounds like a new car or laptop with all the state-of-the-art features, but in this theological sense, anything new is very, very bad. It became a weird time of paranoia. Anyone with an advanced degree (master's or doctorate) was viewed with suspicion, and any question that might suggest changing a traditional biblical interpretation or historical interpretation could get you in a lot of trouble, as became grossly obvious at the Adventists' 1919 Bible Conference.

Inerrant Ellen

At the Bible conference, A. G. Daniells, the church president, said that "word-for-word inspiration" of the Bible had "followers among us."[1] People had begun using Ellen not only as Scripture but also as a someone divinely dictated to.

This didn't groove with a statement the church adopted in 1883, when Ellen was still alive. That statement read: "We believe the light given by God to his servants is by the enlightenment of the mind, thus imparting the thoughts, and not (except in rare cases) the very words in which the ideas should be expressed."[2]

When it comes to inspiration, at least for Ellen, it's the thought that counts. God works through the prophet's own words, and Ellen even edited her work from time to time—which blew the minds of people such as A. T. Jones and many of those at the dreadful 1919 Bible Conference.

Oh yeah, it got much worse.

Ellen was gone, and thanks to followers who never knew her, her voice was changing, receiving supernatural enhancements she would never have been cool with. Historian George Knight points out that at this time: "The church in a fearful and reactionary mood even went so far as to publish a General Conference-sponsored textbook for Adventist colleges that explicitly denied Ellen White's moderate position on thought inspiration and advocated inerrancy and the verbal inspiration of every word."[3]

The irony is painful. While the church lambasted the liberal universities, they pumped their own schools with dodgy material. Let this be a lesson; doing theology out of fear is always a really bad idea. Jesus says, "Watch and pray," not "Watch and panic."

Later on, leaders like B. L. House, in 1926, went so far as to say that "the selection of 'the very words of Scripture in the original languages was overruled by the Holy Spirit.' "[4] Sounds like the Spirit possessed people rather than inspired them. The 1919 Bible Conference continued to reveal how Ellen's writings had been ransacked.

During the conference, C. L. Benson stated, "Out in the field we have stressed the importance of the spirit of prophecy [Ellen's writings] more than the Bible, and many of our men are doing it right along."[5] Adventists were simultaneously losing the Bible *and* Ellen's voice.

When people who had known Ellen, such as A. G. Daniells, tried to point out the dangerous trend, others countered with things like this: "There is a dangerous doctrine that is rapidly permeating the ranks of our people" [and] "ought to be met squarely. It is this: That Sister White is not an authority on history."[6]

Now even the historical sources Ellen used were considered flawless! It kept getting worse. The voice of reason, along with Ellen's voice, drowned in the fears fundamentalism.

As Daniells watched the outcome of the conference, which chose to cling firmly to its extreme views instead of sharing a balanced position with church members, he lamented that people "will hunt around to find a statement in the Testimonies and spend no time in deep study of the Book [the Bible]."[7]

Since then, other harsh battles have been fought in the church. Ellen has often been mishandled and misunderstood, and an eye of suspicion has been cast on anyone who dares to make her human. Thankfully, Ellen's voice is in recovery today, but we still have a way to go.

ENDNOTES

1. A. G. Daniells, quoted in "Inspiration of the Spirit of Prophecy as Related to the Inspiration of the Bible," Report of the 1919 Bible Conference, August 1, 1919, 1, 2, http://docs.adventistarchives.org/docs/RBC/RBC19190801__B.pdf#view=fit.

2. "General Conference Proceedings," *Review and Herald,* November 27, 1883, 5.

3. George Knight, *A Search for Identity: The Development of Seventh-Day Adventist Beliefs* (Hagerstown, MD: Review and Herald® Publishing Association, 2000), 137.

4. B. L. House, *Analytical Studies in Bible Doctrines for Seventh-day Adventist Colleges,* 66, quoted in George R. Knight, *Reading Ellen White: How to Understand and Apply Her Writings* (Hagerstown, MD: Review and Herald® Publishing Association, 1997), 108.

5. C. L. Benson, quoted in "The Use of the Spirit of Prophecy in Our Teaching of Bible and History," Report of the 1919 Bible Conference, July 30, 1919, 39, http://docs.adventistarchives.org/docs/RBC/RBC19190730__B.pdf#view=fit.

6. Claude E. Holmes, *Have We an Infallible "Spirit of Prophecy"?* 1, 11, quoted in Knight, *A Search for Identity,* 139.

7. A. G. Daniells, quoted in "The Use of the Spirit of Prophecy in Our Teaching of Bible and History."

Chapter 77

Ellen and Us

Ellen White never claimed to be a prophet.

Seriously, she didn't.

When confronted with this oddity here is how she replied:

> Some have stumbled over the fact that I said I did not claim to be a prophet; and they have asked, Why is this?
>
> I have had no claims to make, only that *I am instructed that I am the Lord's messenger*; that He called me in my youth to be his messenger, to receive his word, and to give a clear and decided message in the name of the Lord Jesus.
>
> Early in my youth I was asked several times, Are you a prophet? I have ever responded, I am the Lord's messenger. I know that many have called me a prophet, but I have made no claim to this title. My Saviour declared me to be his messenger. "Your work," he instructed me, "is to bear my word. Strange things will arise, and in your youth I set you apart to bear the message to the erring ones, to carry the word before unbelievers, and with pen and voice to reprove from the Word actions that are not right. Exhort from the Word. I will make my Word open to you. It shall not be as a strange language. In the true eloquence of simplicity, with voice and pen, the messages that I give shall be heard from one who has never learned in the schools. My Spirit and my power shall be with you." . . .
>
> Why have I not claimed to be a prophet?—Because in these days many who boldly claim that they are prophets are a reproach to the cause of Christ; and because my work includes much more than the word "prophet" signifies. . . .
>
> To claim to be a prophetess is something that I have never done. If others call me by that name, I have no controversy with them. But my work has covered so many lines that I can not call myself other than a messenger, sent

to bear a message from the Lord to his people, and to take up work in any line that he points out.

When I was last in Battle Creek, I said before a large congregation that I did not claim to be a prophetess. Twice I referred to this matter, intending each time to make the statement, "I do not claim to be a prophetess." If I spoke otherwise than this, let all now understand that what I had in mind to say was that I do not claim the title of prophet or prophetess.[1]

What do you see here? When someone clearly has a prophetic gift, what possible motivation could she have to not claim it?

Simple—she was afraid of losing her voice.

So many words carry baggage. If you tell people you are a Christian, what do they automatically think about you? If you say you like comic books, what impression do people immediately get about you? If you are a boy who likes My Little Ponies (a "Bronie"), people attach certain ideas to your life—not good ones, either.

What happens when you say you are a prophet?

Exactly. People associate a whole bunch of things with you that might not reflect what you are like at all. So how do we prevent ourselves from making Ellen into something she wasn't and isn't? How can we make sure we don't drown out her voice with our own? The only way is to read for yourself, asking the Holy Spirit to give you wisdom and use good tools.

Just as I described in the first chapter, take time to write down all of the ideas you have about Ellen and then read her writings. Whenever she shatters one of those ideas, highlight what she said, and be willing to change that idea.

There are so many stories left untold in this book, like the time she preached on a barroom table in Europe, how she comforted her twin sister when she lost her baby, or her attempts to convince that same twin sister to accept the truths Jesus showed her. Appendix B shows where to find these stories (including the barroom table tale and her letters to her twin sister), but these are only a fraction of what she wrote.

Ellen's voice has spoken in so many places, at so many times, in so many unique situations, that it can be hard to distill it into easily digestible pieces. You have so much more to discover—more miracles, more dangers, more nuggets of wisdom, more crazies (nine whole volumes of them), and more statements that need to be wrestled with. Rediscover her voice for yourself and don't let any author, crabby theologian, or wild-eyed fundamentalist be the final voice for you.

In 1900, Ellen wrote,

What I might say in private conversations would be so repeated as to make it mean exactly opposite to what it would have meant had the hearers been sanctified in mind and spirit. I am afraid to speak even to my friends; for afterwards I hear, Sister White said this, or, Sister White said that.

My words are so wrested and misinterpreted that I am coming to the conclusion that the Lord desires me to keep out of large assemblies and refuse private interviews. What I say is reported in such a perverted light that it is new and strange to me. It is mixed with words spoken by men to sustain their own theories.[2]

Let's treat her carefully, respectfully, honestly, and gently—so she isn't afraid to speak.

ENDNOTES

1. E. G. White, "A Messenger," *Review and Herald,* July 26, 1906, 8, 9; emphasis in original.

2. E. G. White, *Selected Messages,* 3:82, 83

Appendix A:
Ellen G. White Time Line

The early years, 1827–1860

Born on a late fall day in a farmhouse near Gorham, Maine, Ellen Harmon spent her childhood and youth in nearby Portland. She married James White in 1846, and the struggling young couple lived in a variety of New England locations as they sought to encourage and instruct fellow Advent believers by their preaching, visiting, and publishing. After eleven irregular issues of *The Present Truth,* they launched the *Second Advent Review and Sabbath Herald* in Paris, Maine, in 1850. Thereafter they followed a steadily westward course—to Saratoga Springs, New York, and then Rochester, New York, in the early 1850s, and finally, in 1855, to Battle Creek, Michigan, where they resided for the next twenty years.

1827, November 26	Born at Gorham, Maine.
1836 (c.)	Broken nose and concussion at Portland, Maine.
1840, March	First heard William Miller present the Advent message.
1842, June 26	Baptized and accepted into Methodist Church.
1844, October 22	Disappointed when Christ did not come.
1844, December	First vision.
1845, Spring	Trip to eastern Maine to visit believers; met James White.
1846, August 30	Married James White.
1846, Autumn	Accepted seventh-day Sabbath.
1847–1848	Set up housekeeping at Topsham, Maine.
1847, August 26	Birth of first son, Henry Nichols.
1848, April 20–24	Attended first conference of Sabbath keeping Adventists at Rocky Hill, Connecticut.
1848, November 18	Vision to begin publishing work—"Streams of Light."
1849, July	First of eleven numbers of *The Present Truth,* published as a result of the vision of November 1848.

1849, July 28	Birth of James Edson, second son.
1849–1852	Moved from place to place with her publisher husband.
1851, July	First book published, *A Sketch of Experience and Views*.
1852–1855	In Rochester, New York, where husband published *Review and Herald* and *The Youth's Instructor*.
1854, August 29	Third son, William Clarence, born.
1855, November	Moved with the publishing plant to Battle Creek, Michigan.
1855, December	"Testimony for the Church," number 1, a sixteen-page pamphlet, published.
1856, Spring	Moved into their own cottage on Wood Street.
1858, March 14	Great controversy vision at Lovett's Grove, Ohio.
1860, September 20	Fourth son, John Herbert, born.
1860, December 14	Death of John Herbert at three months.

Years of church development, 1860–1868

The 1860s saw Ellen White and her husband in the forefront of the struggle to organize the Seventh-day Adventist Church into a stable institution. The decade was also crucial in that it encompassed the beginnings of the Adventist health emphasis. Responding to Mrs. White's appeal, the church as a body began to see the importance of healthful living in the Christian life. In response to her Christmas vision of 1865, our first health institution, the Western Health Reform Institute, was opened in 1866. The institute later grew into the Battle Creek Sanitarium.

1860, September 29	Name Seventh-day Adventist chosen.
1861, October 8	Michigan Conference organized.
1863, May	Organization of General Conference of Seventh-day Adventists.
1863, June 6	Health reform vision at Otsego, Michigan.
1863, December 8	Death of eldest son, Henry Nichols, at Topsham, Maine.
1864, Summer	Publication of *Spiritual Gifts*, volume 4, with thirty-page article on health.
1864, August	Visit to James C. Jackson's medical institution.
1864, September	Our Home on the Hillside, Dansville, New York, en route to Boston, Massachusetts.
1865	Publication of six pamphlets, *Health: or How to Live*.

1865, August 16	James White stricken with paralysis.
1865, December 25	Vision calling for a medical institution.
1865, December	Mrs. White takes James White to northern Michigan as an aid to his recovery.
1866, September 5	Opening of Western Health Reform Institute, forerunner of Battle Creek Sanitarium.
1867	Purchased a farm at Greenville, Michigan, and built a home and engaged in farming and writing.

The camp meeting years, 1868–1881

Residing at Greenville and Battle Creek, Michigan, respectively, until late 1872, and then dividing her time between Michigan and California, Ellen White spent her winters writing and publishing. During the summer, she attended camp meetings, some years as many as twenty-eight! *Testimonies,* numbers 14–30, now found in *Testimonies,* volumes 2–4, were published during these years.

1868, September 1–7	Attended first Seventh-day Adventist camp meeting, held in Brother Root's maple grove at Wright, Michigan.
1870, July 28	Second son, James Edson, married on his twenty-first birthday.
1870	*The Spirit of Prophecy,* volume 1, published; forerunner of *Patriarchs and Prophets.*
1872, July–September	In Rocky Mountains, resting and writing en route to California.
1873–1874	Divided time between Battle Creek and California, attended camp meetings, and spent some months in 1873 in Colorado resting and writing.
1874, April 1	Comprehensive vision of the advance of the cause in California, Oregon, and overseas.
1874, June	With James White in Oakland, California, as he founded the Pacific Press Publishing Association and the *Signs of the Times.*
1875, January 3	At Battle Creek for dedication of Battle Creek College. Vision of publishing houses in other countries.
1876, February 11	William Clarence, third son and manager of the Pacific Press, married at the age of twenty-one.
1876, August	Spoke to 20,000 at Groveland, Massachusetts, camp meeting.
1877	*The Spirit of Prophecy,* volume 2, published; forerunner of *The Desire of Ages.*

1877, July 1	Spoke to 5,000 at Battle Creek on temperance.
1878	*The Spirit of Prophecy*, volume 3, published; forerunner of last part of *The Desire of Ages* and *The Acts of the Apostles*.
1878, November	Spent the winter in Texas.
1879, April	Left Texas to engage in the summer camp meeting work.
1881, August 1	With husband in Battle Creek when he was taken ill.
1881, August 6	Death of James White.
1881, August 13	Spoke for ten minutes at James White's funeral at Battle Creek.

The 1880s, 1881–1891

Following James White's death in August 1881, Ellen White resided in California, at times in Healdsburg and at times in Oakland. She labored there, writing and speaking, until she left for Europe in August 1885, in response to the call of the General Conference. During the two years in Europe, she resided in Basel, Switzerland, except for three extended visits to the Scandinavian countries, England, and Italy. Returning to the United States in August 1887, she soon made her way west to her Healdsburg home. She attended the 1888 General Conference Session at Minneapolis in October and November; following the conference, while residing in Battle Creek, she worked among the churches in the Midwest and the East Coast. After a year in the East Coast, she returned to California but was called back to attend the General Conference session at Battle Creek in October 1889. She remained in the vicinity of Battle Creek until she left for Australia in September 1891.

1881, November	Attended the California camp meeting at Sacramento and participated in planning for a college in the West, which opened in 1882 at Healdsburg.
1882	*Early Writings* published, incorporating three of her early books.
1884	Last recorded public vision, at Portland, Oregon, camp meeting.
1884	*The Spirit of Prophecy*, volume 4, published; forerunner of *The Great Controversy*.
1885, Summer	Left California for trip to Europe.
1888	*The Great Controversy* published.
1888, October	Attended Minneapolis General Conference.
1889, November	*Testimonies*, volume 5, published, embodying *Testimonies*, numbers 31–33, 746 pages.
1890	*Patriarchs and Prophets* published.
1891, September 12	Sailed to Australia via Honolulu.

The Australian years, 1891–1900

Responding to the call of the General Conference to visit Australia to aid in establishing an educational work, Ellen White arrived in Sydney on December 8, 1891. She accepted the invitation somewhat reluctantly, for she had wanted to get on with her writing of a larger book on the life of Christ. Soon after her arrival, she was stricken with inflammatory rheumatism, which confined her to her bed for some eight months. Although suffering intensely, she persisted in writing. In early 1893, she went to New Zealand, where she worked until the end of the year. Returning to Australia in late December, she attended the first Australian camp meeting. At this camp meeting, plans for a rural school were developed that resulted in the establishment of what became Avondale College at Cooranbong, ninety miles north of Sydney. Ellen White purchased land nearby and built her Sunnyside home late in 1895. Here she resided, giving her attention to her writing and traveling among the churches until she returned to the United States in August 1900.

1892, June	Spoke at opening of Australian Bible School in two rented buildings in Melbourne.
1892	*Steps to Christ* and *Gospel Workers* published.
1894, January	Joined in planning for a permanent school in Australia.
1894, May 23	Visited the Cooranbong site.
1895, December	Moved to her Sunnyside home at Cooranbong, where much of *The Desire of Ages* was written.
1896	*Thoughts From the Mount of Blessing* published.
1898	*The Desire of Ages* published.
1899–1900	Encouraged the establishment of Sydney Sanitarium.
1900	*Christ's Object Lessons* published.
1900, August	Left Australia and returned to United States.

The Elmshaven years, 1900–1915

When Ellen White settled at Elmshaven, her new home near St. Helena in Northern California, she hoped to give most of her time to writing her books. She was seventy-two and still had a number of volumes that she wished to complete. She little realized how much traveling, counseling, and speaking she would also be called upon to do. The crisis created by the controversies in Battle Creek would also make heavy demands on her time and strength. Even so, by writing early in the morning, she was able to produce nine books during her Elmshaven years.

1900, October	Settled at Elmshaven.
1901, April	Attended the General Conference Session at Battle Creek.
1902, February 18	Battle Creek Sanitarium fire.
1902, December 30	Review and Herald fire.
1903, October	Met the pantheism crisis.
1904, April–September	Journeyed east to assist in the beginning of the work in Washington, D.C., to visit her son Edson in Nashville, and to attend important meetings.
1904, November–December	Involved in securing and establishing Paradise Valley Sanitarium.
1905, May	Attended General Conference Session in Washington, D.C.
1905	*The Ministry of Healing* published.
1905, June–December	Involved in securing and starting Loma Linda Sanitarium.
1906–1908	Busy at Elmshaven with literary work.
1909, April-September	At the age of eighty-one traveled to Washington, D.C., to attend the General Conference Session. This was her last trip east.
1910, January	Took a prominent part in the establishment of the College of Medical Evangelists at Loma Linda.
1910	Gave attention to finishing *The Acts of the Apostles* and the reissuance of *The Great Controversy,* a work extending into 1911.
1911–1915	With advancing age, made only a few trips to Southern California. At Elmshaven engaged in her book work, finishing *Prophets and Kings* and *Counsels to Parents and Teachers.*
1915, February 13	Fell in her Elmshaven home and broke her hip.
1915, July 16	Closed her fruitful life at the age of eighty-seven. Her last words were "I know in whom I have believed." *Testimonies,* volumes 6–9, were also published in the Elmshaven years.

Appendix B: Recommended Reading

All right my, friends, so you still want more Ellen? And after everything I've done for you—only kidding. I will give you the name of the book, the author, and a brief rundown on what it's all about. Then you can find the books at the following recommended sellers:

- AdventistBookCenter.com (I highly recommend this one—my friends work here.)
- Amazon.com (Order the Ellen White jigsaw puzzle while you're at it, or not; actually I don't know how I feel about Ellen puzzles.)
- Abebooks.com (If you're broke and need a used copy for cheap, order here.)

OK, now here's what I recommend you get.

Ellen biographies

Ellen G. White, by Arthur White. This six-volume biography by Ellen's grandson is loaded with thousands of pages of stories, letters, travels, and so much more. Many of the stories in this book I first learned about in this series. It's also free online. Oh, and Ellen's bar-table preaching story is found in these brown, hardcover books.

Messenger of the Lord, by Herbert E. Douglass. This is an important book, similar to Arthur White's work, but not as extensive. Check it out!

Meeting Ellen White and *Walking With Ellen White,* by George R. Knight. Both are brief, easy-to-read introductions of who Ellen was and how she lived. More info on her twin sister resides in these books.

Sexuality

As was mentioned earlier, *Flame of Yahweh* by Richard M. Davidson is epic. It's a *huge* book and a bit scholarly, but if you want an in-depth exploration of sexuality by an Adventist scholar, there is nothing better.

Historical background

Ellen White's World, by George R. Knight, is the easiest to read. I highly recommend it—and drew from it many of the fun facts about life in the nineteenth century that I shared in this book.

Food in History, by Reay Tannahill, was a book assigned to me in a class in historical research methods at the University of Nebraska. While not exclusively about the nineteenth century, it will give you an appreciation of how complicated, not to mention strange, our approaches to food have been in the past.

From 1888 to Apostasy, by George R. Knight. This book gives an account of the life of A. T. Jones, but in so doing it also gives a lot of background on Ellen White's struggles in the late 1800s. Use this book in conjunction with *A User-Friendly Guide to the 1888 Message,* also by George R. Knight.

James White: Innovator and Overcomer, by Gerald Wheeler; *Joseph Bates: The Real Founder of Seventh-Day Adventism,* by George R. Knight; and *John Harvey Kellogg,* by Richard W. Schwarz are all biographies of people close to Ellen. Their stories overlap with hers, and you will see more of the world she lived in as a result.

Seeking a Sanctuary, by Malcolm Bull and Keith Lockhart, provides an outsiders' view of Seventh-day Adventist history, including Ellen. Although this book is scholarly, you will find some stunning stories in here.

The Protestant Crusade, 1800–1860, by Ray Allen Billington was written way back in 1964, but it's full of awesome stories about what Christianity was like in the eighteenth and nineteenth centuries—not very flattering, either. Some good stories in here. This is a benchmark work, but since it is out of print, you will have to scour the Internet for a used copy.

My good friend, Michael Campbell, who did his doctoral thesis on the 1919 Bible Conference, maintains a blog at http://www.adventisthistory.org. You should check that out as well.

Apps

EGW Writings
Ellen White Answers
EGW Classics

Defending Ellen

Ellen White Under Fire: Identifying the Mistakes of Her Critics, by Jud Lake. This is a great book if you want to learn the history of Ellen's haters and how the accusations they have don't hold up under scrutiny.

101 Questions About Ellen and Her Writings, by William Fagal. This little book is easy to read and full of short, but solid, answers to a variety of questions that people come up with regarding Ellen. Some of the questions are pretty interesting.

Web sites

http://www.ellenwhite.com (By the way there are over twenty Ellen White audio-books on this site!)

http://text.egwwritings.org

http://www.ellenwhitedefend.com

http://ellenwhitedaudio.org

http://www.ellengwhitetruth.com

http://www.ellen-white.com

Note: There are a lot of crazy Ellen White Web sites out there. They are usually pretty easy to spot—they look cheap and are very wordy. They like to use dramatic words such as "exposed!" and "revealed!" The best thing is to avoid them and read Ellen's works for yourself if you want to know what she said.

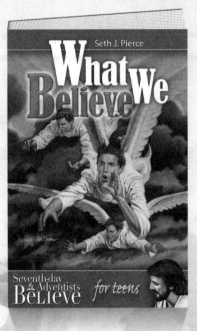
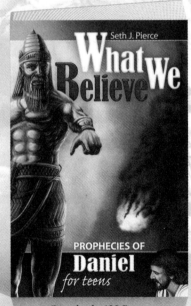